THE QUALITY OF
QUALITATIVE RESEARCH

Clive Seale

SAGE Publications

London • Thousand Oaks • New Delhi

First published 1999   Reprinted 2000

 SAGE Publications Ltd
6 Bonhill Street
London EC2A 4PU

SAGE Publications Inc
2455 Teller Road
Thousand Oaks, California 91320

SAGE Publications India Pvt Ltd
32, M-Block Market
Greater Kailash – I
New Delhi 110 048

British Library Cataloguing in Publication data

A catalogue record for this book is available from the British Library

ISBN 0 7619 5597 6
ISBN 0 7619 5598 4 (pbk)

Library of Congress catalog record available

Typeset by Mayhew Typesetting, Rhayader, Powys

Contents

Preface and acknowledgements

This book, on aspects of methodology, starts from the premise that methodological writing is of limited use to practising social researchers, who are pursuing a craft occupation, in large part learned 'on the job', through apprenticeship, experience, trial and error, rather than by studying general accounts of method. The broad thrust of the argument is that methodology, if it has any use at all, benefits the quality of research by encouraging a degree of awareness about the methodological implications of particular decisions made during the course of a project. Intense methodological awareness, if engaged in too seriously, can create anxieties that hinder practice, but if taken in small doses it can help to guard against more obvious errors. It may also offer ideas for those running short on these during the course of a project. Reading methodology, then, is a sort of intellectual muscle-building exercise, time out in the brain gymnasium, before returning to the task at hand, hopefully a little stronger and more alert.

Because of this rather pragmatic and sceptical orientation, of mine, you will find that a lot of this book (especially the chapters in Part II) contains extended discussions of particular examples of research practice. Consider this, if you like, as a sort of vicarious 'apprenticeship' experience. Any contemplation of other people's research work, if it involves thinking seriously about its strengths and weaknesses, can be like this. Methodological writing of the sort you will find in Part II, however, may help to structure this experience a little more, focusing on particular themes that I believe to be of importance when considering how to produce good-quality research.

Part I, on the other hand, is not all like this. It starts with an example, chosen to illustrate some general points, but it largely contains thoughts about the philosophical, political and more purely methodological issues that many people claim lie behind, indeed ought to determine, the decisions that social researchers often make 'on the ground'. As well as concluding that research practice should in fact be conceived of as relatively autonomous from such abstract and general considerations, I also discuss on some other topics of concern. Broadly speaking, it will become clear to you that I am in favour of a fallibilistic approach to research, within a 'subtle realist' orientation, that does not give up on scientific aims as conventionally conceived, but also draws on the insights of postscientific conceptions of social research. Methodological awareness involves a commitment to showing as much as possible to the audience of research studies about the procedures and evidence that have led to particular conclusions, always remaining open to the possibility that conclusions may need to be revised in the light of new evidence. It does not, however, mean abandonment of authorial responsibility in favour of an 'anything goes' mentality.

In treading this path, I hope carefully and with due consideration of the great variety of conflicting positions that exist, my aim is to present a guide to some of the key methodological discussions on how to ensure quality in qualitative research. I hope that this will assist you in learning from at least some of the examples shown, or at least make principled decisions not to follow in the steps of particular authors in your own research practice. At the end of the book is a series of discussion exercises related to the chapters. These are designed to help integrate the text with courses in research methods, should this be the context in which this book is read.

I have benefited enormously from the careful consideration given by Martyn Hammersley and David Silverman to drafts of the manuscript. It will become clear later in the book that their distinguished methodological writings have influenced me, in different ways, but I am particularly grateful to have had such direct help from them. Paul Coates generously provided philosophical expertise in checking parts of the manuscript. Nevertheless, the final text, errors and all, remains my own responsibility.

Additionally, I would like to record my deep gratitude for the support and tolerance of my wife Donna in the writing of this manuscript. She is always behind my work with these qualities, but particularly so on this occasion.

Clive Seale
Autumn 1998

Part I

GENERAL CONSIDERATIONS

1

Why Quality Matters

CONTENTS

I am going to start with an example because I believe that it helps to show why quality matters in qualitative research. It also shows one type of threat to quality, as well as allowing me to indicate how this might be overcome.

Announcing that qualitative research has now entered a 'fifth moment' in its development, two influential commentators on qualitative research, Norman Denzin and Yvonna Lincoln (1994), propose that the field is now characterized by responses to a 'double crisis'. Qualitative researchers, they say, face a 'representational crisis', since research texts can no longer be assumed capable of capturing lived experience in the way once thought possible. A second crisis, of 'legitimation', arises from this: the old criteria for evaluating the adequacy of researchers' accounts no longer hold. Words like 'validity' and 'reliability' are markers of an earlier, now largely discredited (or at least no longer fashionable) 'moment' in the short history of qualitative social research.

The contemporary sensibilities of the 'fifth moment' were expressed in raw form in a book review written some years earlier by Denzin (1988a), in which he delivered judgement on a work emanating from the 'modernist phase' or 'second moment' of qualitative research: Anselm Strauss's (1987) book, *Qualitative Analysis for Social Scientists*. Denzin reflects:

> this book marks the end of an era. It signals a turning point in the history of qualitative research in American sociology. At the very moment that this work finds its place in the libraries of scholars and students, it is being

challenged by a new body of work coming from the neighboring fields of anthropology and cultural studies. Post-Geertzian anthropologists (Marcus, Tyler, Clifford, Bruner, Turner, Pratt, Asad, Rosaldo, Crapanzano, Fischer, Rabinow) are now writing on the politics and poetics of ethnography. They are taking seriously the question 'How do we write culture?' They are proposing that postmodern ethnography can no longer follow the guidelines of positivist social science. Gone are words like theory, hypothesis, concept, indicator, coding scheme, sampling, validity, and reliability. In their place comes a new language: readerly texts, modes of discourse, cultural poetics, deconstruction, interpretation, domination, feminism, genre, grammatology, hermeneutics, inscription, master narrative, narrative structures, otherness, postmodernism, redemptive ethnography, semiotics, subversion, textuality, tropes. (1988a: 432)

Denzin argues that the modernist assumption of an empirical world that can be studied objectively by qualitative methods is no longer sustainable. He makes the apparently democratic point that scientific emphasis on theory generated by researchers gets in the way of paying close attention to the theories that people use in everyday life. He says that Strauss's modernist demand to make generalizations across cases obstructs a detailed focus on the individual characteristics of particular cases. Denzin observes: 'By making qualitative research "scientifically" respectable, researchers may be imposing schemes of interpretation on the social world that simply do not fit that world as it is constructed and lived by interacting individuals' (1988a: 432). Instead, we live in a postmodern world of multiple selves and endless fragmentation of experience. This, Denzin claims, has profound consequences for the practice of social and cultural research.

We thus see in this review a clash of two 'moments'. On the one hand is the older, scientific view of Strauss. On the other hand, Denzin proposes a postscientific vision of locally relevant, temporary accounts, perhaps collaboratively written by researchers and those whose lives have been researched. No single account should dominate others in this postmodern conception which, nevertheless, is itself a successor to earlier 'moments'.

This divide, which I may have exaggerated a little, points to a central problem for qualitative social researchers that I hope this book will help to solve. Where competing conceptions exist about such basic matters as the nature of the social world and how we may know it, and these appear difficult, if not impossible, to resolve, how is the social researcher going to decide where he or she will stand? I argue in this book that researchers can use methodological debates constructively in their research practice without necessarily having to 'solve' paradigmatic disputes of the sort I have outlined.

So that you can see how this might be done, I will continue to use Denzin's work as an example.

Denzin's alternative

Denzin himself points the way towards this resolution of paradigms or 'moments' since, contrary to the impression I have given so far, he does not say that the modernist grounded theory methodology of Strauss is invalid, or to be dispensed with as being in some way wrong or mis-guided. Such a position would in fact itself be a modernist strategy, signalling that its author is proposing some improved grand narrative for social research. Denzin is careful not to fall into this trap, instead adopting the more liberal view that grounded theorizing is simply one choice among many that qualitative researchers can make: 'it is now clear that qualitative researchers have choices. Twenty years ago they didn't' (1988a: 432).

It therefore seems incumbent on us to evaluate the quality of Denzin's alternative, which we can do by examining one of his own studies (Denzin, 1994), done in the style of deconstructionism which, in his preamble to the study, he claims 'may be employed as a postmodern research strategy for the interpretive study of contemporary society' (1994: 182). The work involves an analysis of the meanings of a Stanley Lumet film (*The Morning After*), in which a Los Angeles actress awakes to find herself next to a murdered man. The film tells the story of her struggle to avoid being framed for the murder.

At one level, Denzin's report reads like a somewhat elaborate film review, briefly giving us the plot of the film and then recording his personal response to it. Thus, he is clearly offended by some of the underlying political messages that he sees. At a certain point Alex (the actress) meets another character (Turner) and they speak as Turner drives:

> *Turner:* (*driving, looking over his shoulder*) A spade in a caddy ran into somebody.
> *Alex:* Spade in a caddy. Is that anybody like Jack in the Box?
> *Turner:* I wish I had the caddy dealership in Watts. Spades, ah, they spend disproportionately on their transportation, also in dressing their young.
> *Alex:* What are you, the Klan anthropologist?
> *Turner:* You can learn a lot about a person by the car they drive.
>   (Denzin, 1994: 194)

Denzin comments: 'In this dialogue, the text criticizes Turner's racism through the two phrases "Jack in the Box," and "Klan anthropologist," thereby neutralizing the unpresentable through an appropriate moral stance. But the effacement of blacks stands' (1994: 194) and later, after exegesis of messages about homosexuality contained in the film, he observes that 'the film . . . asserts that gays and "spics" who, if not evil, are persons about whom jokes can be told' (1994: 195). Denzin, then, is unhappy about the dependence on stereotypes that can be seen in the superficially anti-racist and pro-gay messages contained in the dialogue and characterization, saying that: 'The above analysis reveals how the deconstructionist method may be utilized in the reading of a contemporary cultural text' (1994: 195).

Yet his 'findings' (to use a word from the modernist era) are more ambitious than this. He also wishes to read the film as conveying what it is like to live in the conditions of postmodernity. For this reading, he relies heavily on the ideas of Baudrillard, Lyotard and Derrida. In particular, he draws on Baudrillard's (1988) depiction of America as the location of a media-dominated culture, in which the real has become 'hyperreal', where human beings are judged by 'their ability to match up to media representations' (Denzin, 1994: 188). Additionally, people's identity is decentred and fragmented according to whatever context they inhabit at a particular moment. Alex, the key figure in *The Morning After*, is thus analysed by Denzin as conveying 'a decentred character' who drifts in and out of relationships and widely varying social settings so that she 'is constituted in these relationships' and yet 'has no center' (1994: 192). The film's location in Los Angeles is also significant, as Denzin understands this city to be 'the quintessential postmodern American city' (1994: 184).

Denzin ends his analysis with a vision of the more general effects that can be achieved by the application of deconstructive method, which he now locates as falling within cultural studies rather than sociology, his previously preferred disciplinary identity: 'Cultural studies . . . is a project informed by the politics of liberation and freedom, by a post-Marxism with no guarantees . . . texts [such as *The Morning After* are] ideological efforts to find a common ground in a postmodern world that has neither a fixed center nor a coherent understanding of this thing called human' (1994: 197). He thus is mixing two postscientific tendencies within social theory, those of postmodernism and critical theory. Presumably reluctant fully to embrace the relativist tendencies within postmodernism, he wants to rescue the quest for deconstructive readings of everything by asserting a moral position on heterosexism and racism, positions that he clearly regards as foundational and unassailable.

At one level, it can be argued that evaluating this as a report of qualitative social research is inappropriate. It is a different sort of project, not setting itself up as an authoritative, defensible interpretation of a cultural artifact, but simply presenting one person's response, from which readers are free to vary if they wish. Yet this would be to avoid some important issues. Denzin, as we saw in his review of Strauss's book, clearly feels that his approach can be seen as an alternative strategy for doing qualitative research; at one level, at least, a successor 'science' to Strauss's modernist conception. His reading also contains numerous markers of his desire to persuade readers of the truth value of his deconstructive reading. This is seen most obviously in his assumption of the correctness of the particular moral positions that he adopts. This is not an innocent, liberal-minded, personal response to a film that we can take or leave as the mood suits us, but a claim on our hearts and minds.

It is therefore an interesting exercise to apply the canons of grounded theorizing, the modernist methodology outlined by Strauss (1987), to Denzin's text, as if it were a more conventional research report rather than the exotic new animal that Denzin himself announces. First, we may ask how well grounded are Denzin's concepts in his data? Secondly, have his theories emerged from data, or are they preconceived and forced on the data? Thirdly, has he actively searched, through theoretical sampling perhaps, for negative instances in order to develop his theory by a method of constant comparison? (These terms are explained and illustrated further in Chapter 7 of this book.) If we can answer these questions, we may go some way towards learning what is valuable in Denzin's choice, while retaining a sense of what is valuable in Strauss's alternative. In this way we can learn from both, without having to resolve the matters that divide the two 'moments' that they represent.

First, it is clear that Denzin does not use theoretical concepts without showing the reader the phenomena to which they refer. To take just one concept, that of the decentred self, it is clear that Alex's life exhibits this condition, and Denzin's text describes several illustrative passages from the film to show this. On the second question, however, Denzin's analysis is powerfully driven by a pre-existing set of theories, rather than emerging from an original reading of 'data'. He has chosen this film to illustrate the truth of certain ideas derived from Baudrillard. He might have chosen some other film to do this, but the theoretical messages about our supposed postmodern condition would have been the same. The text is, in this sense, highly overtheorized, in the manner of the 'theoretical capitalist(s)' that Glaser and Strauss (1967: 10), in their original account of grounded theorizing, had wanted to overthrow. We might feel that their postmodern equivalents appear now to be renewing their ascendancy over qualitative research.

On the last question I also find Denzin's report lacking. A fallibilistic approach, which I advocate in this book as desirable in qualitative research, is not well served by presenting a personal interpretation and then simply saying that people are free to disagree if they so wish. It requires a much more active and labour-intensive approach towards genuinely self-critical research, so that something of originality and value is created, with which, of course, people are then always free to disagree, but may be less inclined to do so because of the strength of the author's case. Take, for example, Denzin's belief that in a postmodern world our lives and fragmented, changing identities are overdetermined by media representations. Clearly, this belief is something that he has taken from Baudrillard. Rather than regarding this as given, Denzin might have generated a rather different form of research project investigating people's relationships with media representations, through interviewing or observational methods. This might have led him to some novel insights about the applicability of concepts like hyperreality, grounded in data about people's experience.

Take, too, his view that this particular film contains subtly racist and heterosexist messages. At present, we are given Denzin's own reaction as evidence that this is the effect of particular passages of dialogue, and we are shown the dialogue itself in order to persuade us to go along with Denzin's interpretation. How much more interesting and revealing it might be to seek to understand the responses of ordinary cinema goers to these passages in the film. At the same time, Denzin's deconstructive method is a useful preliminary exercise in imagining the sort of questions one might ask of such cinema goers, and in formulating the more general research questions that might inform such a project, which would itself be a very different type of exercise from the review that Denzin presents.

Conclusion

We should not, of course, take this too far. It can be argued that Denzin is engaged in a different project from that of Glaser and Strauss, one of social or cultural commentary rather than social research perhaps, somewhat distanced from the need to develop ideas through a genuinely fallibilistic approach to the interaction of ideas and data. It should not, then, be judged in terms of how well he does what his predecessors did.

One could take the view that it is simply a matter of preference as to which 'moment' one adopts, or which approach one takes. However, this seems a characteristically postmodernist way of dealing with the issue, avoiding concerns about the purpose of social research. It also seems questionable to promote Denzin-style analysis as necessarily morally or politically superior to its modernist predecessors (see Chapter 2). If we reject preference or moral superiority as adequate reasons for adopting 'fifth moment' analysis, we are left with the view that such work may be a useful source of ideas, but cannot be proposed as a wholly adequate successor to more scientific conceptions of social research.

At the same time, an unproblematic return to modernist assumptions seems impossible. The widespread appeal of alternative conceptions of research is based on some fundamental dissatisfactions with the scientific world view. This book takes this tension as its starting point.

Quality does matter in qualitative research, but I agree with Denzin that the modernist headings of 'validity' and 'reliability' are no longer adequate to encapsulate the range of issues that a concern for quality must raise. Instead, we need to accept that 'quality' is a somewhat elusive phenomenon that cannot be pre-specified by methodological rules. This in fact is the 'threat' to quality that I referred to at the start of this chapter: the idea that research must be carried out under the burden of fulfilling some philosophical or methodological scheme. Practising social researchers can learn to do good work from a variety of examples, done within different 'moments', without needing to resolve methodological disputes before beginning their work. At the same time, the quality of qualitative research is enhanced if researchers engage with philosophical and methodological debate, so that the pursuit of quality becomes a 'fertile obsession' (Lather, 1993) as methodological awareness develops and feeds into practice. But before I discuss this, we should consider further the sources of disquiet with scientific conceptions of qualitative method.

KEY POINTS

- A variety of conceptions of qualitative research exist, with competing claims as to what counts as good-quality work.

- Rather than opting for the criteria promoted by one variety, 'paradigm', 'moment' or school within qualitative research, practising researchers can learn valuable lessons from each one.

2

Postscientific Critiques

CONTENTS

Two broad currents of criticism and disquiet have served to dislodge
modernist visions of quality in qualitative research, opening up the field
to a more flexible and pragmatic relationship between research practice
and methodology. Political perspectives have involved objections to the
hidden values which modernist commitments to guiding ideals like
objectivity and rationality have involved. In the wake of this, postmodernism appears to have shaken the foundationalism on which much
qualitative research has depended. Denzin's research practice, exemplified in the previous chapter, contains elements that address both
sources of criticism. I shall consider each in turn.

Political perspectives

Marxist, feminist and other perspectives from critical theory argue that
the quality of research should be judged in terms of its political effects
rather than its capacity to formulate universal laws or apparently objective truth. The overriding criterion for judging the quality of a study is
its capacity to emancipate, empower or otherwise make free a particular
oppressed group of people (Lincoln and Denzin, 1994). Techniques of
'member validation' (discussed in Chapter 5), in which the perspectives
of participants in a research study are incorporated in its validation, have
at times been linked to the achievement of such political goals (Guba and
Lincoln, 1994), on the grounds that if people whose lives have been
researched endorse a study this is an indicator of its value. Methods of

communicating research findings are linked with this: action research attempts an interactive cycle between practical struggles, the formulation of research questions and the reporting of research findings in a way that informs further practical struggle (Schwandt, 1996). Feminist standpoint epistemology (Harding, 1986) argues that starting research from the concerns of women is likely to be more objective than starting anywhere else, as such an oppressed group will possess insights otherwise concealed by the biases of dominant versions. More broadly, the dominance of policy makers in setting research questions has long been a source of concern to practising researchers, whose livelihood often seems to depend on conforming to the world view of people in power.

These views have considerable appeal and, if adopted with due regard to other aspects of rigour, offer advantages that have been ignored in other research traditions. Political sensitivity is a necessary part of the methodological awareness that social researchers should possess. There is, however, a fundamental problem that political versions of research quality like this must face: the fact that there is no general consensus on what is politically desirable. Unfortunately, a common response to this problem has been to ignore political diversity in favour of vigorous promotion of particular value positions, or advocacy of the supposed interests of particular groups. This itself clearly has the potential for sustaining oppressive social relations. Additionally, it is a mistake to assume that oppressed groups have the best insights into the sources of their oppression (although they can explain some of its consequences), which the uncritical advocacy of member validation and standpoint epistemology can assume. If this were the case, oppression might not be so common. It is at least as likely that oppressors will understand how oppression works (Hammersley, 1995b), though they might not wish to reveal this to a researcher.

At times, the goals of politically critical researchers look strikingly similar to the conventional goals of a liberal education. Thus Schwandt (1996) argues that:

> social inquiry ought to generate knowledge that complements or supplements rather than displaces lay probing of social problems . . . [it] can be judged in terms of whether [it] . . . is successful at enhancing or cultivating *critical* intelligence in parties to the research encounter . . . [and] on the success to which his or her reports of the inquiry enable the training or calibration of human judgement. (Schwandt, 1996: 69)

The idea that these things are desirable in the population is of course a value position itself, consonant, for example, with the cultural values of late modern USA, where the advantages of individualism and democracy are largely unquestioned. Societies which value conformity, based on uncritical trust in authority and tradition, are routinely stigmatized in such a view. Many in such cultures would view as potentially oppressive the Western values promoted by Schwandt's version of research. Given, however, that social research is a largely Western phenomenon, one would expect most social researchers to endorse Schwandt's value position.

Placing to one side, for the moment, the issue of whether emancipation is a universal good, we can also note that there is some dispute over whether the emancipatory potential of research is inevitably linked to particular research methods. Buchanan (1992), who feels that there is such a link, argues that quantitative, 'positivist' research aims to control and predict, while qualitative research aims at a more ethical goal of helping people lead less alienated lives. As is usual with such attempts to dictate the meaning of research practice, it is not difficult to think of examples where the opposite is true. For instance, quantitative social surveys have often been used to document the consequences of oppression and inequality (Booth, 1886–1902; Rowntree, 1901; Russell, 1986; Arber and Ginn, 1991). Pursuing a similar line to that of Buchanan, Oakley (1981) once claimed that qualitative, depth interviews with mothers resulted in data that were more valid in exposing people's true feelings and opinions than were structured interviews, thus enabling her research better to represent women's views on a public stage. The equation of feminist research practice with qualitative method has, however, been questioned by other feminist researchers, who argue that issues of method should not be conflated with the politics of research (Jayaratne, 1983; Reinharz, 1992; Maynard and Purvis, 1994). These authors argue that feminist political perspectives are relevant in influencing the sort of questions researchers ask, or the issues they address, but not in determining the methods used to answer them (beyond a general commitment to ethical practice). It is of interest to note that in more recent work, Oakley (1989) has found that quantitative methods can be effective in generating findings to promote women's interests.

Another attempt to link a political position to a method is contained in the view that researcher and researched need to share the same social status if authentic accounts are to be revealed. Thus there is debate between feminist methodologists about the desirability of men doing research on women, or of middle-class white women doing research on the lives of black or working-class women. Clearly, there are arguments for saying that trust may be more likely in circumstances where researchers and researched share similar experiences. Trust can lead to particular sorts of account, which may be of value for certain research purposes. For other research purposes, however, it can be relevant to see the effects of distrust, since public as well as private accounts are potentially of interest to social researchers (Cornwell, 1984). Additionally, there is no guarantee that trust results from conditions of equal social status. People may find it easier to reveal secrets to strangers. The experience of feminist women interviewing non-feminist women has also disrupted this view (Millen, 1997). Maynard and Purvis (1994) present a version of feminist research which reflects a decoupling of this aspect of method from the politics of research.

The attempt to gauge good research practice from political positions is reminiscent of attempts to link philosophical considerations to issues of method. I argue in Chapter 3 that this is a mistake. Just as philosophical debates can be used as a resource by researchers wishing to generate ideas and reflect on techniques, so can political disputes. These can act as a helpful sensitizing context if the researcher does not allow them to overdetermine practice. A general awareness that a research study may have both intended and unintended political consequences seems desirable. The danger of prioritizing particular political goals in research is that these also come to dominate researchers' interpretations of the social world being investigated. Convinced by prior reasoning that oppression exists, that it takes particular forms and that it is universally undesirable, some qualitative research proceeds to 'discover' matters that someone who does not share the same political views would not find. One sees this, for example, in Waitzkin (1979) and Graham and Oakley (1981). (I analyse the latter study in more depth in Chapter 9.) Quite conventional approaches to validity and reliability, such as the avoidance of anecdotalism, attention to sampling issues and searching for data that challenge an emerging theory, seem appropriate responses here.

Calls for 'relevance' are a less dramatic version of the critical political perspectives viewed above, and in Hammersley's (1992b) formulation of subtle realism (which I discuss in Chapter 3), relevance is one criterion by which the quality of research can be judged. Relevance as a criterion, compared with the more glamorous goals of emancipation or empowerment, appears thin and weak. The researcher concerned with relevance may recognize that a research study may be relevant to different groups in different ways, and that unforeseen relevance may emerge in unpredicted quarters. The perspective of relevance acknowledges that the same policy makers and practitioners who commission research will use research findings as rhetorical resources in debates about practice, where carefully established research findings will compete on an equal basis with anecdotes, hunches and other fleeting thoughts (Green, 1998). Alternatively, they may simply ignore relevant research information. A research report may be relevant not because it points people in a particular practical direction, but simply because it allows people to see their practice from a novel point of view. Reading conversational analysis of one's own speech, for example, is a little like seeing slow-motion film. It enables otherwise taken-for-granted skills to be perceived and made into objects of thought for the first time (Silverman, 1997a, b). Because this stimulates a more reflective mood it may lead to changed practices, but these will not be directed by any normative exhortations by the researcher. Additionally, one can argue that relevance to the existing research literature, or to general social theory, is legitimated by a concern for relevance, in which case one is a long way from a vision of social researchers as vanguards of revolution.

Multiple voices

In Chapter 3, using the postpositivist rationale of subtle realism, I describe the construction of an imagined research community, negotiating and then applying standards of judgement about the quality of social research. Political perspectives, such as critical theory or feminism, propose alternative communities having an equal, if not dominant, voice in judging the quality of research, informed chiefly by the requirements of emancipatory political programmes. Such critics are not impressed by the performance of the liberal democratic research community. More recently, however, in the wake of the declining popularity of Marxist perspectives, a politico-philosophical movement has emerged that questions all claims to quality, authority or trust, including Marxist and feminist ideologies, exercising a profound influence over certain genres within social research. It begins from a position that decries generalization across social contexts as an act of despotism (Lyotard, 1993) and dismantles attempts to outline transcendental ways of getting at truth (Foucault, 1992). Broadly speaking, this is a perspective that stands in opposition to the modernist aspirations implied by the construction of research communities wielding quality criteria, preferring to see the world as a babble of competing voices, none of which ought to lay claim to privileged status. If the social researcher has a task in this postmodern vision, it is to deconstruct the rhetoric of authority and to facilitate polyvocality (Game, 1991). New textual forms have emerged under this *avant garde* movement which, paradoxically perhaps, proclaim their authority as containing the spirit of postmodern times (Denzin, 1997).

The view that we live in postmodern times has encouraged, in relation to the research communities I have discussed thus far, a radical scepticism about the claim of any author to speak truth, to the extent that, at times, the project of social research in any form has seemed hard to maintain. In anthropology the effect has been particularly marked, being famously signalled by the collection edited by Clifford and Marcus (1986). This has been carried into sociological ethnography by Atkinson (1990, 1992) and Van Maanen (1988), who present analyses of the literary qualities of research reports, although both, in the end, pull back from the extreme view that sees no difference between research and fiction. Ethnographers had long recommended the production of reflexive research reports designed to aid readers in applying their critical faculties to the text. But the turn to language that has transformed many approaches in the human sciences intensified the reflexive attitude to the point of a crisis of writers' confidence. Research reports have increasingly been viewed as episodes of story telling, at best being partial truths, up for negotiation with different audiences wielding differing standards of judgement. This perception was encouraged by a number of key events, including the publication of Malinowski's diaries (1967) which revealed this founder of anthropological method to have deviated disturbingly from his own methodological recommendations. The attempts by Freeman (1983) and Lewis (1951) to replicate earlier anthropological studies by Mead (1943, first published in 1928) and Redfield (1930) resulted in further disappointment for scientifically inclined anthropologists when it seemed impossible to get the same results, appearing to lend support to the idealist view of multiple realities (these disputes are discussed in Chapter 10).

In the initial phase of this growing postmodern sensibility, ethnographers turned on their own realist texts to examine their uses of rhetoric in persuading readers to trust their accounts. This involved an approach similar to that of the literary critic concerned to show the stylistic conventions of particular genres. Unlike the material analysed by literary critics, however, research texts had hitherto claimed to report on a real world rather than to construct a fiction. The exposure of rhetorical ploys and other writerly devices in research texts seemed to undermine these referential claims. Instead, it came to be perceived that research texts construct new worlds. Coupled with the after-effects of political critiques of the white, liberal democratic research community emanating from feminist and other sources, doubts about the desirability of a strong authorial presence gathered pace. In response to this, one can argue that studies of how research texts are actually received by various audiences do not always support a view of readers as uncritical cultural dopes who allow research texts to determine how they see their worlds. Nor does the exposure of rhetorical ploys itself undermine all of the referential claims of a text, though it may seem to do so.

Initially, however, the critique of modernist authorship involved the abandonment of research as a legitimate activity. The growth of theory-driven studies was exponential. I am tempted to say, nevertheless, that the career interests of members of the research community made it inevitable that solutions would be proposed. People turned their minds to the production of new forms of reporting from the field that would replace the apparently discredited realist genre. I do not propose a detailed description of these here, as they will be discussed further in Chapter 11, but suffice it to say that these alternatives often attempt to de-emphasize the authority of authors, for example by presenting lengthy transcripts of interviews with minimal authorial commentary (for instance, Crapanzano, 1980; Dwyer, 1982). Alternatively, episodes of poetry and drama may be interspersed with more conventional prose, so that the boundaries with fictional genres are further reduced (Mulkay, 1985; Richardson, 1992). Above all, they are peppered with references to methodological anxieties, which can appear to overwhelm the enterprise of telling a good story.

Geertz (1988) makes some thoughtful critical comments in reviewing the new ethnographic writing styles, founded on anti-foundationalism, that have emerged:

> what is, to me anyway, finally most interesting about . . . these attempts (and most of the others – they appear almost by the week – I have read) . . . is the strong note of disquiet that suffuses them. There is very little confidence here and a fair amount of outright malaise. The imagery . . . is of estrangement, hypocrisy, helplessness, domination, disillusion. [Doing ethnography] is not just practically difficult. There is something corrupting about it altogether. (1988: 97)

The solution to this is not to stay blind to the issues raised by postmodern doubts about the validity of textual claims to truth. Clearly, research writing contains a strong element of art and rhetoric, and it is important to be sensitive to the politics involved in adopting a strong authorial presence. As with political perspectives on research practice, however, I argue that these debates can be used as resources by practising researchers. Close adherence to the postmodern view creates the weaknesses which Geertz identifies, but if taken as sensitizing debates such views can be useful. There is, in fact, a shared spirit between these contemporary pronouncements and earlier recommendations of inductivism (Glaser and Strauss, 1967), or in favour of the phenomenological attitude for making familiar things appear strange (Schutz, 1944), or humanistic interpretivist recommendations to 'take the role of the other' (Lofland, 1971). These all involve a moral commitment to use research activity to aid intersubjective understanding, to understand or to give 'voice' to people inhabiting hitherto hidden areas of social life, resisting tendencies to impose one's own common-sense world view on 'the field' and therefore on other people. In this respect there are continuities with calls by critical theorists for an emancipatory research practice. This also involves a subtle realism which maintains a view of language both as constructing new worlds and as referring to a reality outside the text, a means of communicating past experience as well as imagining new experiences.

Additionally, the view that research texts can be treated as if they were no more than works of fiction seems to abandon a particular segment of the reading public, who will continue to insist on 'non-fictional' texts for certain purposes. There are plenty of essayists, journalists and 'new journalists' (Denzin, 1997) who will rush to fill this gap. Journalism shares similarities with qualitative research writing genres, but there are also important differences, and these are generally based in a commitment to greater depth of thought, more sustained periods of investigation and a more rigorously self-critical approach in the service of higher ideals than scandal mongering, entertainment or immediate emotional and dramatic appeal.

In terms of research practice, the textual and political awareness promoted by critical theorists and postmodern critique need not involve the abandonment of a strong authorial voice. In learning to play a new piece of music from a written score, it is a good idea to play it loud so that mistakes can be heard and corrected. Clearly, in research the concept of a correct version is dubious, but there is a great deal to be said for 'playing loud' nevertheless. You are then at least 'heard' by your potential critics, rather than hiding behind the sounds made by others. The aim of giving the dispossessed access to authorship and to a public voice is desirable too, but it need not diminish the contribution that can be made by researchers themselves, else researchers become no more than stenographers (Snow and Morrill, 1993; Van Maanen, 1988). Hammersley (personal communication) has put it like this: 'abandoning a strong authorial voice is to abandon one's responsibilities as a researcher or to operate surreptitiously as a ventriloquist'.

There are other responses to the idea of the postmodern in addition to those contained in the new ethnographic writing practices. Discourse analysis, for example, unlike realist ethnography, is a qualitative method which attempts to apply a deconstructive approach consistent with postmodern sensibilities. Seeing the world as a text, the discourse analyst describes rhetorical effects, often associating this with some general commitment to emancipatory goals (for example Burman and Parker, 1993; Yardley, 1997). One can reasonably ask conventional questions about the validity of a discourse analytic study (see the discussion of Foucault in the next chapter). Potter and Wetherell (1994) do in fact generate some confident responses to the issue of judging the validity or quality of a discourse analysis. In general, then, there is little evidence in discourse analytic studies of the crisis of authorial confidence seen among ethnographers. Instead, a common textual strategy appears to be to refer to the existence of validity debates but then to get on with the analysis. Here, for example, are Potter and Wetherell (1994) giving advice to their readers:

> More than in many other kinds of social research, the evaluation of discourse analytic studies depends on the quality of the write-up . . . it is up to you to examine . . . our work; in a sense you will need to perform your own discourse analysis to judge its persuasiveness as a critical investigation. (1994: 63)

To the philosopher concerned to construct some overarching rationale for truth claims this is infuriating, as it offers no external foundations for judging truth, leaving us with a relativistic spiral of discourse analyses of discourse analyses. Yet I believe that Potter and Wetherell's advice reflects a healthy and realistic approach to research authorship that avoids the paralysis of will that Geertz identifies. Research done without absolute foundations in philosophical schemes, or indeed without clearly defined political purposes, can nevertheless benefit from a broad awareness of these general debates and produce works of some lasting value that reach beyond purely local concerns.

Conclusion

Political and postmodern objections to modernist conceptions of qualitative research practice are flawed in various ways if they are taken to be foundational for social research, but should not be dismissed. Political sensitivity, as well as an awareness that scientific criteria can no longer be assumed unproblematically to support researchers' authority to pronounce on truth, is inevitably a part of the contemporary sensibilities of social and cultural researchers. It is possible, too, to catch critics of modernism in more generous mood, pointing the way towards more collaborative and conciliatory approaches to issues of quality. In their conclusion to their *Handbook of Qualitative Research*, Lincoln and Denzin (1994) state:

> The history of qualitative research is defined more by breaks and ruptures than by a clear evolutionary, progressive movement from one stage to the next. These breaks and ruptures move in cycles and phases, so that what is passé today may be in vogue a decade from now. Just as the postmodern, for example, reacts to the modern, some day there may well be a neomodern phase that extols Malinowski and the Chicago school and finds the current poststructural, postmodern movement abhorrent. (1994: 575)

And Denzin's (1988a) review of Strauss, with which I started this book, begins 'This is a very good book' (1988a: 430), going on to extol the virtues of this (albeit 'passé') paradigm.

In this spirit of reconciliation between research genres (see also Seale, 1998a), I argue in this book that it is possible to have an encompassing view of quality in qualitative research that respects the contributions made at different 'moments' in its history. This is largely because I regard research as a craft skill, relatively autonomous from the requirement that some people seem to want to impose that it reflect some thoroughly consistent relationship with a philosophical or methodological position. At the same time, I believe that social researchers should engage in philosophical and methodological reflection as an integral part of their practice. The chapter that follows, then, is a discussion of some philosophical considerations that underly research practice, together with suggestions as to how researchers might relate their practice to such a discourse.

KEY POINTS

- The idea that the quality of research should be judged in terms of political goals faces the problem of lack of agreement on what these should be, yet sensitivity to the relevance of research for practical projects is desirable.

- Postmodern deconstructions of the authority of research texts are a helpful check on assumptions of infallibility, but need not lead to the abandonment of attempts to find a strong authorial presence.

3

Trust, Truth and Philosophy

CONTENTS

[There is] a limited contribution that general ideas and information can make to practice, and in this case to research itself as a form of practice. (Hammersley, 1992b: 203)

What does it take to trust an author? Social researchers and other writers in the human sciences increasingly encounter a problem that is also a more widespread feature of social relations in late modernity: lack of trust in authority, whether political, scientific or from some other source, to speak the truth. The factors underlying this general growth of scepticism are various: exposure through global media to conflicting versions of truth; public perceptions of harm done by experts in the name of science, progress or rationality; officially sponsored exhortations to consumerism and individualism. Paradoxically, the rise of mass higher education, which has encouraged a culture of critical thinking, has involved social researchers as academics themselves in creating the conditions under which their textual claims to readers' trust is undermined.

The options for researchers working in these conditions of chronic, radical doubt are twofold. Frustration, despair and cynicism about the production of artifacts of any lasting value is one option. Involvement with pragmatic, short-term activities can often then be maintained without recourse to deeper thought. On the other hand, scepticism can be allied to a creative optimism, leading researchers to address the political issues, personal troubles and social problems of the day in new and exciting ways, without necessarily laying claim to some universal foundation for absolute truth as a basis for ultimate security. The creation of research reports that reflect a self-questioning methodological awareness (see Chapter 11) can address some of the demands made by a critical readership.

It is tempting to see methodological writing on social research as little more than an epiphenomenon, thrown up by the underlying shifts and conflicts within communities of researchers and readers. These are themselves driven by that active, sustained engagement with a changing social world, commonly called social research, which continually encounters (and produces) new objects for study. There is a strong sense in which methodological prescriptions – and this has become particularly evident in qualitative social research – have only marginal relevance for research practice, which is fundamentally a craft skill rather than an application of some free-standing rational scheme. Yet methodological writing, if grounded in research experience, can provide concepts that sensitize researchers to the practical issues they confront in specific projects. These concerns include the problem of trust, which in turn relates to perceptions of the quality of research studies.

Responses to the problem of trust in the quality of qualitative research have taken several forms. A popular approach has been the adoption by authors of professionalized friendliness. Authors demonstrate this in exhortations to treat research subjects democratically, conducting interviews as if between equals, going to extravagant lengths to avoid 'exploitation', proving superior skills in eliciting emotional disclosure or bypassing false fronts in research subjects (for example Oakley, 1981). This sometimes merges with quite powerfully expressed political positions, creating a sense of security in moral rectitude. These strategies are analogous to the 'facework' done by other representatives of abstract systems in late modernity, in which a trustworthy demeanour is cultivated in order to encourage the leap of faith required of clients before productive engagement can occur (Giddens, 1990, 1991).

Another approach to the problem of trust has been to seek philosophical justification for research styles, laying claim to a strong relationship between particular epistemological or ontological positions and particular approaches to research (Smith and Heshusius, 1986; Guba and Lincoln, 1994). It is imagined that somewhere in the realm of philosophy there exists a variety of 'answers' to the problems that researchers face. Sometimes, too, authors claim intellectual distinction with baser textual strategies, using obscure language to mystify novice readers, or making extremist statements of certainty about matters that are obviously controversial. It is surprising, however, how commonly these flawed strategies attract acolytes, who are presumably seeking a sheltering canopy from the uncertainties of more open thought.

Quality in qualitative research is an elusive phenomenon. Most of us can look back and point to works that many people feel to be of good quality. While there may sometimes be a feature common to several studies that has helped produce this perception of value, the feature may be absent in other good studies, or be positively detrimental to quality in others. In addition, authors can surprise readers with new textual or other research strategies. Methodological writing can examine past practice for potential lessons, but can only hope to influence rather than control future practice. In this chapter, I propose now to consider key philosophical concerns that may be thought of as influencing social research practice and offering contrasting foundations for judgements of the quality of social research.

Positive science

The positivist vision in social research is an optimistic, moral commitment to a realm of ideas felt to have a universal validity, located in a world that is independent of local human concerns, though it is ultimately created by human labour. Positivism, taken broadly, offers an opportunity for people to gather together in an imagined community committed to human progress and emancipation through the application of reason and the methodological prescriptions that are said to flow from this.

Positivist social scientists have attempted to replicate the success of the natural scientists in controlling the natural world, and so have been committed to approaches perceived to be characteristic of natural science. This involves the separation of theories from observable facts so that the truth of theories can be tested in a world of these independently existing facts. The world of observable facts is felt to be knowable through human sensory experiences (the empiricist position of Hume). Positivism has also often involved commitment to value neutrality, a preference for measurement and quantification of observable events and a search for statistical regularities that can be understood as causal laws.

The overthrow of positive science is a part of qualitative researchers' creation myth (Hammersley, 1995b), laying the basis for alternative accounts of quality in social research. It is said, for example, that positivist philosophy of science cannot account for the interaction between theory and fact, between observer and observed, which has become evident in some advanced areas of natural science and is more obviously present in social science. Thus, it is argued, the vision of an objective observer is untenable and the core assumptions of positivist empiricism are undermined (Guba and Lincoln, 1994). The interpretivist position, which informed early practitioners of qualitative research, begins from the premise that methodological monism is no basis for the study of the social world. The objects of social science are different from

those of natural science, in that they are capable of independent voli-
tion. Interpretivists (for example Schutz, 1970) often claim that the
positivist scientist misses the progress to be made in the objective
exploration of human subjectivity. Less explicitly discussed, but feeding
much of the feeling that characterizes rehearsals of the creation myth,
are sensations of discomfort at the technical appearance of numbers
rather than words, of disquiet at the prospect of being governed by
deterministic causal laws rather than being free to act as one chooses.
This returns us again to the individualistic social climate that has
accompanied the growth of interest in the qualitative alternative.

The creation myth involves an oversimplified version of positivism
(Hammersley, 1992b). This is particularly evident if we turn from
positivist mimicry of the methods of natural science to the more purely
philosophical variants that emerged under the heading of logical
positivism in the early part of the twentieth century. The appearance of
monolithic consensus is then overturned, as idealist, anti-empirical and
even relativist tendencies within some versions of positivism are
detected (Hammersley, 1995b). The notion that such philosophical
accounts can strictly determine methodological practice appears increasingly absurd in the light of a rigorous analysis of their logical consequences (Marsh, 1982). Additionally, elements which in some contexts
are called positivist are present in several versions of qualitative
research. Analytic induction (Znaniecki, 1934; see also Chapter 6)
involves the search for universally true causal laws. Conversation
analysis, in its rejection of any exploration of subjectivity, its preference
for observable behaviour only, and its insistence on single correct
interpretations, shares this much with some versions of positivism
(Fontana, 1994), albeit of a 'cautious' type (Silverman, 1989).

To account for these problems a modified creation myth has begun to
emerge, once again externalizing the 'problem' by creating a new
subject, 'postpositivism', to contrast with updated constructivist or
postmodern versions of the qualitative paradigm (Guba and Lincoln,
1994; Denzin, 1997). Its targets are researchers who maintain 'positivist'
elements such as quantification and the search for causal factors, while
incorporating interpretivist concerns with subjectivity and meaning (for
example Brown and Harris, 1978), or advocates of pragmatic combinations of quantitative and qualitative methods (LeCompte and Goetz,
1982; Miles and Huberman, 1994), or methodologists who argue for
subtle realism (Hammersley, 1992b). Popper's fallibilistic approach
(1963), emphasizing the creation of falsifiable theory that is modified by
the empirical testing of its explanatory power, is another example of
'postpositivism'. The Popperian social researcher maintains a pragmatic
separation of theory and data, though the positivist vision of universal
truth recedes. Categorization of all these positions as 'postpositivist' is a
rhetorical device, with a potential for symbolic violence at least equivalent to that which the term 'positivism' once had. Yet postpositivist

approaches contain much that is appealing to practising researchers concerned about the nihilistic tendencies of more radical approaches.

Knowing a real world

Positivist social research, regardless of debates about the method by which observations are made, has generally involved application of the hypothetico-deductive model to a world considered to exist independently of the human mind. Propositions, logically deduced from theoretical statements, are operationalized in research projects, tested against the objectively observed, factual nature of the real world, thus determining the truth or falsity of propositions, which in turn influences the content of theories. Inductive theory development is an aim of many natural scientists, who in past times sought to distinguish their method from pure logical deduction based on the ideas of classical texts, preferring empirical investigation. Durkheim's rules of method, sometimes characterized as positivist, also contain a strong inductivist element in the call to 'systematically discard all preconceptions' (Durkheim, 1982: 72) when doing science. In spite of this history within a positivist tradition, induction has nevertheless been proposed as an alternative by anti-positivist qualitative researchers (Glaser and Strauss, 1967). Here, investigators are exhorted to enter the field with as few preconceptions as possible, relying on an accumulation of impressions which, with the aid of a facilitative human mind, eventually speak for themselves, so that new theories emerge from the real world.

Clearly, neither of these alternatives satisfies the constructivist point that objective knowledge of the world is impossible, since all observation is driven by pre-existing theories or values which determine both how objects are constituted in sense experience and why some objects are selected rather than others. Blaikie (1993) and Kelle (1997) draw on the work of the pragmatist philosopher Peirce to describe abduction, retroduction and qualitative induction as alternative ways of conceiving a middle road between induction and deduction, demonstrating a better acceptance of the formative role played by the human mind in structuring observations. These also aim to represent the continual cycling back and forth between theorizing and data production that is characteristic of many scientists' experiences, without abandoning the view that theorizing can be influenced by systematically structured encounters with a real world that is in some sense beyond theory and outside language. Kelle outlines this view:

> With qualitative induction a specific empirical phenomenon is described (or explained) by subsuming it under an already existing category or rule; whereas abductive inference helps to find hitherto unknown concepts or rules on the basis of surprising or anomalous events. Abductive inference combines

in a creative way new and interesting empirical facts with previous theoretical knowledge. Thereby, it often requires the revision of pre-conceptions and theoretical prejudices – assumptions and beliefs have to be abandoned or at least modified. Thereby, the theoretical knowledge of the qualitative researcher does not represent a fully coherent network of explicit propositions from which precisely formulated and empirically testable statements can be deduced. Rather it forms a loosely connected 'heuristic framework' of concepts which helps the researcher focus his or her attention on certain phenomena in the empirical field. (Kelle, 1997: 4.4)

Contrasts between induction and deduction have their parallels in contrasts between realism and idealism. In both cases, the issue concerns the nature of the relationship between the human mind and the world. The idealist position has terrific appeal for those who wish to believe that the world of ideas is paramount, so that if a person's idea of the world changes then so does the world. Idealism suggests that neither God nor sensory experience can guarantee any other foundation for truth, which is solely a creation of the human mind. A solipsistic version of this suggests, further, that the only mind I can know is my own. The problem with this, though, is that it offers no basis for human communication and can therefore give us no grounds on which to construct a common language for scientific statements, let alone judge their quality. If we are all living in individual mind-worlds of our own, there is no possibility of knowing each other, or of jointly producing anything. One may, then, opt for a version of idealism involving conceptions of a collective mind, yet appreciation of cultural diversity makes it hard to sustain a single version of this. Once one is faced with the problem of multiple versions, however, the pitfalls of relativism seem close at hand. One person's version may be as good as any other's; all is relative to the perspective of the beholder.

One way out of this is to argue that relativism can be adopted as an interesting way of thinking, of particular value if one is trying to understand another person or culture (Hacking, 1982). This does not require the thinker to subscribe to relativism on a foundational basis (which is logically impossible in any case), but simply to adopt it as an attitude of mind when, for example, doing fieldwork. This is particularly attractive to researchers wishing to avoid the ethnocentrism that characterized much early anthropology (Asad, 1973; Clifford, 1986). Here the similarities with inductivism are apparent, in encouraging open-mindedness for example. In support of this is the view that relativism is not a foundational problem for practical consciousness (Silverman, 1993); people navigate the world in spite of the existence in it of philosophers who believe that it may have no independent existence, or that we are all living in different worlds. Why should it therefore be a problem for researchers, who do not have to set themselves the task of solving abstract philosophical problems?

The appearance of realist and idealist positions as irreconcilable opposites has led some (for example Altheide and Johnson, 1994) to advocate a quasi-mystical immersion by researchers in an 'empirical world of lived experience' (1994: 489). I am arguing, by contrast, in a spirit similar to Hacking, that philosophical positions can be understood by social researchers as resources for thinking, rather than taken as problems to be solved before research can proceed. In the early days of the qualitative revolution an appeal to philosophy and theory as foundational (for example Filmer et al., 1972) was appropriate, helping to overturn the complacency of those in the dominant quantitative orthodoxy. My conclusion that this is now unhelpful arises from critical engagement with the ideas of later qualitative creation mythologists (for example Lincoln and Guba, 1985), and is usefully applied to idealist, relativist, constructivist and postmodernist perspectives in social research. Yet the idea that philosophical positions can be used as resources can also be applied productively to realist, objectivist and positivist positions. These, too, remain valuable assets for the craft of social research, as long as they do not overdetermine method.

Take the philosophical ideal of objectivity, which has received a considerable hammering from certain quarters. The old version of this involves an appeal to a form of reasoning that is superior to common sense, practical consciousness. This is because, as Schutz has put it, 'By making up his mind to become a scientist, the social scientist has replaced his personal biographical situation by . . . a scientific situation' (1970: 16). Objectivity is the attempt to separate these two biographical modes, so that scientific thought comes to inhabit a realm in which personal values or subjective preferences for particular moral positions or values are kept separate from the interpretation of facts.

The assault on objectivity takes many forms, among which is the philosophical point that these same facts can never be neutrally produced, leading to the view that scientific statements are no more value free than those produced in everyday life. There are also political objections to objectivity: the superior status claimed by science on the basis of value freedom has in practice become implicated in exploitive social relations; the separation of scientific and personal biography is in fact never possible. All of these points, while sensitizing us to the limits and dangers of attempts to provide objectivity, can miss the point that, like relativism, objectivity is a resource that can be used productively as an attitude of mind by social researchers.

Cain and Finch (1981), for example, while adopting a politically sensitive approach to research, advocate this use of objectivity as a valuable resource. Data may always to a degree be constructed through pre-existing values and theories, but procedures employed both to collect and to analyse data can strive to eliminate influence from the personal biographical perspective of the individual researcher. At the very least, the researcher can make explicit to readers what this personal perspective is, so that readers can make their own judgements about the extent to which it has influenced the text (a strategy sometimes referred to as 'reflexivity'). Importantly, to the extent that objectivity is thereby 'done', the text then achieves a life of its own which is indeed 'superior' or at least separate from the biographical circumstances of its production. This is a non-foundationalist approach to objectivity which maintains the contribution that the search for objectivity can make to the quality of research, without implying an unrealistic commitment to fixing knowledge as true for all time.

A middle way is also possible between the extremes of objectivism and relativism, realism and idealism and the deduction/induction dispute. This is founded on a pragmatic acceptance of social research as a collection of craft skills, driven by local, practical concerns, such as the expectations which particular audiences may have. At the same time, pragmatic social researchers can use philosophical and political debates as resources for achieving certain mental attitudes, rather than a set of underlying principles from which all else must flow, creating unnecessary obstacles to flexible and creative inquiry. In this sense, social scientists can be as pragmatic in their scientific thinking as we all are in everyday practical consciousness, as we prefer to bracket out deeper existential or ontological questions in order to get on with life. Of course, fateful moments throw us out of practical consciousness, requiring episodes of philosophical thought. These are often moments where the individual turns to ritual, using symbolic tokens to attach personal biographical concerns to stories of broader scope that are told by members of imagined communities (Seale, 1998b). This is another role for methodological debate among researchers, as episodes of ritualized discussion (for example the work of the creation mythologists) can refresh a mind that may have been dulled by routine application of technique. One can, then, understand such debates as conversations stimulating methodological awareness among researchers, rather than laying foundations for truth.

Subtle realism (Hammersley, 1992b), analytic realism (Altheide and Johnson, 1994), Kantian soft or 'transcendental' idealism and critical realism (Bhaskar, 1989) are all markers of an approach to social research which accepts that, although we always perceive the world from a particular viewpoint, the world acts back on us to constrain the points of view that are possible. The researcher treading this middle way is continually aware of the constructed nature of research, but avoids the wholesale application of constructivism to his or her own practice, which would result in a descent into nihilism. Research, then, constructs 'transitive objects' (Williams and May, 1996: 85), such as the concepts of social science, to represent the real. Knowledge is always mediated by pre-existing ideas and values, whether this is acknowledged by researchers or not. Yet some accounts are more plausible than others, and human communities in practice have created reasonably firm grounds on which plausibility can be judged, whether or not these grounds can be supported in some ultimate sense by means of philosophical reasoning. Judgements about the plausibility of research accounts inevitably involve a temporary subscription to the view that language is referential to a reality outside the text. This is a long way from a simple correspondence theory of truth, but it contains elements of this. Neither does it claim that truth solely lies in the consistency of claims with some other set of claims, though this can legitimately be an element in judging truth claims. It involves opposition to the pure constructivist view that states that there is no possibility of knowing a real world that exists separately from language.

To detach oneself from philosophy in this way, it is sometimes helpful to notice the insecurity of philosophical conceptual divisions. Hammersley (1992b, 1995b) identifies idealist and constructivist tendencies in some versions of positivism. He and Van Maanen (1988) also point out that much qualitative work – early Chicago school studies for example – are stolidly realist and even empiricist in their claims to describe the real lives of hitherto ignored characters. It is also possible to see realist elements in the ideas of certain icons of the constructivist movement. Thus Barrett notes that Foucault 'is not relativist in any way – contradictory to some misreadings of his work – and his statements about epistemology and truth are themselves loaded to the brim with truth claims' (1991: 145). Foucault, in his various historical works (for example 1967, 1977) was in fact concerned to describe how particular regimes of truth emerged in particular sites; the status that his account assumes, however, is fairly conventional. Discourse analysts (for example Yardley, 1997), as research practitioners influenced by the Foucauldian account of discourse, often exhibit an uncomfortable split between a deconstructive attitude towards others' texts and an attempt to make their own texts believable (see also Chapter 2).

There are many examples of pragmatic, subtle realism in the research literature, some of these additionally showing writers drawing on philosophical debate as a resource rather than allowing it to overdetermine their practice. Here are a few, some of which come from surprising sources. Martin Trow in 1957, for example, opposing the view of Becker and Geer (1957) that the truth of interview data could be judged by reference to observational data (a conventional justification for triangulation), makes an argument which for its day is surprising in the degree to which it acknowledges the influence of researchers' mental constructs:

> The fact that social scientists are constantly making inferences from their data does not especially disturb me . . . Our progress in social science will not come through an effort to get 'closer' to the source of data, and thus try to minimize or do away with the process of inference by dissolving it back into data collection and somehow apprehending reality directly. That simply isn't possible. (Trow, 1957: 337)

Bloor, on the other hand (see Chapter 6), chose to apply the realist (and indeed positivist) technique of analytic induction to his data on medical decision making, while recognizing quite explicitly that in doing so he adopts a realist viewpoint as a useful mental device, temporarily bracketing out the wider philosophical issues (though he misrepresents Ayer's true position):

> the question of whether or not inductive thought is possible is, I am aware, philosophically contentious. I would like to sidestep this issue. Let me take up the position that Ayer has described as 'naive realism': it seemed to me that I was thinking inductively (what's good enough for Professor Ayer is good enough for me). (Bloor, 1978: 546)

Armstrong, in other respects associated with Foucauldian constructivism (Armstrong, 1983), used a study of inter-rater reliability to reach a position which is exactly halfway between the two extremes of idealism and realism. He and others (Armstrong et al., 1997) report that six experienced analysts of qualitative data were asked to identify five main themes in a series of depth interviews with sufferers of cystic fibrosis and to mark the transcripts where these occurred. All identified a similar set of concerns as being the first theme: the relative invisibility of genetic disorders perceived by sufferers. On theme two, the perception that the general public was ignorant about genetic disorders, most also agreed, as they did with theme three, the adequacy of health service provision. The fourth theme was tackled by the different analysts in somewhat different ways, while the fifth theme showed considerable divergence. The authors conclude that in spite of debate about the philosophical assumptions that underlie exercises in inter-rater reliability, in practice data do appear to speak in similar ways to different people, though each analyst might have used the themes to construct a differing narrative about the people interviewed.

Finally, methodological writers influenced by the contemporary turn to language in social theory are often to be found making realist points to modify the free play of ideas and preserve a commitment to empirical investigation and reporting:

> to recognize the poetic dimensions of ethnography does not require that one give up facts and accurate accounting for the supposed free play of poetry. 'Poetry' is not limited to romantic or modernist subjectivism: it can be historical, precise, objective. (Clifford and Marcus, 1986: 26)

> There is danger that in rejecting a naive adherence to representation . . . as unproblematic . . . (research) texts lose all sense of reference to the social world, but become overwhelmingly *self*-referential. The problems arise if a particular insight or innovation is taken to extremes. (Atkinson, 1992: 50)

We can assert both the textuality of ethnographic facts and the factuality of ethnographic texts. (Van Maanen, 1995: 22)

The old positivist approach assumed the uncontroversial existence of shared meanings, but ended up imposing meanings that were resisted by many individuals. The alternative qualitative paradigm, investigating how shared meanings are constructed and celebrating their diversity, can lead to a condition of profound uncertainty and distrust. It seems time for qualitative researchers to establish a new consensus around exploring shared meanings for positive purposes, drawing on the strengths of a constructed, imagined research community.

Constructing a research community

At the heart of the advocacy of subtle realism lies the idea of a research community with agreed standards of judgement for the plausibility, credibility and relevance of research reports. Distinguishing claims from evidence, providing the strongest evidence for more important claims and exposing the judgements of the researcher for readers to scrutinize are all methods for addressing the standards applied by a community of critical peers. In arguing for this, Hammersley (1992b) pursues an argument similar to that of Popper (1972), who claimed the authority of an imagined 'third world' of objective knowledge, humanly constructed but, by virtue of being a joint endeavour of a community of scientists, having an existence independent of the biographies of individual scientists. Hammersley is also similar to Popper (1963) in advocating a fallibilistic approach, regarding 'truths' as provisional until there is good reason for contradictory versions to gain support.

Clearly, however, this has the potential to support a rather conservative approach. We can observe that this community of researchers is not in fact an imagined thing of the mind, but a reality. Particular people do concrete things in the world and call them research. These people come from particular cultural backgrounds and bring specific, exclusive prejudices to bear in the standards that they maintain. In practice, the social research community is no different from the rest of society in its divisions of status and power, acting at times to oppress and silence particular groups who are unable to influence the discourses of social research (Harding, 1986). Hammersley's stress on whether findings are consistent with knowledge that is currently accepted in the relevant research community ('plausibility') initially looks rather dubious in this light. Against this, nevertheless, the advocate of subtle realism might point to the role of evidence in testing theories for both credibility and plausibility, which exerts a persuasive force on the research community and can result in the revision of accepted wisdom and the eventual overthrow of dominant paradigms.

The idea of a self-critical research community acting together to pro-duce positive knowledge for the benefit of others retains its appeal for many researchers. The continuing desire to participate in a shared language, constructing and negotiating standards for judging quality, incorporating political and cultural differences always involves an act of trust in the judgements of others, though this can be made easier by the application of certain methodological procedures. These procedures, discussed in more depth in later chapters of this book, are based on this view of a research community existing as a key audience for social researchers concerned about the quality of their efforts. They include, for example, peer debriefing and auditing of research studies described by Lincoln and Guba (1985). Acceptance of the researcher's case can then partly depend on the capacity of the researcher to expose to the reader judgements and methodological decisions made in the course of a research study (Swanborn, 1996).

Political critiques of the research community as an arbiter of quality depend on evidence about how it manages its affairs in practice, as well as value judgements about what counts as a beneficial result. The latter is inevitably going to vary, since the meanings of words like 'democracy' or 'equality' or 'health', which researchers might wish to promote, are not fixed. All that we are usually left with, once individualistic, paranoid and egotistical tendencies have finally played themselves out, are some rather well-worn principles for encouraging cooperative human enter-prises. Thus it can be said that in any joint human enterprise there are likely to be some people who use the activities of the group for harmful purposes and others who play safe by attaching themselves to the centre. Some will stand outside the group in perpetual criticism, which may be experienced as destructive, or be successful in pointing out harmful consequences, whether intended or not. As in any such activity, there are also those who use strategies of compromise and cooperation to engineer creative solutions to problems, using the resources of the group for their own purposes as well as contributing to the efforts of others. This involves a degree of self-confidence and openness to criticism, which can contribute a positive spirit to the community enterprise and result in artifacts of some lasting value. Such are the ways in which a research community might work.

Conclusion

The view that methodological debates about validity are a 'fertile obsession' (Lather, 1993) rather than a route to final settlement of truth claims is an attractive one. It is consistent with my view of the relative autonomy of research practice from philosophical and political debates and from other generalized discussions. In arguing this I am not recommending unreflective research practice. Research is in large part a craft skill, learned through personal experience of doing research and from an appreciation of what is good in other people's research studies. In the last analysis, the quality of research does not depend on unthinking adherence to rules of method, but exposure to methodological debates can help loosen thoughts that are stuck. A good study should reflect underlying methodological awareness, without this awareness being continually made explicit so that it is a screen obscuring the artifact itself.

Like it or not, a research community exists, to which researchers in practice must relate and which possesses various mechanisms of reward and sanction for encouraging good-quality research work, however defined. There are systems of qualification, promotion, grant application and peer appraisal designed, however inadequately they may work in practice, to promote good work. The search for distinction in this community can at times involve a great deal of posturing and self-deception, yet from this imperfect human enterprise there occasionally arise works in which many people place their trust and acknowledge to be good.

This chapter, like the previous one, has reviewed some general ideas that might guide researchers in doing such work. The chapter that follows will examine some versions of quality that are related to the philosophical and political positions that I have discussed, but which are somewhat more grounded in particular research practices.

KEY POINTS

- Research is a craft skill, relatively autonomous from the need to resolve philosophical or epistemological debates, but it can nevertheless draw on these as resources in developing methodological awareness.

- Paradigm warfare, drawing on philosophical discussion to justify divisions between schools of research, potentially obscures the strengths of disfavoured research traditions.

- Subtle realism provides a pragmatic philosophical rationale for researchers locating their practice within a constructively self-critical research community.

4

Guiding Ideals

CONTENTS

> The criteria for judging a good account have never been settled and are changing. (Clifford, 1986: 9)

One response to idealist and constructivist accounts of research practice has been to claim that the imposition of criteria for judging quality is inappropriate (Smith, 1984). If there is no possibility of direct knowledge of the world, if language does not correspond to a stable external reality, if multiple realities can be constructed by different minds, the imposition of criteria is no more than an attempt to gain an artificial consensus. Feyerabend (1975) has outlined the attractions of this anarchist position, arising from an urge to overthrow rationalism in favour of the creative free spirit which his reading of the history of science suggests lies behind most scientific insights. His justification for this position is similar to that of discourse analysts identified in Chapter 2, who identify but paradoxically embrace the relativism that lies at the heart of their practice:

Always remember that the demonstrations and the rhetoric used do not express any 'deep convictions' of mine. They merely show how easy it is to lead people by the nose in a rational way. An anarchist is like an undercover agent who plays the game of Reason in order to undercut the authority of Reason (Truth, Honesty, Justice and so on). (Feyerabend, 1975: 32–3)

One response to anti-criteriology of this sort is to deny that it is a defensible philosophical position (Hammersley, 1992a). Superficially, this may seem like an attempt to call an anarchist to rule, an enterprise that is almost as self-defeating as relativism. Surely, we may feel, exposure to such texts as Feyerabend's, arguing that we should dispense with rigid criteria, can engender a helpful mental attitude for the research practitioner wishing to loosen trapped thoughts. Episodes of anarchic thinking can help to generate creative insights, and it may be that overcontrolled adherence to reporting conventions can stultify the expression of novel ideas.

But other conceptions of scientific practice say that this does not consist of originality and brilliance of insight alone. Rather, the Baconian vision described a cumulative process, so that the findings of each generation of scientists would build on those of the previous generation. The routine, regulated production of scientific knowledge (Salvarsan was discovered when Ehrlich tested the 666th compound for efficacy against syphilis) has its place. Qualitative social research has looked less like this than most other branches of science, although there have been calls for qualitative studies to build on the theoretical insights and findings of previous studies (for example Dingwall and Murray, 1983). Additionally, there are, quite simply, certain errors that novice researchers regularly make if the urge to anarchic thought is the only methodological influence, which can be avoided by attention to experienced advice. A concern with criteria need not suppress creativity or new ideas; the context of discovery can be approached with considerably more freedom than can the context of justification.

I argue, then, for a position of intense methodological awareness, rather than the two extremes of complete anarchy or strict rule following. Anarchic moments have a place within a disciplined context, emphasizing principled, methodic and systematic thinking. Qualitative researchers need to demonstrate an educated awareness of the consequences of particular methodological decisions during a research study, whether they relate to the production of data or the choice of writing style. In this respect I agree with Schwandt (1996), who argues that the term 'criterion' might usefully be replaced with 'guiding ideal' or 'enabling conditions'. Additionally, methodological awareness can be acquired from exposure to almost any intelligent methodological discussions, be they from the likes of Smith or Feyerabend, or texts from the positivist tradition in social research.

Positivist criteria

The positivist tradition contains some rigorous, well-argued and stimulating methodological discussions; such material should be required reading for qualitative researchers wishing to enhance the quality of their practice. These discussions are found under the headings of 'validity' and 'reliability', reflecting the confidence that such writers had in a monolithic, consensus vision of scientific progress, which now lies in tatters. Although these writers thought that they were outlining methods for establishing universal truths, I argue that it is now feasible to read positivist methodology as incorporating a vision of science as a human construction, outlining techniques for persuading particular audiences of truth claims, though often with an openness to falsifiability that resonates with late modern scientific sensibilities. Engagement with positivist methodological discussion can thus be a valuable resource for qualitative social researchers who otherwise believe themselves to be working within different paradigms.

Validity in this tradition refers to nothing less than truth, known through language referring to a stable social reality. A qualitative creation mythologist might have added that language is seen as 'unproblematically' doing this, yet this is not the case. Positivist methodology problematized the status of language, but did so in particular and, to later eyes, exclusive ways. This can be seen in positivist approaches to measurement validity.

Measurement validity

The positivist attempt to measure phenomena is based on a distinction between concepts and indicators, central to what is sometimes called operationalism (Rose, 1982). Leaving aside more purely philosophical discussions of operationalism (where, for example, the concept-indicator distinction makes less sense), Rose exemplifies operationalism in quantitative research practice by showing how a concept (such as 'alienation') may be broken down into its constituent parts (say, powerlessness, self-estrangement, loneliness and so on). This is a descent of the ladder of abstraction, ending in measurement devices (such as questionnaire items) which identify things that indicate the constituent concepts. Thus, a person answering a fixed-choice item asking whether he or she feels lonely often, sometimes or never adds to or subtracts from his or her alienation score. The resultant measure should then stand in an isomorphic relation to reality (Kerlinger, 1964). The success of this strategy depends crucially on widespread agreement about the meaning of linguistic terms, such as 'lonely' or 'often', as well as there being a well-understood connection between responses to a questionnaire, and things that obtain at other points in the respondent's life. It is not hard for qualitative researchers to think of ways in which these conditions might not obtain (Cicourel, 1964), but neither did positivist methodologists find these thoughts hard to have, and they engineered some interesting solutions.

First, there is the deceptively simple point that, on the face of it, some indicators are likely to be better than others for certain purposes. To indicate alienation in the general population, for example, a questionnaire item involving the word 'loneliness' is probably better than one using the word 'alienated', since the former is a word in more common usage which many would feel draws on a consensus of shared meaning based in everyday experiences. In measurement theory, then, the concept of face validity depends on a view that we live in human communities that have constructed a system of linguistic symbols to refer to our common experiences, so that we can talk to each other in meaningful ways about these. Positivist methodology here taps this quite plausible account of language in human social life. Thus Cannell and Kahn explain this commitment:

> In the construction of questions the primary criterion for the choice of language is that the vocabulary and syntax offer the maximum opportunity for complete and accurate communication of ideas between the researcher . . . and the respondent. The language of the question must conform to the vocabulary level of the respondent . . . the choice of language should be made from the shared vocabulary of respondent and researcher. (Cannell and Kahn, 1954: 553)

Further, positivist methodology claimed that it is possible to explore variability in meanings through rigorous piloting of questionnaire items. If we take a group of people who are similar in various respects to the people who are going to answer a question, ask them that question and then ask them to discuss why they answered in particular ways, revealing what the question meant to them, we are better able to choose words that have a common currency. The investigation of shared meaning through such piloting exercises is a basic recommendation of this research genre, sharing much of the spirit of later interpretivist inquiries into subjectivity. But piloting has been very frequently omitted by practitioners of poor-quality survey research, so that researchers end up imposing what Cicourel famously called 'measurement by fiat' (1964), drawing conclusions about meaning and about concept-indicator links without adequate evidence. Because Cicourel was promoting a qualitative alternative in the face of what, in 1964, was a largely unquestioned quantitative orthodoxy, he used this weakness to make some generalized claims about the inadequacies of the positivist approach to measurement:

> Each set of utterances is a time object and cannot be equated with another set of utterances in answer to the same question unless it can be shown or assumed

that the same or similar conditions accompanied each event . . . Standardised questions with fixed-choice answers provide a solution to the problem of meaning by simply avoiding it . . . The meaning of questions with fixed-choice answers . . . is dependent on interpretive rules. (Cicourel, 1964: 101, 108)

However, this ignores more rigorous research practices in relation to meaning, supported in positivist methodological prescriptions, addressing precisely the problems that Cicourel describes. In extensive efforts to explore the effects of question wording, survey researchers have explored and sought to gain shared agreement about the application of interpretive rules. Additionally, elaborate postpositivist strategies for dealing with the issue of meaning have been developed to address these problems, involving a mixing of qualitative and quantitative methods (Brown and Harris, 1978; Marsh, 1982), discussed further in Chapter 9.

The dependence of positivist methodology on a socially constructed consensus about meaning becomes apparent in discussions of content, predictive, concurrent and construct validity (American Psychological Association, 1954; Cronbach and Meehl, 1955). The discussion of face validity above subsumes most of the concerns raised under the heading of content validity. Predictive and concurrent validity share the same logic: if the results of a measure are agreed by some other measure taken at the same time (concurrent) or in the future (predictive), then the validity of the measure under question is enhanced. Put crudely, if we invent a questionnaire measuring, say, pupils' academic ability, we would expect it to correlate with teachers' assessments (concurrent) or with exam success (predictive). Fundamentally, such exercises are an attempt to persuade readers that particular measures tap shared meanings. This is obviously an uncertain business, as the criteria chosen to validate a measure may themselves be invalid. Exam success, for example, is felt by many people to be no great indicator of academic ability. However, through repeated testing of measures against a variety of criteria which, for the relevant audiences, plausibly indicate the underlying concept, a general sense of confidence that a measure is indicating its intended object may be sustained. One can argue, of course, that such efforts impose meanings that emanate from the researcher's lifeworld, rather than being based in an exploration of the meanings that people construct in interaction, or that these meanings are oppressive to particular groups. These objections make evident the rather fragile nature of the consensus attempted by these techniques, as well as exposing the political insensitivity that can result from such an approach if it is followed thoughtlessly.

A further elaboration of this line of thought about measurement validity is to be found in the concept of construct validity (Cronbach and Meehl, 1955). This was designed to address the problem of there being inadequate criteria to establish the predictive and concurrent validity of certain measures. If a researcher wants to test whether a new measure indicates the required object, construct validity involves an investigation of its behaviour in relation to a variety of other measures, which are believed on theoretical or other grounds to be related to it in particular ways. For example, if it is believed (on the basis, say, of previous studies) that social class influences educational achievement and one wishes to create a new measure of educational achievement, one would have doubts about the validity of this new measure if no correlation were found between it and a measure of social class. Clearly, this line of reasoning depends on several tenuous assumptions: are we right to believe that a relationship between the two constructs ought to be found? Is our measure of class valid?

At first sight, this seems to double the number of problems apparent in the more simple techniques of predictive and concurrent validity. Yet construct validity does not depend on just one test; in fact, confidence in the construct validity of a measure builds up over time, across a number of research studies in which the behaviour of a measure is investigated in relation to a great variety of theoretical propositions so that, as it were, it becomes like a new linguistic term, gaining general currency in the research community because it has been shown to be robust across a number of testing situations. The idea that measures exist in a 'nomological network' is designed to convey this spirit. Later techniques such as Campbell and Fiske's (1959) notion of convergent and discriminant validity continue the self-critical but fertile obsession with validity that was the hallmark of high-quality positivist approaches to measurement.

Like the exploration of the effects of question wording, all of these more formal techniques for establishing measurement validity reflect an active commitment to establishing and testing validity claims which can serve as an example of rigour to researchers working within other traditions. They were invented because positivist researchers wanted to show that they had questioned the basis for researchers' claims about the social world in the most thorough manner they could imagine. For qualitative creation mythologists to claim that this reflects advocacy of blind, rule-following behaviour seems contrary to the spirit of the classic texts in which these ideas were originally expressed, where they are presented, rather, as a part of argumentative endeavour dependent in the last analysis on human judgements about the credibility and plausibility of claims.

The qualitative tradition has at times drawn on such positivist discussions. Triangulation (see Chapter 5) is a technique advocated by Denzin (1970) for validating observational data which originated from Campbell and Fiske's (1959) ideas about converging and diverging measures. LeCompte and Goetz (1982) point out that the advantages claimed by participant observers under the heading of 'naturalism', whereby lengthy immersion in the field is said to enhance the accuracy of a research account, are directly parallel to positivist researchers' claims for measurement validity. However, such parallels are less often drawn by qualitative researchers occupying the idealist, constructivist or postmodern positions described in Chapter 2, who feel distanced from the apparently naive realist assumptions that lie behind the advocacy of triangulation and naturalism.

Internal validity

The discussion of internal and external validity initiated by Campbell and Stanley (1966, see also Cook and Campbell, 1979) marked an explicit commitment to Popperian fallibilism by quantitatively oriented social researchers. Internal validity concerns the extent to which causal propositions are supported in a study of a particular setting. The researcher's task is to consider and try to overcome a variety of 'threats' to these propositions. For example, in trying to show that X had caused Y to vary, could the researcher be sure that some other factor had not intervened? Campbell's (1969) paper 'Reforms as experiments' traced through some of the nine threats listed in his earlier paper in relation to the particular example of a police crackdown on speeding drivers in Connecticut in 1960. The governor of Connecticut had triumphantly pointed to the accident statistics, showing a reduction in the year after the crackdown and claiming this as a causal effect of the police initiative. Yet there are clearly a number of threats to such a conclusion. The weather or car design could have improved; drivers could have become more careful in response to the high accident statistics; a look at the accident statistics over a long period of time revealed the year before the crackdown to have been an unusually high 'blip' in any case, which would in all likelihood have been followed by a regression to the mean. Each of these points illustrates a different one of the nine threats, which are themselves of general relevance to researchers facing particular research problems, helping them to generate objections that might be made to their conclusions.

Various things might be done by researchers concerned to sustain causal arguments, such as creating a control group, or statistically controlling for confounding variables (see for example Rosenberg, 1968). The point for our purposes, however, is that Campbell's discussion showed validity in the quantitative tradition to be a matter which could never be finally settled by the application of some technical procedure. This perception of the significance of Campbell and Stanley's work is shared by Mishler:

> Campbell and Stanley [understood] that validity assessments are not assured by following procedures but depend on investigators' judgements of the relative importance of the different 'threats' . . . [N]o general, abstract rules can be provided for assessing overall levels of validity . . . These evaluations [of threats] depend, irremediably, on the whole range of linguistic practices, social

norms and contexts, assumptions and traditions that the rules had been designed to eliminate . . . 'rules' for proper research are not universally applicable [and] are modified by pragmatic considerations. (Mishler, 1990: 418)

In fact, the use of the 'threats' requires an imaginative effort by the researcher to enter the minds of potential critics. They are devices for encouraging methodological awareness, as well as setting up an internal dialogue that ensures that research findings are presented to their public in as good order as possible, so that external dialogue with real critics, from within or outside some scientific community, can begin at a higher level than might otherwise be the case.

Causality in qualitative research Before leaving the topic of internal validity, we should address the issue of the desirability of causal analysis in qualitative research. I do not think the argument that fallibilism is promoted by Campbell and Stanley's scheme depends on a resolution of this issue, but it is one that has made for some mental blocks when qualitative researchers try to learn from their quantitative counterparts. The argument here seems to rest on a view that causal analysis represents a deterministic view of human action. Some early versions of the qualitative alternative emphasized the active aspects of human social life, as is seen in the choice of the word 'actor' rather than 'subject' to describe people, and terms such as 'action theory' (Filmer et al., 1972) to describe melds of symbolic interactionism, ethnomethodology and phenomenology proposed as frameworks that could inform the practice of qualitative social research. For the most part, the qualitative alternative has been presented as a vehicle for answering questions about *what* is happening in a particular setting (as in naturalistic ethnographic approaches) or *how* realities of everyday life are accomplished (the ethnomethodological and discourse analytic projects). The issue of *why* things happen in the way they do is more rarely addressed as an explicit project, though a place for this in qualitative research is increasingly argued as the threatening shadow of determinism appears to have receded (Silverman, 1993; Gubrium and Holstein, 1997).

One can argue that many 'what' and 'how' accounts contain hidden assumptions about why things happen. In qualitative research it is often the case that examples of causal thinking impinge on the text, sometimes in spite of the writer's avowed rejection of more explicit causal analysis. Take, for example, a more or less randomly chosen sentence from Geertz's (1993, first published 1973) famous account of Balinese cockfights, which analysed these events as cultural scripts, explicitly rejecting ideas about the causal functions of ritual:

> Jealousy is as much a part of Bali as poise, envy as grace, brutality as charm; but without the cockfight the Balinese would have a much less certain understanding of them, which is, presumably, why they value it so highly. (1993: 447)

Here, the cockfight is proposed as a cause of better self-understanding; this in turn is proposed as a cause of the high value placed on cockfights. Take another couple of sentences, again more or less at random, from another classic ethnography:

> The general region from which the immigrant came was also important in the organization of Cornerville life. The North Italians, who had greater economic and educational opportunities, always looked down upon the southerners, and the Sicilians occupied the lowest position of all. (Whyte, 1981: xvii)

Whyte, in this passage of 'description', is proposing a causal relationship between region of origin and Cornerville pecking order. Further, he is suggesting that economic and educational differences between Italian regions are antecedent variables. Once one is sensitized to the idea of cause, it becomes evident that in ordinary language it is difficult to speak a thought without some notion of cause entering the picture. Qualitative researchers, it seems, are no different in this respect. However, sustained attention to causal analysis is rare in qualitative research (although see Fielding and Fielding, 1986; Hammersley, 1992b for discussions of examples of this in the research literature).

Writers generally depend on carrying readers along with their sense of having been close to the field, so that causal asides of the sort exemplified above are accepted as the product of the successful application of *verstehen*. Rationalizations for this (seen, for example, in LeCompte and Goetz, 1982) depend on the argument that immersion in a setting facilitates direct apprehension of causal relationships, which quantitative researchers can only infer. (This does not, though, address the philosophical objection that causal reasoning is the product of mind rather than sense data.) Qualitative work provides a different form of data, and may indeed make it possible to trawl through a variety of candidates for constant conjuncture, but the logical operations necessary to infer cause, as outlined by writers such as Campbell and Stanley, in terms of assessing threats (such as mistaking an association for a cause) remain the means by which the validity of causal arguments are sustained. The search for negative instances or deviant cases that falsify emerging causal propositions should here be central to qualitative researchers' efforts.

External validity

External validity, which Campbell and Stanley (1966) proposed in conjunction with their discussion of internal validity, concerns the extent to which causal propositions are likely to hold true in other settings, an aspect of the generalizability of findings. Extremist accounts (as we saw in Chapter 2) designate the act of generalizing from one setting to another as, potentially, one of despotism (Lyotard, 1993). More moderate views acknowledge the difficulties that are inherent in applying the lessons of one setting to another, but maintain that there is little point in conducting research studies whose significance cannot extend beyond their local context. Again, the fallibilistic approach of postpositivist methodology has much to offer on this front, Campbell and Stanley pointing out various threats to generalizability in the same spirit as their threats to internal validity. There have also been attempts to apply this logic to qualitative research (LeCompte and Goetz, 1982). There have also been attempts to substitute qualitative alternatives to the rationale for empirical generalization that underlies the notion of external validity (for example Mitchell, 1983; see Chapter 8). Hammersley (1991) questions the very basis for the distinction between internal and external validity, suggesting that if a relationship is proposed as causal this is also a proposition of general relevance. If X is shown to cause Y in a particular context, it must do so in other similar contexts. The issue of whether the proposition applies in another setting then becomes one of replication.

It seems necessary to construct a rationale for generalization which addresses the distinction between a nomothetic natural science, concerned with laws and generalizations, and an ideographic social science that would focus solely on descriptions and understanding of specific events. We need explanations for events based on case studies which might have a broader resonance for people seeking to understand other, similar events. In this respect, thick descriptions of particular settings are appropriate, giving sufficient detail about the context of events so that readers can vicariously experience what it was like to be in the setting. Readers can then conduct their own 'thought experiment' in seeking to transfer the lessons learned from this setting encountered through a research text. Adopting this pragmatic approach to generalizability allows one to apply the fallibilistic approach of Campbell and Stanley, as issues of the empirical typicality of the setting are then brought into play, and can be addressed. Specific techniques for doing this, as well as a more extended discussion of theoretical generalization, are given in Chapter 8.

Reliability and replicability

Qualitative researchers, working within the tradition that is often characterized as 'positivist', pursue conceptions of reliability and replicability that are rooted in a realist view of a single external reality knowable through language. Exercises in inter-rater reliability, for example, seek to ensure that different observers make the same interpretations of particular objects. Multiple differing interpretations are unacceptable, as it is assumed that a single valid version is the goal of research. Replication of studies (itself rarely seen in qualitative social research) is designed to establish corroborating evidence for findings whose truth status is in doubt. If different studies, employing the same methodology, discover the same thing, then faith in the account as a true one is enhanced.

This simple logic is turned on its head once the constructivist view of multiple realities is adopted, whereby attempts at reliability or replicability are regarded as exercises to promote an artificial consensus. Different people, so this argument goes, are bound to have different accounts of the world; the qualitative researcher's role is perhaps no more than to facilitate the expression of these accounts. However, the status of even these accounts is then brought into question, as clearly they are themselves no more than a selection of possible versions. Once again, we seem to be caught between extreme poles.

The position of subtle realism is helpful in guiding us to a middle way on these topics. LeCompte and Goetz (1982), for example, show how this might be done. (Their ideas are discussed more fully in Chapter 10.) These authors distinguish between 'internal' and 'external' reliability. The first of these is the type of reliability addressed in the study by Armstrong et al., (1997), where different researchers were asked to identify themes in transcripts of some qualitative interviews, described in Chapter 3. Certain core themes were identified by all, but some themes were less shared. As Armstrong argues, since things have not been resolved at the ontological level, exercises in inter-rater reliability (or, by extension, replicability) have their place in generating trust and exposing a research text to some testing circumstances. Even if we do not finally adjudicate between competing accounts, it helps to see a little more of the accounts that are kept relatively silent in a text, and this is the function served by reporting the results of reliability and replication exercises. Internal reliability, then, refers to the extent to which different researchers identify similar constructs.

External reliability is altogether more demanding, referring to the overall replication of research findings in re-study exercises. These have proved particularly difficult for qualitative researchers but, as I argue in Chapter 10, these difficulties often arise from particular practical problems associated with qualitative research that are not shared by quantitative researchers, rather than insuperable philosophical problems. Replication exercises can be helpful, like those involving internal reliability, in helping readers perceive social settings or problems from a variety of different points of view. The expectation of complete replication is a somewhat unrealistic demand.

Interpretivist criteriology

I have started to introduce the modifications proposed by qualitative researchers to positivist criteria of validity and reliability. LeCompte and Goetz (1982) argue that a concern with validity and reliability is one that should be shared by all social researchers, claiming indeed a unity of the social scientific endeavour, although they point out that the specific techniques for establishing validity and reliability are somewhat different in, say, an ethnography compared with an experiment. Subsequent interpretivist criteriologists have progressively moved away from the assumption of shared underlying commitments, leading to conceptions of 'validity' and 'reliability' that are very far removed from positivist and even realist perspectives. Yet the urge to generate criteria for judging good-quality studies seems irrepressible, partly due to the requirement that qualitative and quantitative social researchers impress the worth of their efforts on sceptical audiences, such as research funding bodies. In the second half of this chapter, I shall review various interpretivist attempts at criteriology, before considering the place of these in constructivist or postmodern conceptions of the research process.

A sometimes bewildering variety of new concepts confronts any reviewer of this field of methodological writing. For example, Altheide and Johnson's (1994) review of interpretivist positions on validity identifies 'successor validity, catalytic validity, interrogated validity, transgressive validity, imperial validity, simulacra/ironic validity, situated validity, and voluptuous validity' (1994: 488). A glance at Kirk and Miller (1986), however, shows Altheide and Johnson to have omitted from this list 'apparent', 'instrumental' and 'theoretical' validity. Additionally, Kirk and Miller demonstrate the ease with which new forms of reliability can be conceptualized, dividing this in their scheme into the 'quixotic', the 'diachronic' and the 'synchronic'.

Proliferation of concepts characterizes the field and, I believe, reflects the difficulties which qualitative methodologists have had in making their ideas 'stick'. This is in marked contrast to parallel authors in the quantitative tradition, where a consensus around certain ideas (for example the distinction between validity and reliability, or between internal and external validity) has apparently been more easy to sustain. In qualitative research the project of criteriology experiences particular contradictions because of the difficulty in regulating and constraining an endeavour whose guiding philosophy often stresses creativity, exploration, conceptual flexibility and a freedom of spirit. A review of all the concepts that have been proposed by qualitative criteriologists would, therefore, be a major enterprise with dubious value; rather, I propose to focus on two authors, Lincoln and Guba, whose work has been particularly influential, as well as demonstrating changes over time that reflect the growth in constructivist and postmodernist influences.

Lincoln and Guba (1985) argue that establishing the trustworthiness of a research report lies at the heart of issues conventionally discussed as validity and reliability. This is a perception which I share. They claim that four questions have, from within the conventional paradigm, been asked of research reports:

(1) *Truth value*: How can one establish confidence in the 'truth' of the findings of a particular inquiry for the subjects (respondents) with which and the context in which the inquiry was carried out?

(2) *Applicability*: How can one determine the extent to which the findings of a particular inquiry have applicability in other contexts or with other subjects (respondents)?

(3) *Consistency*: How can one determine whether the findings of an inquiry would be repeated if the inquiry were replicated with the same (or similar) subjects (respondents) in the same (or similar) context?

(4) *Neutrality*: How can one establish the degree to which the findings of an inquiry are determined by the subjects (respondents) and conditions of the inquiry and not by the biases, motivations, interests, or perspectives of the inquirer? (Lincoln and Guba, 1985: 290).

Further, they are of the opinion that 'The criteria that have evolved in response to these questions are termed "internal validity," "external validity," "reliability," and "objectivity"' (1985: 290). While broadly accurate, we should note that the first of these stretches the original meaning of internal validity, which in the quantitative paradigm reflects preoccupations with establishing the adequacy of causal statements, rather than the broader issues raised in Lincoln and Guba's first item. This may reflect their claim, made earlier in their book, that the 'naturalistic paradigm' involves a rejection of the view that cause and effect can be distinguished.

They then go on to criticize attempts by qualitative methodologists such as LeCompte and Goetz (1982) who wish to sustain a commitment to these 'conventional' criteria, since they depend on axioms such as 'naive realism and linear causality' (1985: 293). For example, 'truth value' assumes a 'single tangible reality that an investigation is intended to unearth and display' (1985: 294), whereas the naturalistic researcher makes 'the assumption of multiple constructed realities' (1985: 295). 'Applicability' depends on generalizing from a sample to a population, on the untested assumption that the 'receiving' population is similar to that of the 'sending' sample; the naturalistic inquirer, on the other hand, would claim the potential uniqueness of *every* local context, requiring empirical study of both sending and receiving contexts for applicability to be established. They are similarly critical of the other two 'conventional' criteria. Consistency, they say, depends on naive realist assumptions; neutrality depends on an artificial separation of values from inquiry.

Instead, Lincoln and Guba propose their own four-point criterion list (see Table 4.1) for naturalistic inquirers. First, 'credibility' should replace 'truth value'. Through prolonged engagement in the field, persistent observation and triangulation exercises, as well as exposure of the research report to criticism by a disinterested peer reviewer and a search for negative instances that challenge emerging hypotheses and demand their reformulation, credibility is built up. Additionally, Lincoln and Guba advise researchers to 'earmark' a portion of data to be excluded from the main analysis, returned to later once analysis has been done in order to check the applicability of concepts. But 'the most crucial

TABLE 4.1 Lincoln and Guba's translation of terms

Conventional inquiry	Naturalistic inquiry
Truth value (Internal validity)	Credibility
Applicability (External validity)	Transferability
Consistency (Reliability)	Dependability
Neutrality (Objectivity)	Confirmability

technique for establishing credibility' (1985: 314) is through 'member checks', showing materials such as interview transcripts and research reports to the people on whom the research has been done, so that they can indicate their agreement or disagreement with the way in which the researcher has represented them.

Secondly 'transferability' should, they say, replace 'applicability' or external validity as conventionally conceived. This is achieved not through random sampling and probabilistic reasoning, but by providing a detailed, rich description of the setting studied, so that readers are given sufficient information to be able to judge the applicability of findings to other settings which they know.

To replace consistency, or reliability as conventionally conceived, Lincoln and Guba propose 'dependability', which can be achieved by a procedure that they call 'auditing'. A fuller account of this is given in Chapters 10 and 11, but suffice to say that it involves 'auditors' in examining an 'audit trail' for adequacy. This consists of the researchers' documentation of data, methods and decisions made during a project, as well as its end product. Auditing is also useful in establishing 'confirmability', Lincoln and Guba's fourth criterion, designed to replace the conventional criterion of neutrality or objectivity. Auditing is an exercise in reflexivity, which involves the provision of a methodologically self-critical account of how the research was done, and can also involve triangulation exercises. The authors conclude by pointing out that trustworthiness is always negotiable and open ended, not being a matter of final proof whereby readers are compelled to accept an account. This, they claim, 'stands in marked contrast to that of conventional inquiry' which claims to be 'utterly unassailable' (1985: 329) once relevant procedures have been carried out. This overdrawn contrast clearly suits the creation mythologizing in which Lincoln and Guba participate.

Constructivist 'criteria'

Many of the procedures outlined by Lincoln and Guba are useful for qualitative researchers to know about and to incorporate into their work where relevant; they will be discussed in greater detail in the chapters that follow. But it is evident that their criteria depend on a contradictory philosophical position, since their belief in 'multiple constructed realities' (1985: 294) rather than a 'single tangible reality' (1985: 295), which lies at the heart of the constructivist paradigm, is not consistent with the idea that criteria for judging the trustworthiness of an account are possible. Relativism does not sit well with attempts to establish truth, even if the term is placed in inverted commas.

Acknowledging this problem, in later work (Guba and Lincoln, 1989, 1994) they give an account of a fifth criterion, 'authenticity', which they believe is consistent with the relativist view that research accounts do no more than represent a sophisticated but temporary consensus of views about what is to be considered true. In detailing the components of authenticity, Guba and Lincoln reveal a sympathy for political conceptions of the role of research which was already evident in their earlier commitment to the value of member checking (a procedure whose strengths and considerable limitations are discussed further in Chapter 5). Authenticity, they say, is demonstrated if researchers can show that they have represented a range of different realities ('fairness'). Research should also help members to develop 'more sophisticated' understandings of the phenomenon being studied ('ontological authenticity'), to be shown to have helped members appreciate the viewpoints of people other than themselves ('educative authenticity'), to have stimulated some form of action ('catalytic authenticity') and to have empowered members to act ('tactical authenticity'). Of course, the view that fairness, sophistication, mutual understanding and empowerment are generally desirable is itself a value-laden position which a Foucauldian deconstructionist might very well enjoy taking apart. It represents a pulling back from the relativist abyss. As they say, 'The issue of quality criteria in constructivism is . . . not well resolved, and further critique is needed' (1994: 114).

These authors, along with many others in the qualitative social research community, have travelled on a path beginning with a rejection of 'positivist' criteria and the substitution of interpretivist alternatives. Dissatisfied with the limitations of these, constructivism has been embraced, introducing an element of relativism. Political versions of the value of research have then been imported to save facing the logical implications of relativism, which of course ends in a nihilistic vision and abandonment of the research enterprise. This is a path which, roughly speaking, Denzin too has trodden (Denzin, 1970, 1989, 1997) and which is reflected (as we saw in Chapter 1) in his finale to the *Handbook of Qualitative Research* edited by himself and Lincoln (Denzin and Lincoln, 1994), in which the two authors (Lincoln and Denzin, 1994) describe qualitative research as having reached a 'fifth moment' in its development. Postmodernist and constructivist influences, they argue, have resulted in a 'crisis of legitimation', but the central commitment of qualitative researchers remains:

This center lies in the humanistic commitment of the qualitative researcher to study the world always from the perspective of the interacting individual. From this simple commitment flow the liberal and radical politics of qualitative research. Action, feminist, clinical, constructivist, ethnic, critical and cultural studies researchers are all united on this point. They all share the belief that a politics of liberation must always begin with the perspectives, desires, and dreams of those individuals and groups who have been oppressed by the larger ideological, economic, and political forces of a society, or a historical moment. (1994: 575)

As a criterion for judging the quality of research, it is immediately obvious that this is open to dispute (see also Chapter 2 of this book). It is not difficult to imagine a well-conducted study that enabled people in positions of power to achieve their aims. The vision of society as no more than a system inhabited by oppressors and oppressed also seems naive (see also Hammersley, 1995b). Research can at times be more relevant to direct political projects, at others less relevant, but its quality is an issue somewhat independent of this.

Permissive criteria

Criteriology is, at root, an impossible project if it is intended to reflect an internally logical line of argument that simultaneously reconciles philosophical and political positions with the great variety of research practices which people may wish to pursue. The challenge appears to be to construct some general account of what one might hope to find in a good study that is, on the one hand, open enough to include this variety, and, on the other hand, not so loosely specified as to be of no value in providing guidance.

Although the urge to categorize leads Guba and Lincoln (1994) to place Hammersley in a 'postpositivist' camp and it is one which he himself appears to embrace (see Hammersley, 1992a), I believe that this is an author whose attempt at criteriology achieves a good balance between directiveness and permissiveness. His position is, for the most part, a pragmatic compromise between various extremes, outlined originally in relation to ethnography, but capable of application to other forms of qualitative social research.

Hammersley (1992b) draws on quantitative accounts of validity and reliability as well as interpretivist criteriology, while rejecting aspects of both to produce a reformulation. This involves just two broad areas of concern: truth and relevance. Regarding the first, where the underlying philosophical justification is that of subtle realism (see Chapter 3), he argues that there are three important considerations when assessing arguments based on research. First, the reader should assess whether the claims made are plausible given existing knowledge about a topic. Where an argument varies from existing knowledge, the researcher should be concerned to provide particularly strong evidence in support of claims. This relates to the second point, which demands that core arguments require better supporting evidence than peripheral ones. Hammersley's third point relates to his analysis of the different sorts of claims which it is possible to make: definitions, descriptions, explanations and theories require different levels of evidence. What is required to support a theory, for example, is more demanding than what is required to support a description.

On the issue of relevance, we have already seen in Chapter 2 that Hammersley departs from the full-scale political commitment that Lincoln and Denzin have found themselves advocating. Broadly speaking, Hammersley is in favour of research that is value relevant, but not research that is value laden. Additionally, the value relevance of research may not be immediately obvious to researchers or readers, so this criterion is of lesser importance than the issue of truth.

Here, then, we have 'criteria' that are at a fairly generalized level, capable of incorporating a wide variety of research practices. Yet, one can argue, they give only limited guidance to researchers seeking to learn procedures and methods that will help improve the quality of their work. For this, we must turn to more detailed specifications. Here again, it is possible to formulate a list in a way that allows for considerable interpretive freedom, incorporating various research practices done with a variety of philosophical commitments. Reproduced in Appendix A is an example of one such attempt to specify criteria.

The list in the appendix reflects its origins as an attempt to provide guidelines for the referees of journal articles considering final reports of research for publication. It therefore places considerable emphasis on the adequacy of reporting. There are many other such 'checklist' approaches to criteriology. They proliferate, for example, in the field of health studies: Cobb and Hagemaster, 1987; Secker et al., 1995; Fitzpatrick and Boulton, 1996. The important point to note about the one reproduced in the appendix is that the wording of the criteria leaves many things open to human judgement, while providing a helpful checklist of things which a self-critical researcher, or sceptical reader, might look for in a report. They are questions that might reasonably be asked of conventional ethnography or interview studies, or of discourse and conversation analyses, or action research projects. One might argue that they fail to include criteria of political relevance, but they ask questions that politically committed researchers might nevertheless wish to address, and a number of items reflect concern to establish the viewpoint of people on whom research is done, if not actively to promote what is thought to be their interests. Additionally, and this is important in relation to the general argument of this book, they reflect an underlying fallibilism that involves continual openness to alternative viewpoints and the obligation to consider research reports as always being provisional versions of the social world.

Conclusion

In this chapter I have reviewed positivist criteria for judging the quality of research studies, and have considered the phenomenon of interpretivist criteriology, which merges with political and constructivist attempts to specify quality. Positivist criteria are more fallibilistic than qualitative creation mythologists often like to claim, and I have argued that exposure to any well thought-out methodological discussion, from whatever tradition, is likely to increase a desirable aspect of research practice: methodological awareness. If there is one thing that produces poor studies, it is a researcher who is blind to the methodological consequences of research decisions.

Positivist discussion of measurement validity, internal and external validity, reliability and replicability is a necessary starting point if methodological awareness is to be developed. Although qualitative creation mythologists have contributed to a perception that these arose within a different research tradition, recognition of the artificial and somewhat rhetorical character of the qualitative–quantitative divide ought to lead qualitative researchers to read the classic texts of quantitative methodology. Interpretivist criteriology appears ultimately to founder on the contradictions inherent in constructivist and postmodernist influences, whereby the belief in multiple realities is inconsistent with attempts to judge the adequacy of singular versions. Yet on the way to this apparent impasse, as we see in the work of Lincoln and Guba, some interesting and useful procedures have been described which, from whatever philosophical perspective one is working, are likely to assist researchers seeking creatively for ways of enhancing the quality of particular projects. Finally, with Hammersley's criteria and the checklist approach that followed, we saw that it is possible to propose criteria for improving quality, if this is done in a relatively open and permissive way, that preserves the enterprise of qualitative research as a creative and exploratory enterprise that cannot be contained by the strict imposition of methodological rules.

The chapters in Part II of this book are loosely structured around the themes identified in this chapter, which are themselves related to some of the more philosophical considerations raised in Chapters 1–3. Initially, the relationship between claims and evidence will be considered, particularly from the point of view of early qualitative methodologists whose approach to this was not dissimilar from their quantitative 'positivist' counterparts. A discussion of grounded theory moves us forward to the techniques that appeared at around the time that qualitative criteriology was gaining pace, and an account of the use of numbers in qualitative research allows consideration of generalizability. The discussion of reliability and replicability that follows allows greater exposure to constructivist criticisms of earlier positions on this. The final chapters involve exploration of the implications of constructivism and postmodernism for research writing practices. In the second part of the book extensive use is made of examples from particular research projects, in furtherance of the view that the 'answers' to many of the methodological puzzles that arise when considering the issue of quality in qualitative research lie in research practice itself.

KEY POINTS

- The quality of research is not automatically determined by the imposition of generalized quality criteria, but such schemes can help sensitize researchers to the issues that a particular project may need to address.

- Positivist methodological criteria appear naive if linked to a crude realist agenda, yet discussions of validity and reliability within this tradition offer a helpful starting point for qualitative researchers wishing to develop methodological awareness. More directly relevant help is available in the writings of interpretivist and constructivist 'criteriologists'.

- The trustworthiness of research accounts can be enhanced by attention to their plausibility, given existing knowledge, and their credibility, based on supporting findings with adequate evidence for central claims.

Part II

RESEARCH PRACTICE

5

Converging on a Point?

CONTENTS

The subtle realist position outlined by Hammersley (1992b) and dis-cussed in the first part of this book has at its core a concern with the relationship between claims and evidence. If a research account makes claims about the nature of the social realm that it seeks to describe or explain, then readers should expect to find evidence in support of these claims. Good evidence is particularly necessary for key claims and on these rest the status of a research account as providing more sophis-ticated understandings than are available to individuals in the study settings. Seeking for evidence within a fallibilistic framework that at no point claims ultimate truth, but regards claims as always subject to possible revision by new evidence, should be a central preoccupation for qualitative researchers, and a number of techniques have been proposed in order to achieve this.

In this chapter and the next I shall review these under four headings: triangulation, member validation, analytic induction and the search for negative instances. Although these, for the most part, were initially developed within traditional frameworks (for example crude realist or empiricist frameworks) that many might claim are inconsistent with subsequent paradigms (for example constructivism), I argue that they are nevertheless capable of improving the quality of contemporary research practice. This is because they involve systematic attempts to test out researchers' assumptions and arguments, so that these become both more convincing and at the same time more inclusive of a variety of perspectives.

The first two of these techniques have in common, at least when they were originally proposed, a desire to converge on a single version of reality by gathering more than one perspective on this. Triangulation attempts this quite explicitly; member validation does so by prioritizing the perspective of the people whose lives researchers attempt to describe, so that it also has the potential for incorporation in more political versions of research. Yet, as I will show, the crudely realist assumptions of both techniques do not preclude their use within rather different epistemologies.

Triangulation

The idea of triangulation derives from discussions of measurement validity by quantitative methodologists. Campbell and Fiske (1959) argued that 'In contrast with the *single operationalism* now dominant in psychology, we are advocating . . . a *methodological triangulation*' (1959: 101; their italics) and proceeded to outline their ideas for the convergent and discriminant validation of measurement instruments. Subsequently, Webb et al. (1966) used the idea to advocate multiple operationalism, employing several methods at once so that the biases of any one method might be cancelled out by those of others. Its use in qualitative research, however, was first advocated and then popularized by Denzin (1970), whose textbook has been through several editions (1978, 1989) in which the original concept has been modified. Other textbook definitions at times contain distant echoes of this background in the quantitative research tradition, as where Hammersley and Atkinson describe it as a method whereby 'links between concepts and indicators are checked by recourse to other indicators' (1983: 199). The term itself is designed to evoke an analogy with surveying or navigation, in which people discover their position on a map by taking bearings on two landmarks, lines from which will intersect at the observer's position. If only one landmark were taken, the observer would only know that they were situated somewhere along a line. Triangulation used in this way assumes a single fixed reality that can be known objectively through the use of multiple methods of social research (Blaikie, 1991).

Denzin's (1978) version outlines four types of triangulation. Data triangulation involves using diverse sources of data, so that one seeks out instances of a phenomenon in several different settings, at different points in time or space. Richer descriptions of phenomena then result. Investigator triangulation involves team research; with multiple observers in the field, engaging in continuing discussion of their points of difference and similarity, personal biases can be reduced. Theory triangulation suggests that researchers approach data with several hypotheses in mind, to see how each fares in relation to the data. The fourth is methodological triangulation, and is the most widely understood and applied approach. This, for Denzin, ideally involves a 'between-method' approach, which can take several forms but, classically, might be illustrated by a combination of ethnographic observation with interviews. Additionally, methodological triangulation is frequently cited as a rationale for mixing qualitative and quantitative methods in a study.

It will be helpful here to see some examples of methodological triangulation before turning to some of the criticisms that have been made of this approach. Rossman and Wilson (1994) describe a project to investigate the impact on school organization of state authorities' introduction of minimum competency tests in schools. This combined qualitative interviews with school teachers and other educationists in 12 school districts with a postal questionnaire of a larger sample. Analysis of the questionnaire results suggested that curricular adjustments were more common in school districts where teachers reported that their relationship with state educational authorities was 'positive'. The qualitative interviews sought and found corroboration of this. Thus, for example, in a district where no changes occurred in the curriculum, a local administrator said: 'The state has become someone we have to beat rather than a partner to work with' (1994: 320–1). The authors go on to say:

> On the other extreme was a district that accepted the state's increased role in monitoring educational outcomes and worked hard to find creative instructional techniques to improve student performance. The qualitative descriptions of how these two districts responded to the state mandate corroborated and offered convergence to the quantitative findings. (1994: 321)

Another example is from West (1990) who found, in qualitative interviews with parents of children with epilepsy, a predominantly gloomy account, in which they depicted themselves as struggling to cope, with little help from doctors. This, he found, was at variance with another study (Voysey, 1975) which found parents presenting glowing accounts of adjustment and positive acceptance in line with 'official' versions of how they ought to feel. Voysey's study was ethnomethodological, showing how accounts in interviews constituted the parents as responsible family members. West's concern, however, was to assess the validity of these accounts as a resource for discovering what was really going on in families, and in particular their interactions with doctors. Put crudely, he wanted to know whether he or Voysey was right, so he observed parents in medical consultations to see if they looked as bad as they had been depicted in his interviews. He found doctors using euphemisms, evading parents' concerns, being reluctant to discuss the side effects of drugs which they wanted children to take, and otherwise demonstrating a lack of helpfulness that was similar to that which had been depicted in interviews. West concludes that the observational study revealed 'a picture which in major details corresponds with the accounts parents provided of their experience of medical care' (1990: 1237). Voysey, he suggests, elicited 'public' accounts because she visited the families only once for the interview, and thus was perceived as a representative of officialdom, whereas he spent time getting to know his respondents and was therefore trusted with more authentic accounts.

The capacity of observation to validate interview data, acting as a benchmark of truth in this respect, was claimed by Becker and Geer (1957) some time before Denzin's popularization of the term triangulation. Becker's methodological writings (Becker, 1970a) are peppered with such points, which are broadly designed to show the naturalistic advantage of ethnography. Thus he says that observers must collect many types of evidence before concluding that a thing is true (1970b), and that ethnographers doing fieldwork are able to make numerous observations across different times and places and can cross-check these so that it is hard for respondents to lie (1970c). The anthropologists Kirk and Miller (1986) endorse the idea that the length of time spent in the field, involving as it must a continual reality testing of theories about what is going on, is a guarantee of the validity of fieldwork evidence. This is largely, they say, because multiple points of view are adopted by the observer over a period of time, so that a phenomenon is described from many different angles. Glaser and Strauss make similar points: 'theory generated from just one kind of data never fits, or works as well, as theory generated from diverse slices of data on the same category' (1967: 68).

All of these authors demonstrate that Denzin's advocacy of triangulation, whether of method or of data, was always likely to strike a chord with qualitative researchers working in a tradition based on a somewhat crude realist and empiricist perspective, largely relying on naturalistic observational methods to guarantee authenticity. Yet even within this tradition there were seeds of disquiet, which have implications for the advocacy of methodological triangulation, especially if based on observation as a benchmark. This can be seen in Trow's (1957) response to Becker and Geer's arguments in favour of observation as the basis for adjudicating the truth status of interview accounts. Trow notes that the privacy of the interview situation can allow people to say things they would not reveal in the natural settings of everyday interaction, where significant others might hear and disapprove. Additionally, a more complex version of the relation between methods and truth, though one that is still crudely realist in its assumptions, was presented by Zelditch (1962). He suggested that observation could be considered as the benchmark if the aim were to describe particular incidents, but interviews might be regarded as better if the aim were to describe norms of conduct. Sample surveys would be the benchmark if the frequency with which a phenomenon occurs were to be described.

Criticisms of triangulation

Denzin assured the popularity of the concept in part by crystallizing existing tendencies, in part by addressing growing epistemological doubts about the security of naturalistic methods. Thus, in his preamble to the topic in the 1978 edition of his book on method, he states:

> the human-personalistic . . . element intrudes into every step of the scientific process . . . the values, definitions and ideologies of each scientist significantly determine the translation of rules of method into the scientific process . . . The act of doing research is an act of symbolic interaction . . . complete agreement between methods and their users can never be expected . . . Triangulation, or the use of multiple methods, is a plan of action that will raise sociologists above the personalistic biases that stem from single methodologies. (1978: 294)

One can say, then, that Denzin envisaged triangulation as a technique to help the researcher replace a personal biographical perspective with a scientific one that was, in some sense, above or outside the personal, thus giving it wider currency in a scientific community. Yet he did not see this as a particularly secure place nor, perhaps, was it desirable to imagine that a complete separation between the personal and the scientific was possible. Research itself was 'an act of symbolic interaction' and might therefore be treated for some purposes as indistinct from other interventions in the world, such as those made by ordinary members. This position was to inform his later advocacy of postmodern ethnography (Denzin, 1988a, 1988b, 1994, 1997).

Although retrospectively we might perceive these subtleties in Denzin's work, it is easy to see that some researchers might read triangulation as a means to guarantee validity. Indeed, triangulation appears cast in this role on the lists of criteriologists (Fitzpatrick and Boulton, 1996; LeCompte and Goetz, 1982). Criticisms of the technique are therefore helpful in promoting a better awareness of its strengths and limitations, though they are often cast in extremist terms that suggest too complete a rejection of the method.

The ethnomethodological critique Cicourel's ethnomethodological position (1964, 1974) offers the most extreme vantage point from which to
view triangulation. His own critique of the term is typically paradoxical,
in that he proceeds by enthusiastically advocating the advantages of
'indefinite triangulation' (1974: 124). This rhetorical ploy (which I think
could usefully be read now as a joke, though this was probably not
Cicourel's intention) proceeds by showing that what he means by this is
in fact the precise antithesis to the consensus on truth sought in conventional triangulation. His illustration comes from his own practice:

> The triangulation procedure varies with the research problem. When gather-
> ing information on language acquisition in the home setting we left a tape
> recorder playing for about one hour during lunch. A transcription of the tape
> was done by a typist who had been instructed to render a verbatim record.
> Then the transcript, the first version of this scene, was read by the mother
> while she listened to the tape; her comments produced another version of the
> interaction. The typist was next asked to listen again to the tape and to
> describe what she thought was 'going on', correcting her original transcript as
> she deemed necessary. In this elaboration and correction a different version of
> the scene was always produced. My phonetic transcription of the tapes
> created still another version . . . The reader could now say that we should
> have simply combined the different versions to produce the 'best' one
> possible, but the point is that different versions could have been produced
> indefinitely by simply hiring different typists and providing the mother with
> different transcripts. (1974: 124)

This is an amusing little demonstration of the constructivist objection to
realist tendencies in discussions of triangulation. For the sake of the
mothers and typists involved, I hope that this is fictional; although this
would matter very little for the point Cicourel is trying to make, which
is that we are all, including social researchers, engaged in story telling
at all times.

More serious-minded critics claim that triangulation only makes sense
from within a positivist framework. Blaikie (1991), for example, who
fails to see any joke in Cicourel – 'But the question arises as to why it
should be called triangulation' (1991: 130) – argues that the idea 'has no
relevance for genuine interpretivists and ethnomethodologists' (1991:
131) since it involves subscription to inappropriate ontological and
epistemological positions. He is referring here to the realist versus
idealist debate covered in Chapter 3. Readers will recall that I argued
there, as if against Blaikie, that all-or-nothing commitment to a philosophical position was unwise for practising social researchers. At a
more concrete level, Blaikie proceeds with his critique by means of an
example, taken from Jick (1979).

Jick gathered accounts from interviewees about the levels of stress
and anxiety they experienced as employees as a result of organizational
mergers. He sought to validate these self reports by seeing whether

people who visited an archive library, containing memoranda about the organization, were also those who reported high stress levels. He hypothesized that people who made such visits would be doing so out of anxiety, seeking perhaps to reconcile current news reports about mergers with statements made by the organization in the past. Unhappily, Jick found no correlation, and speculated that this might be due to anxious employees being also people of low educational level, relying on verbal reports rather than library visits to assess organizational plans. Blaikie comments that such speculation 'is like trying to navigate in a fog' (1991: 126).

Jick clearly did not know what was going on in these visits to the library, and would have benefited from investigating the phenomenon of visiting more closely before constructing a theory about its meaning by fiat, and then a triangulation strategy on top of this. But let us imagine that he had interviewed a sample of library visitors, found that their reasons for the visit were as predicted, and then presented data to show a correlation between self-reported anxiety and frequency of visits. It is not hard to imagine this as the outcome of a more rigorously designed strategy of triangulation, which would enhance confidence in the reliability of self-reported anxiety levels. Furthermore, it is not the case that triangulation must always lead to convergence and confirmation. As part of a fallibilistic, reality-testing approach to research it can lead to new theories. Thus Jick makes his new speculation about levels of education, a theory that might be tested by further data analysis or collection; Blaikie himself offers an alternative theory: that the better-educated trade unionists or political activists were the people who were visiting the library the most. Here is another explanation to test, which might improve understanding of what is going on, rather than being a reason to ditch triangulation exercises.

One can, then, mount an argument, as does Silverman (1993), claiming that triangulation exercises can deepen understanding as a part of some fallibilistic approach to fieldwork, but are themselves no guarantee of validity. The urge to adjudicate between accounts, so that some are judged true and others false, Silverman claims, should be resisted, the preference being for an approach that takes an interest in how different accounts (or patterns in data) are produced. This, however, is a rather narrow vision for social research, confining it to investigating the production of meaning in local settings, disallowing the analysis of language as referential in a more or less accurate way to events outside the setting in which the language is produced. If adjudication between accounts is disallowed, there is no reason for us to take notice of research accounts except in so far as we might investigate how they were produced, if we feel so inclined. The similarities between Silverman's broadly ethnomethodological position and postmodern relativism are apparent, stemming from an excessive bracketing out of the possibility of realist accounting.

Let us imagine what West (1990) would have been required to do under Silverman's regime. West could have gathered the two sorts of 'accounts' which he did, but would have been disallowed from adjudicating whether the gloomy accounts he was given, or the optimistic accounts given to Voysey, accurately described what happened in the consultations. Instead, he would have analysed how the impression of gloominess was achieved. Compulsory bracketing of the issue of whether gloomy accounts were true denies the analyst the chance to treat respondents as competent reporters of experience (although in other respects ethnomethodologists such as Silverman regard members as more skilful than many sociologists). West's study of consultations might then have concentrated on how evasiveness was accomplished by doctors. One could say that the better data for his purposes were his observations, since he wanted to see whether doctors avoided parents' concerns, but this would have been an uneconomical means of discovering this. Interviews are widely used in social research because respondents can act as the eyes and ears of researchers; interviewees can recall and summarize a wide range of observations in seconds, which would take weeks and months of observational work to achieve. They can also speak about things that cannot be observed. Triangulation exercises can then help in adjudicating the accuracy of interview accounts by increasing sensitivity to the variable relationship between an account and the reality to which it refers.

The philosophical critique Another objection to triangulation goes as follows: even if all the different methods employed converge on the same thing, apparently agreeing with each other, how can we know that they are correct (Bloor, 1997)? Perhaps some hitherto unthought-of method would reveal something different. In fact, this problem is analogous to that of induction: how can we reliably reason on the evidence of past experience that the sun will rise tomorrow? Logically, of course, we cannot. Taken at this level, the objection to triangulation as a validation exercise is also unanswerable. Yet we operate in the world all the time on the basis of what it is plausible to believe and it will do us little good to assume that the sun will not rise tomorrow. Similarly, we can argue that triangulation exercises help to build plausibility for a particular account as part of a fallibilistic research strategy in which evidence is sought for central claims.

To demonstrate this property of triangulation, I shall take an example of a discourse analytic study (Gill, 1993) and show how the plausibility of the study's conclusions might have been assisted by method triangulation. Gill's study aimed to show how five radio disc jockeys (DJs) and programme controllers explained the lack of female DJs in radio. 'In this way we should learn something about how this inequality is perpetuated' (1993: 75). The analysis focuses on listing the different arguments offered by interviewees to explain and, by implication, justify the exclusion of women. Thus, there was the argument that women do not apply for such jobs, perhaps because they had no interest in such work, or because they perceived that it was a 'man's world' in radio. Then there was the view that audiences had a negative reaction to female presenters, citing the existence of research studies to support this, used by the speaker to distance himself from this view. Another argument contained the view that women did not have the necessary skills; another that women's voices were too shrill and therefore lacked authority.

Gill would clearly like to see more women DJs, and cleverly points out the self-deceptions and contradictions contained in these accounts. Such a study will have been economical on time, involving just five interviews, and is useful in showing the range of arguments available to people in the setting. Let us imagine, however, a study which begins from the position of adjudicating the truth status of the interviewees' accounts. Such a study would be far more extensive and time consuming than Gill's, but would ultimately give a deeper understanding of the social processes at work in radio employment practices. For example, records of applications could be examined to establish the proportion of female applicants; interviews with women could have helped to establish the degree of support for claims about audience reactions to the voices of women presenters, or perceptions that radio is male dominated; an analysis of skills required by DJs and a comparison of these with their distribution in the population might have been attempted.

Additionally, the case is sometimes made that triangulation can serve purposes other than the validation of one account. Cain and Finch (1981), for example, argue that multiplication of methods can help to deepen understanding of different aspects of an issue. Dingwall (1997b) takes the view that triangulation offers a way of explaining how accounts and actions in one setting are influenced or constrained by those in another. Silverman (1993) also has no problem with this use of triangulation, saying that this can help 'to address the *situated work* of accounts' rather than 'using one account to undercut the other' (1993: 158). This postpositivist version of triangulation gets away from the idea of convergence on a fixed point (though I have argued, contra these authors, that this too is worth retaining for some purposes).

Applying this to Gill's study, one can imagine a participant observation study to see the extent to which the views presented by DJs and programme controllers in the public context of one-off research interviews were also used in the daily settings encountered by radio workers, perhaps focusing in particular on job interviews. Such a study might reveal other accounts, perhaps less publicly acceptable. This, though, would require a considerable enterprise of fieldwork and trust building, which was probably not feasible within Gill's original research brief.

Triangulation, then, if used with due caution, can enhance the credibility of a research account by providing an additional way of generating evidence in support of key claims. One does not have to regard it as an 'indefinite' process of infinite regress if it is accepted that the sort of knowledge constructed by social researchers is always provisional, but is nevertheless attempting to convince a sceptical audience.

Member validation

As we saw in Chapter 4, member validation is proposed by Lincoln and Guba (1985) as 'the most crucial technique for establishing credibility' (1985: 314). In that chapter we saw also that the commitment of these two writers later developed into a more politicized conception of the goals of social research, as being appropriately devoted to emancipation. However, the origins of the desire to check the accuracy of research accounts with respondents, as well as other techniques for member validation, lie in the more conventional aim of presenting a convincing account, using the views of the people on whom research has been done as a check that the account has correctly incorporated differing perspectives. In this respect, it is consistent with an attempt to converge on a single version, though as we shall see this need not be its only use.

A variety of ways has been proposed for using the reactions of those whom a researcher has studied to validate a research account (see Table 5.1). Bloor (1997) lists three main types of member validation:

first, the validation of the researcher's taxonomies by the attempted prediction of members' descriptions in the field . . .; secondly, the validation of the researcher's analysis by the demonstrated ability of the researcher to 'pass' as a member . . .; and, thirdly, the validation of the researcher's analysis by asking collectivity members to judge the adequacy of the researcher's analysis. (1997: 41)

Frake (1961, 1964) outlined the first of these, in an anthropological study, in which he also advised that researchers might present hypothetical situations to actors and compare their reactions to these with those predicted by the social scientific account under test. Goodenough (1964) advocated the second, arguing that a society's culture was what one needed to know in order to operate within it as a successful member. The adequacy of anthropological accounts of cultures, then, could be established if a person behaving in the way outlined in the account generated the predicted responses. Fielding (1993) has proposed a similar argument in a sociological context.

TABLE 5.1 Types of member validation

---

1 Use researchers' concepts to predict members' descriptions.
2 Show that the researcher's account can lead to successful 'passing' as a member.
3 Ask members to judge the adequacy of the researcher's account:
  (a) Strong version (e.g. members evaluate the final research report);
  (b) Weak version (e.g. members comment on the accuracy of some interim document, such as an interview transcript).
4 Regard successful action research as a form of member validation.

Apart from practical difficulties in carrying out validation exercises of the type outlined in the first two of these types, there are flaws in any argument for viewing them as unproblematic guarantees of validity, as is noted by Emerson (1981). Members can allow some quite deviant behaviour without overtly taking exception. Also, the second depends on a view of human behaviour as being strictly rule governed, whereas in fact there is a considerable creative and unpredictable component in most settings. These criticisms, however, appear to envisage a rather unthinking application of the procedures.

The first two methods, and the second in particular, are consistent with Schutz's (1970; first published 1953) 'postulate of adequacy', which stated that:

> each term in . . . a scientific model of human action must be constructed in such a way that a human act performed within the real world by an individual actor as indicated by the typical construct would be understandable to the actor himself as well as to his fellow-men in terms of commonsense interpretation of everyday life. (1970: 17)

This was proposed because Schutz regarded social science as a collection of second-order constructs, built on the first-order constructs that actors used in everyday life. Nevertheless, it is important not to equate the postulate of adequacy with the view that lay people should be able to understand the linguistic terms of social science (however desirable this might be on other grounds). It is clear that Schutz did not expect actors to understand the meaning of second-order constructs, only to understand the actions that they describe, if performed in an everyday context. Giddens (1979), therefore, is mistaken in his criticism of the postulate of adequacy when, having quoted the extract from Schutz reproduced above, he states:

> [Schutz] seems . . . to assert that concepts of social science can only be declared to be adequate in so far as they can be translated in principle into the everyday language of lay actors. If this is in fact what Schutz means, it is hardly a defensible viewpoint. In what sense does the notion of 'liquidity preference' have to be capable of translation into the ordinary language concepts of actors engaged in economic activities? . . . [consider] the behaviour of

very small children, to which we might very well want to apply technical terminologies of action; if the children in question are too young to have mastered more than rudimentary linguistic skills, there would obviously be no possibility of testing the adequacy of such terminologies in terms of a translation process. (1979: 246–7)

Although Giddens' point is inadequate as a critique of Schutz, it nevertheless alerts us to one of the problems inherent in the third procedure outlined by Bloor, that of seeking agreement from actors as to the truth of a researcher's account of their world. This is taken up, for example, by Glaser and Strauss (1967) and Turner (1981), who argue that a good grounded theory should be accessible and understandable to lay people. Clearly, though, it is unreasonable to expect members easily to understand social scientific concepts that are not part of their everyday reasoning. Thus we can see the general outlines of a debate about the status of member validation in theory that has also been played out by researchers in practice.

It is the third type listed by Bloor that has received the most attention from practising researchers and it should be noted immediately that there are weak and strong versions of this. A 'weak' version, for example, might consist of asking an interviewee to comment on the accuracy of an interview transcript. A slightly stronger version is to show people the researcher's description of them or their setting or an event within it, to be used later in more complex analysis. This was done, for example, in my own study of equal opportunities practices in schools, where case studies of the practices in individual schools were written up and presented to teachers for comments as to their accuracy, before being incorporated in a final report that sought to summarize the state of play in schools as a whole (Pratt et al., 1982). Rosaldo (1993) also reports an instance of such limited checking, though in this case he checks an explanation rather than a description, from his anthropological fieldwork in the Philippines. Wanting to know what compelled his Ilongot informants to episodes of head hunting, he:

> explored exchange theory, perhaps because it had informed so many classic ethnographies. One day in 1974, I explained the anthropologist's exchange model to an older Ilongot man named Insan. What did he think, I asked, of the idea that headhunting resulted from the way that one death (the beheaded victim's) canceled another (the next of kin). He looked puzzled, so I went on to say that the victim of a beheading was exchanged for the death of one's own kin, thereby balancing the books, so to speak. Insan reflected a moment and replied that he imagined somebody could think such a thing (a safe bet, since I just had), but that he and other Ilongots did not think any such thing. (1993: 3–4)

But the strongest version of this type of member validation is presentation of the full report to members followed by monitoring of their responses. A number of reports exist on such exercises, showing both advantages and disadvantages, and will be summarized below.

Before doing this, however, we can note that Bloor's list is somewhat limited. Member validation can be understood as the research community seeking communication with (and perhaps reassurance from) members of the wider community with whom (or on whom) research is done. As such, it can be equated with the interpretivist moral commitment to understanding others' perspectives, as well as political commitments to democratic research practice, and, ultimately, can be seen as a precursor to postmodern conceptions of the researcher as the facilitator of polyvocality. Once we enter this territory, we depart considerably from any crude realist assumptions that might originally have been involved in member validation. Indeed, the technique now begins to appear less concerned with convergence on a single version, more with voicing multiple perspectives. Thus for Rosaldo, member checking is a sign of a more wide-ranging restructuring of the relationship between researchers and informants. In place of the confident pronouncement by anthropologists of the truths of 'objectivism – absolute, universal and timeless' (1993: 21) are the 'truths of case studies that are embedded in local contexts'. Here, he argues, it is crucial for social analysis to 'grapple with the realization that its objects of analysis are also analyzing subjects who critically interrogate ethnographers – their writings, their ethics, and their politics' (1993: 21).

Taken broadly, one can say also, in accord with Guba and Lincoln's (1989, 1994) conception of 'authenticity' (see Chapter 4), that strategies of action research are instances of member validation. Indeed, the pragmatic criterion of being able to pass as a member (the second type of member validation listed by Bloor) is rather similar to the Marxist view that the test of a theory lies in whether it promotes political change. Further, the similarity of objections both to member validation and to action research helps to emphasize what both share. Just as Emerson's objection to member validation is that deviant behaviour is often allowed to pass and so cannot be a test of the theory that has infomed this behaviour, so it has been said in objection to the Marxist view of action research that theories can be false but still be used to promote political change in the direction they predict (Hammersley, 1995b).

It is thus clear that a variety of strategies have been described for this form of validation, together with some debate about whether such exercises are feasible or desirable in theory. Examination of how such exercises work out in practice, however, is of use in assessing advantages and disadvantages. I will focus on examples of a particular form of member validation, that of showing research accounts to members, because it is the method that is most often reported in the literature and researchers' experiences of this are relevant to other forms.

Examples of member validation

Psychiatric emergency teams   Emerson and Pollner (1988) describe what happened when, in their study of psychiatric emergency teams (PET teams), they showed their report to team members. This was a 'strong' version of this form of member validation (see Table 5.1). The report showed, for example, that an informal method of categorizing referrals for the teams operated, whereby some work was categorized as 'shit work' if it involved coercing clients or an inability to help clients therapeutically. They also found that although there was a general principle of treating the most serious cases first, at other times team members treated people who were nearby or whose problems looked easy to solve. The reports therefore did not contain abstract or difficult social scientific concepts whose meaning would be obscure to members.

The authors list five problems which they encountered. The first concerned problems of 'textual reference', involving members not having read key parts of the report, or having misunderstood the intention of authors. Thus 'we sometimes gained assent to what we never felt we had asserted' (1988: 191); the opposite of this also occurred, where they felt criticized for things they had not said. In response to a 'denunciation' of the research report by one member, another more supportive member objected: 'The paper you are quoting from has absolutely nothing to do with this presentation. It's a totally different subject' (1988: 191). These feelings may be familiar to anyone who has received and disagreed with another person's comments on their written work.

The second problem concerned 'ambiguity of response'. It was not always easy to know whether a comment indicated agreement or disagreement with the report. For example, one member said that the report of how PET teams prioritized their referrals gave him a sense of unease: 'I get a sense that we were crazy in the way we made our decisions . . . There is no coherent or integrated knowledge – no consistency to the way we make decisions' (1988: 192). It is hard to know whether this constitutes agreement with the text, or whether it is some further reflection on the messages of the text. Additionally, in group discussion the comments became responses to other members' responses, thus becoming very confused as to the precise reference point in the text.

Thirdly, the 'relational context' influenced responses. By this, the authors mean that people with whom they were friendly appeared to be less willing to criticize their report. One person, with whom they had a one-to-one session before presenting their results to a group of PET team members, appeared to them to have been reassuring about the basic accuracy of their report. He referred to points at which he had been uncomfortable with the accounts, but had mitigated these by referring to his occasional inability to get a 'good grasp' of the text, thus leaving open the possibility that his feelings had been due to this rather than a firm sense of disagreement. On reflection, after the more critical group meeting, the researchers felt that they should have listened harder to these expressions of discomfort by their friend.

The fourth point is called the 'transactional context' by Emerson and Pollner. By this, they refer to the sorts of questions being asked by the researchers. In their eagerness to elicit the degree of agreement, their formulations were sometimes couched in such extreme terms that made it hard for their respondents to disagree: '[Was there] any place where you had a sense like, were those guys here? Or were they just dreaming it up?' (1988: 193). Clearly, this is asking for a perception of vast discrepancy and is unlikely to get much from someone who is determined to be friendly.

Last, the authors refer to the 'organizational context' in which member validation exercises occur. It may be politically dangerous for members to agree with a report, as indeed it was for some PET team members whose funding might have been threatened by a report indicating inconsistent or officially inappropriate decision-making procedures. 'Specifically, it became problematic as to whether a response is a reaction to the account per se, or an action designed to facilitate or inhibit organizational consequences' (1988: 194).

Because of these features of member validation exercises, Emerson and Pollner argue that it is naive to imagine that they constitute moments of truth, where all is finally revealed. Instead, they are occasions for the production of more text, which itself must be interpreted using powers of human judgement and knowledge of how the 'validation' accounts were produced. In this sense, the authors have sympathy for a view of member validation as 'indefinite triangulation' (Cicourel, 1974: 124) described earlier in this chapter. Yet the relativist spiral described by Cicourel is also unattractive to these authors, who argue that a great deal can be learned from exercises like the one they report. Such exercises are themselves occasions 'in which local practices and dynamics are elaborated and even intensified . . . [they] allow a setting to reveal further aspects of its organization' (1988: 195). Thus they learned more about the contested nature of PET in the exercise, since the political context in which funding decisions are made was brought to the fore by the prospect of publication of the research report. During previous fieldwork this had not been so obvious.

Surgeons' decision making In a study of decision making by surgeons, Bloor (1978) employed what I have called a weak version of member validation, by showing surgeons reports of the criteria that each of them appeared to be using when deciding whether or not a child should have a routine operation. This is 'weaker' (perhaps 'less ambitious' would be a better term) than the exercise reported by Emerson and Pollner because the final report, summarizing and commenting on all surgeons' practices, was not in question. The document was an intermediate one, summarizing a series of observations. One might argue, then, that a better level of agreement might be expected by members than in the study of PET teams, as the text was descriptive of a precise and limited phenomenon in which the reader was the key actor.

Perhaps reflecting this lower level of abstraction, there were occasions where a gratifying level of agreement was recorded, expressed here by one of the doctors:

> I think it was a fair assessment, a fair summary. It put into words many of the things we do which are more second nature I think. You know, I think you've done quite well summarizing (laughs) me: some of these things. 'Well', I think, 'you know that *is* right', when I see it written down. And when you're doing it, well I suppose you have these things in the back of your mind but . . . (1978: 549)

This comment effectively captures the capacity of a research account to shift people from practical everyday consciousness, in which routines are followed without reflection using tacit knowledge, to discursive consciousness, whereby the basis of everyday routine appears as an object of thought and possibly reflection. It may be the moment of 'truth' that might precede the state of 'ontological authenticity' to which Guba and Lincoln (1989, 1994) refer. Other surgeons, however, made more or less minor points that were satisfied by revisions after a full discussion. For example, a disagreement was resolved when a generalization that Bloor had made was modified to take account of a rare type of patient, who had not appeared during the period of observation and whose treatment varied from the general decision rule for that surgeon. This appeared to mark the validation exercise as a success, leading to greater confidence in the findings than had been found possible by Emerson and Pollner who, on reflection, might be seen as having been more ambitious, both in presenting a full final report and in doing this in a politically sensitive group setting.

Nevertheless, Bloor noted problems. One was the simple fact that he suspected that some surgeons had taken only a superficial interest in the exercise, so their apparent agreement might have been based on a lack of concern with accuracy. This is markedly different from the highly charged context of the PET team exercise. Secondly, Bloor comments in similar ethnomethodological spirit to Emerson and Pollner that he has no way of knowing whether the member validation interview was itself valid. A later exercise that Bloor conducted revealed other features of member validation, more in tune with Emerson and Pollner's experience: members changed their minds, for example, or brought their own agendas to the interpretations they made of text. The results of this exercise, and others he has done, have led Bloor to conclude for both member validation and triangulation that their uncritical application makes:

one unwarranted assumption; namely, that the techniques of validation can be treated as unproblematically generated, whereas in practice . . . all validating techniques are social products, constituted through particular and variable methodological processes. (1997: 48–9)

This places Bloor firmly in the postpositivist camp, whereby such techniques are used as potential aids to deeper or more multi-layered understanding, rather than final adjudications of truth.

The annihilation of place: member validation as rhetoric   A further example of member validation in a charged political context comes from Porteous's (1988) study of the gradual destruction of a village community by the siting of a large industrial complex nearby. This time, however, the example reveals a relatively insensitive application of the technique, which is used to try to generate authority for the researchers' account rather than to deepen understanding. Porteous's research report focuses on the villagers' plight, and documents their efforts to present reasoned arguments about justice and human rights to a local council apparently determined to promote the interests of industrialists at the expense of residents. Porteous confesses that the village is his birthplace and states:

> I am naturally distressed that a place that has great meaning for me is being erased . . . and I feel with some passion that ordinary people deserve, at least, an opportunity to tell their stories. (1988: 77)

He continues by outlining the purpose of showing his research report to villagers, councillors and industrialists, which was 'to counteract this deviation from academic detachment' (1988: 77). Later, he says that such a validation exercise is 'one of the ethical imperatives of qualitative social research' (1988: 85). Here, then, is a highly politicized research account, putting forward the views of an 'underdog' community to be adjudicated as true or false in a conventional sense, with none of the 'bracketing out' of the discourse or conversation analyst.

The result was perhaps predictable. None of the officials replied, beyond some who sent a note acknowledging receipt. The villagers, however, responded quickly and enthusiastically:

> the way you have been able to explain the feelings which we *all* have regarding the unfeeling and uninterested way we have all been treated . . . 'they' call it progress and creating jobs but it is so wicked to have everything cut and dried for themselves and . . . we are not given an opportunity to state our feelings . . . I wonder myself, how, if the positions were reversed, would they feel? . . . in every context of the word . . . they have murdered our village. (1988: 86)

Porteous comments: 'It is such comments which make the difficult work of committed qualitative research worthwhile' (1988: 86).

It is difficult to agree with Porteous that the validation exercise has improved his 'academic detachment'. The depiction of his work as 'difficult' is also questionable. Generating accounts that do not challenge the common-sense evaluations of respondents is one of the easier tasks in social research, seeming an obvious thing to do to people new to social research and emotionally satisfying if you happen to identify with respondents' perspectives. The exercise confirms that his account is in line with the views of villagers, but does little to reassure readers that councillors' and industrialists' views have received an equally sympathetic treatment. This is an example that shows the abandonment of a fallibilistic and self-critical approach, using the technique of member validation in a flawed way to boost the authority of the writer.

Member validation and discourse analysis The relevance of member validation for discourse analysis is discussed in Yardley (1997), who observes that such validation is a technique better suited to research devoted to 'phenomenological or advocacy approaches in which the investigator works with the participants to understand and describe their view of the world' (1997: 40). She suggests that participants are unlikely to appreciate or concur with, or even understand, a deconstruction of their rhetorical ploys that is typical in discourse analysis. Inevitably, the researcher will stand as 'expert' in relation to the person whose speech is analysed.

Nevertheless, one can see the potential use of showing a discourse analytic account to members by imagining that Gill (1993; see also my discussion earlier in this chapter) had shown her analysis of disc jockeys' rhetorical strategies for justifying the exclusion of women from radio broadcasting to the DJs themselves. One of Gill's points regarded the self-contradictory nature of the accounts she gathered. Thus a DJ argued at one point that audiences were regretfully 'chauvinist' in their attitudes. Employment practices had, unfortunately, to take account of this. At another point, the DJ argued:

> As I said to you before (.) people are sensitive to voice (.) they pick up a lot in the voice. They can see it as exuding friendliness, sarcasm, anginess or whatever and if it happens to be (.) and if a woman's voice sounds grating or high (.) shrill, then that will switch them off. (1993: 86)

Gill comments that while the earlier account had been critical of the audience, here listeners are characterized as 'perfectly reasonable' (1993: 87) in disliking 'shrill' voices because they are 'sensitive', a desirable quality. Gill, as a discourse analyst, claims to 'bracket out' the issue of whether an account truthfully describes its object. The contradiction is noteworthy as part of an analysis of rhetoric. However, members normally do not do this and would no doubt experience Gill's analysis as a charge against their moral probity and rationality. Such a contradiction would be experienced as a failing in need of remedial action, and any member validation exercise could be expected to produce further repair work, perhaps using new discursive strategies to make good the 'damage' produced by Gill's account. This might reveal hitherto unnoticed strategies, so that member 'validation' could be understood as an opportunity for further data gathering in a spirit similar to Cicourel's outline of indefinite triangulation. Clearly, it would be impossible to use the technique to judge the truthfulness of the discourse analysis, though this might be a useful approach in applying the weak sense of member validation where the accuracy of transcripts might be checked by members.

I should not leave this discussion of the validation of discourse analysis without noting Potter and Wetherell's (1987) persuasive account of criteria for validating this form of work, which concern the coherence and fruitfulness of the analysis as well as its capacity to account for new problems. However, these are not related to the issue of member validation so are not discussed here.

Conversation analysis as self-validating　Finally, we can turn to a method-ology that some have argued is self-validating (in the sense that it requires no separate validation exercise) because the mode of analysis focuses on demonstrably true interpretations of members' reasoning. Conversation analysis (CA) is not, of course, originally conceived as a validation exercise, but concerns about validity have been addressed in a novel fashion through this research method. Potter and Wetherell (1987) present an early outline of these ideas in their description of validation through proving 'participants' orientation' (1987: 170), but a fuller discussion is contained in Peräkylä (1997), who points out that CA is built on the principle that a speaker's turn displays a particular interpretation of the previous speaker's turn. As Sacks put it:

> while understandings of other turn's talk are displayed to co-participants, they are available as well to professional analysts, who are thereby afforded a proof criterion . . . for the analysis of what a turn's talk is occupied with. (Sacks et al., 1974: 729)

Member validation is thus an ongoing feature of conversation. Unlike approaches to language that emphasize the variability of meanings for words, CA takes words to have precise and singular meanings in particular contexts. In this sense, CA allows for a highly 'positivist' reading of social reality, emphasizing singular, fixed interpretations that can be adjudicated as either true or false. This varies considerably from other aspects of CA, which are avowedly anti-positivist in rejecting the possibility of adjudicating between members' accounts, as we saw earlier (Silverman, 1989). Peräkylä gives the example of A calling B on the telephone. A comments that B's line has been busy. The conversation analyst (here Pomerantz, 1980) comments that this is a 'fishing device' design to discover more about B's previous phone call. B obliges by telling A that it was her father's wife who called before, and that when she calls B always talks for a long time as her father's wife can afford to pay for long calls. This news from B is seen as validating the interpretation of A's comment about the busy line as a 'fishing device'.

This line of argument is quite persuasive, and also supports the value of showing data in full so that the basis for researchers' interpretations is fully documented for the reader. I argue in Chapter 10 that this is a particular strength of CA. But let us imagine that we told A that this was our interpretation of her utterance and that she disagreed, saying perhaps that it was her way of explaining why she had taken so long to call B, about which she felt somewhat guilty. The fact that the utterance in practice performed as a fishing device to someone reading a transcript at a later date was purely incidental and unintended. CA in fact sets its face against exploring speakers' intentions (Silverman, 1997b, 1998b), so this application of more conventional 'member validation' would be deemed illegitimate. But it does show that even the absolutist interpretive standards of CA might be modified by the fallibilistic approach implied by more conventional member validation exercises.

Conclusion

Member validation offers a method for testing researchers' claims by gathering new evidence. If approached with a readiness to revise claims in the light of what is revealed, rather than an attempt to confirm mutual value positions between researcher and researched, it can enhance the credibility of a research report, giving it greater sophistication and scope. The examples reviewed show a variety of uses, some of which are more successful in their aims than others. In the PET team example, we see an ambitious attempt at validating a full research account in a highly charged political context, leading to some problems but also occasional new insights. A less ambitious attempt (or 'weak version' – see Table 5.1) is demonstrated by Bloor's study, where significant inaccuracies of data recording and analysis were corrected by the surgeons' responses. Porteous's use of the technique, I have argued, is an example of its misuse, as it fails to test the fallibility of the researcher's account. While these three examples demonstrate attempts to use member validation to converge on a single version, its use in discourse analysis may be more fruitfully understood as a way of generating richer data. Finally, the view that CA is to an extent self-validating through members' work is shown to have some force.

Both member validation and triangulation can assist in enhancing the quality of a research account, by helping to back up key claims with adequate supporting evidence. One does not have to subscribe to a particular epistemological position to perceive the variety of uses to which both types of 'validation' exercise can be put, improving the quality of research by adding to its richness and depth of understanding.

KEY POINTS

- Both triangulation and member validation were originally proposed as techniques for converging on a single true version. Though this is still an important use for them, they can also be understood as generating multiple perspectives.

- Triangulation of method is the most used version of the technique, helping to deepen and enrich understanding of particular settings or events.

- A variety of forms of member validation are possible, as well as 'strong' and 'weak' types. It may be more realistic to use 'weak' forms where convergence on an account is desired. 'Strong' forms are likely to generate additional questions for researchers to answer, rather than confirming a particular version.

6

Accounting for Contradiction

CONTENTS

Seeking out and attempting to account for negative instances that contradict emerging or dominant ideas is a core approach in a fallibilistic analytic strategy devoted to improving the quality of research accounts. Willingness to seek out disconfirming evidence, and to allow this to modify general ideas, constitutes the essence of a scientific attitude. One can also see some parallels between this and moral commitments to hearing, or giving voice to, an otherwise silenced 'Other' in postmodern conceptions of research practice. It is, for example, the core idea in Campbell and Stanley's (1966) outline of quasi-experimental research design as a defence against threats to the validity of conclusions. It is consistent with views (for example Clifford and Marcus, 1986) that de-emphasize the authority of authors to pronounce on social reality, preferring instead an approach that supports multiple perspectives and polyvocality. At the same time, it is likely to enhance the credibility of any one voice that can be shown to account for other voices, thus enabling the postmodern ethnographer to avoid a descent into unconfident solipsism (Geertz, 1988). The moral imperative felt by some to seek out the views and experiences of oppressed members is also enhanced if this activity is understood as a searching for instances that tend to contradict the researcher's assumptions, which are likely to emanate from a position of relative social advantage. The search for negative instances reflects an ongoing scepticism about truth claims that should be a part of all good research work. Additionally, we can say, broadly, that the strategies outlined in the previous chapter might be incorporated as methods of searching for negative instances, in the one case through triangulation, in the other through seeking members' views.

Becker (1998), in a discussion of the value of negative instances (which he likes to call 'deviant cases'), points to their role in developing theory. He also notes that the search for these is like a 'not-so-rigorous analytic induction' (1988: 207), of use in a variety of methodological genres (historical or statistical studies, for example). This is why I discuss analytic induction (AI) in the same chapter as negative instances, since AI can be understood as a special application of the more general approach. AI is more narrowly focused, seeking to identify the essential conditions for a particular event (such as opiate addiction or embezzlement) to occur. 'Not-so-rigorous' use of negative instances, on the other hand, is useful in producing more complex, holistic accounts of the multi-layered dynamics within particular social contexts, without a narrow focus on the causal antecedents of particular phenomena.

Searching and accounting for negative instances

Becker (1970c) presents perhaps the classic statement of the value of negative instances in qualitative research, when he argues that evidence that these have been encountered and explained is a good reason to trust in the results of studies based on fieldwork:

> Any conclusion based on these data has been subjected to hundreds and thousands of tests. Not only has the observer seen many actions and heard many statements that support his conclusion, but he has seen and heard many, many more actions and statements that serve as evidence negating alternative likely hypotheses. (Becker, 1970c: 53)

Clearly, however, I am proposing that the search for negative instances should also be applied by researchers using methods other than ethnographic participant observation. This is also the view of Coffey and Atkinson (1996) who, in their review of a wide variety of qualitative methods, express the desirability of a commitment to falsifiability:

the requirement to try ideas out through repeated interactions with the data means that those ideas must be tested rigorously with comprehensive examinations of the evidence. It is never enough to illustrate good ideas with supportive examples. The grounding of theory in empirical evidence requires comprehensive searching and systematic scrutiny. (1996: 191)

The division of theory from observed data, or of arguments from evidence, is fundamental to this use of negative instances. Obviously, if we take the view that all observations are theory driven, or that evidence is only constituted as such from the standpoint of a particular argument, there is little point in regarding the realm of observation and evidence as exerting an independent influence on researchers' ideas. An extreme non-foundationalism contains no space for arguing the value of a search for deviant cases. This is why I have opted for a more or less realist philosophical orientation for the practical purposes of doing research. This retains a sense in which bias can occur, which is restrained by the fallibilistic attitude towards negative instances. As Hammersley and Gomm (1997) have argued, research accounts are, in a weak sense, researchers' constructs, but that is not their only mode of existence. The search for negative instances helps to guard against culpable error, arising from too great an attachment to the personal perspective or values of the individual researcher. Research is a process whereby the investigator should expect to change his or her mind about things which may currently be cherished, an event that is facilitated greatly if methods of data collection and analysis incorporate an active search for negative instances.

Studies lacking negative instances

There are numerous examples of research studies that demonstrate the benefits of an active search for negative instances and I will review some of these here. First, however, I will describe two studies which, while perceptive in various ways, might have benefited from a more actively fallibilistic approach.

'Hearing' talk as a negative instance   The first of these is an example already discussed, Gill's (1993) study of radio disc jockeys in which she reports the following data extract:

> PC: It's also very much a man's world so they're picked on if they are here (.) you know a woman has got to assert herself pretty definitely if she's working in radio. (1993: 79)

Gill 'hears' this as *not formulated as sexism'* (1993: 79) – pointing out that the choice of words deflects attention away from the 'notion of structural inequality or institutional practices', instead identifying the phenomenon described as 'the behaviour of *individuals*' (1993: 79). She is concerned to read the interviews as 'accounts which justified the exclusion of women' (1993: 90). This leads to exclusive interpretations of data extracts like this. Let us imagine, for instance, that she allowed herself to hear this extract as a clear acknowledgement of sexist practices by PC. This is, no doubt, how PC might say he intended his words if he encountered Gill's contrasting interpretation. Though initially appearing to contradict the general thrust of the analysis, which suggests that every speech is a form of denial of sexism, Gill might use this extract to create a stronger analysis that is sensitive to people's capacities to mould their self-presentations to the immediate demands of particular interactions. PC's words might be understood as a further discursive or rhetorical strategy to prove non-sexist credentials to an interviewer, in a context where PC knows that this admission will cost him little. It is, potentially, a negative instance which deepens and strengthens the analysis.

Adding to textual analysis A further example of a qualitative study that might have benefited from a more rigorous approach to the analysis of negative instances is that of Ben-Ari (1995), who presents an analysis of acknowledgement pages in around 200 anthropological monographs. He notes, for example, three features in his data: first, authors more often acknowledge their seniors rather than their juniors; secondly, acknowledgements are sometimes made to the people who have been studied; and thirdly, they are sometimes made to the family and friends of the author. Here are three examples of Ben-Ari's reporting of these things:

> In their acknowledgements, anthropologists invariably make references to people within their professional community. These references often include remarks directed at 'juniors' or 'equals', but by far the most common statements are those addressed to 'seniors': teachers and older colleagues, supervisors and mentors, guides and intellectual influences. (1995: 136)

> Fieldwork, of course, is a social process that invariably involves the ethnographer in a heavy web of obligations toward the 'other'. Ethnographers express their awareness of this situation with thanks to those researched:

>> An anthropologist's first debt is to the people who allowed him to study them, and I here wish to put on record my deep gratitude to them. (Gellner, 1969: xii). (1995: 148)

> Acknowledgments in ethnographies rarely lack reference to another category of people with which anthropologists maintain close ties but which do not as a rule belong to the profession – family and friends:

>> Throughout my apprenticeship my parents gave me unstinting support in every possible way. My wife, who shared only a brief part of the pleasures of fieldwork, cheerfully endured the long periods of analysis, writing, tension and proofreading. (Kuper, 1970: ix). (1995: 152)

This is a fairly standard presentation of data in a qualitative research report: the general statement followed usually by one or two illustrative examples. In more rigorously coded work, one might see counts of instances being presented. However, let us for the moment focus on Ben-Ari's interpretation of the facts that he reports. The first finding, he says, reflects the author's desire to be perceived as being at the centre of an important network, dropping names as a strategy for 'securing other people's attention' (1995: 137) 'to improve an anthropologist's career chances' (1995: 138). The second finding, he says, reflects the author's desire to establish the credibility of his or her text, by showing through such expressions of warmth that successful fieldwork relations have been established; this enhances the sense that the author has 'been there' and is a textual strategy 'directed towards professional readerships'. The third finding is similarly designed to create an impression on readers since 'such passages . . . create images of ethnographers as social persons (1995: 153); indeed, they specifically 'convey a sense of [anthropologists] as total persons not limited to their professional selves' (1995: 156). These last two interpretations rest on a view that these are imperatives that are particularly pressing in anthropology, where 'being there' is a key marker of methodological credibility, and the method of fieldwork is particularly dependent on the possession of an empathetic and well-rounded character, such a person being the sort who might be successful in gathering confessional accounts from members.

Clearly, Ben-Ari is presenting an analysis that is in tune with contemporary scepticism about writers' authority. An engagingly light-hearted cynicism is expressed in his interpretations, which are finely judged to appeal to an audience already primed for such messages by the ethnographic critique of ethnography that has emerged in recent years (for which see Chapters 2 and 11). In this respect, Ben-Ari appears to be on safe ground with his intended audience, just as Gill may have felt secure in her assumptions about her readers' sympathies.

Let us imagine some threats to the validity of these interpretations, in the spirit of Campbell and Stanley's (1966) sceptical approach. It is based on the sort of comment that an author might have made to Ben-Ari, were he to have conducted a member validation exercise. Perhaps Ben-Ari would have been exposed to the view that authors acknowledge their seniors not because they wish to gain career advantage but because they wish to express a debt of gratitude for having learned valuable things that have contributed to the work. Since important senior people are more likely to have taught and influenced the author than are junior people, it is inevitable that these are the people who feature more often. Authors acknowledge the people they study, and their family and friends, because these are in fact people from whom they have received practical assistance, and an acknowledgement is one way of repaying people for this. In this respect, anthropology is no different from any other discipline.

TABLE 6.1 Three uses for deviant cases

---

1 Deviant cases that provide additional support for the analyst's conclusions, perhaps by showing participants acknowledging that an event is unusual.
2 Deviant cases that require modification of the analyst's emerging ideas.
3 The deviant case is considered exceptional for good, explainable reasons.

Source: after Peräkylä, 1997

How might Ben-Ari have defended his particular interpretations against the threats posed by such alternatives? He might have interviewed the writers and the readers of these pieces in order to establish whether authorial intentions and audience reactions supported his version of name dropping. He might have compared the extent of name dropping in authors who were already successful, compared with those who were still 'on the make'. He might have studied a random sample of acknowledgements from monographs in other disciplines to establish the relative frequency with which respondents or friends and family were acknowledged. In short, he would have actively sought for instances that might at first contradict, but would eventually have deepened his analysis, giving it broader scope and greater credibility with a readership that did not share his underlying assumptions.

Studies that account for negative instances

Let us then see how certain authors have applied the principle of accounting for negative instances. Peräkylä (1997) presents a helpful three-point categorization of these, which I summarize in Table 6.1.

I would also add that while I have tended to stress in the account so far that it is desirable to search actively for negative instances, these may arise in addition without any active search, being thrown up in the course of data collection and coding. A number of the examples given below are like this.

Deviant cases give additional support For his first example, Peräkylä cites Pomerantz's (1980) conversation analytic study of 'fishing' in telephone calls, in which Pomerantz argued that callers sometimes 'fish' for information about the identity of other callers while the phone has been busy by mentioning the fact of an engaged line. A statement like 'I've been trying you all day; the line has been busy for hours' is normally 'heard' as a request for information. Pomerantz gives an example where this information was not forthcoming, so that the caller later reiterated her request with a clear 'Who were you talking to?' This constitutes an acknowledgement that something unusual happened when the other party to the call ignored the 'fishing' move, providing additional support for Pomerantz's view of the purpose of such moves.

Similar examples of the first type of deviant case come from my own work concerning reports by relatives and others about people who had died alone (Seale, 1996). My analysis showed that in the majority of cases where this had occurred, people were concerned to demonstrate their moral adequacy to interviewers by emphasizing that this was an unwelcome event, and that had they been able they would have wanted to be present at the death. I related this to psychoanalytic ideas about ontological security (basic security about being in the world), suggesting that speakers sought to demonstrate that they inhabited a secure place in a moral community in order to deal with the threat which dying alone posed for their own sense of security about the proper order of things.

Yet five accounts showed speakers denying their allegiance to the ideals of accompaniment that I had identified, mostly in the form of people who said they had not wanted to be present at the death of a person who died alone. Closer examination, however, revealed that these were associated with alternative strategies for establishing the speaker's membership within the moral community by taking steps to provide plausible reasons for their stance.

One such person was the son of an 83-year-old woman, who said that 'death is a private thing' when asked why he had not wanted to be there. This was associated with a view that it was beneficial to be unaware of unpleasant events, turning this idea to the subject of his mother's unawareness of her dying: 'You've nothing to worry about if you don't know.' But this speaker had mentioned early in the interview that his wife suffered from 'early senile dementia so I can't work'. Clearly, this information had affected the interviewer, as she wrote at the end: 'Respondent's wife suffering from premature senility but never mentioned as causing problems re: (care of) mother.' The speaker had provided the interviewer with sufficient reason to absolve him from any blame.

Another son who had not wanted to be there provided a rather similar form of justification. He said that he had had a heart attack in the month before his father died, being therefore 'unable to visit' him. He had been visiting him less in the months before his death because his father was 'oblivious' to his presence due to his mental confusion. He noted that he had been erroneously informed by staff that his father 'had got a week' when his father had actually died before this. With these facts established, he then felt able to say that he 'didn't mind not being there at the actual death'.

Two other people referred to the wish to avoid distress. One spoke of his own potential distress, using the unawareness of the dying person in a fashion similar to the second son above: 'I experienced the neighbour's death last month, so if my wife's death was anything like that – (my presence) didn't make any difference as she was in a coma.' The other referred to the distress of the wife of the deceased: 'I'm glad my grandma wasn't in the room – it would have distressed her to see him die.' This last instance may be more properly understood as a comment on another's reputation that served to underline the speaker's own.

The fifth deviant case concerned the wife of a publican. She was quite explicit that her reason for wanting to have been there at the time of death had nothing to do with the ideal of accompaniment. Her husband's long-standing alcoholism had left her feeling little warmth for him; her reason for wishing she had been there was to save her employee the distress of finding the body.

I felt that these apparently deviant cases, where speakers appeared to locate themselves outside the ideal of accompaniment, were satisfactorily explained as aberrations. The speakers in each instance successfully demonstrated their moral adequacy by alternative means. In doing this, they showed an orientation towards the event as deviant from normal behaviour, requiring explanation, so strengthening the general case that accompaniment of dying people is perceived as a generally desirable moral norm.

Deviant cases lead to modification of ideas Peräkylä also illustrates his second category from a conversation analytic study of telephone calls, this time Schegloff's (1968) finding that in only one out of 500 calls the caller spoke first. Until then, Schegloff had believed that there was a norm obliging the answerer to speak first (as in 'Hello' on picking up the phone). When this general rule was broken by the answerer remaining silent, the caller reissued the 'summons', originally indicated by the telephone bell, by demanding that the answerer identify themselves. Thus Schegloff came to understand these opening moments of calls as a summons followed by an answer.

Examples of analytic induction (such as the work of Cressey, 1950, 1953), give plentiful instances of the modification of ideas by accounting for negative instances. As these are discussed later in this chapter, I will not repeat the review here. I can, however, give an example which illustrates modification of ideas, but which also illustrates another desirable feature of good research work, which is rarely found in qualitative social research: a study that builds cumulatively on the findings of a previous study. In this case, the researcher took the findings of another researcher as a set of ideas to be tested in a related setting, finding deviant cases which led to a modification of the original researcher's conceptual scheme.

The study was done by Dingwall and Murray (1983), testing Jeffery's (1979) observation that in hospital casualty departments staff categorized patients as 'bad' if they had problems deemed to be trivial, or were drunks, tramps or victims of self-harm. On the other hand, if patients had problems that allowed doctors to practise and learn new clinical skills, or that tested the professional knowledge of staff, they were categorized as 'good'. Jeffery's study, then, was a classic interactionist study of typifications, based on ethnographic fieldwork. Dingwall and Murray, in contrast, studied children in casualty departments rather than adults, finding that they constituted a negative instance if Jeffery's analysis was applied. Children often exhibited the qualities of the 'bad' adult patients, being uncooperative for example, or suffering from mild or self-inflicted injuries. Yet staff did not treat them harshly.

This led to a considerably more elaborate analytic scheme than that proposed by Jeffery, suggesting that the labels applied by staff depended on a prior assessment of whether patients were perceived as being able to make choices (children were not, adults were, on the whole). Children were therefore generally 'forgiven' behaviour that in adults would be deemed reprehensible on the grounds that children are understandably irresponsible. Additionally, staff assessed whether the situation was such that patients were able to make choices. Thus, some adults might be categorized as being present in casualty inappropriately, rather than being 'bad' patients if the events that had led them there were not their 'fault' (for example they had had poor advice to go to casualty from a person in authority). This new analytic scheme had the potential to account for a far greater variety of situations than the original scheme proposed by Jeffery, illustrating the potential that negative instances have for improving the quality of qualitative research studies.

Deviant cases are explainable The third category is illustrated by Peräkylä by an example from his own work (Peräkylä, 1995) on the delivery of diagnoses in medical consultations. He found that doctors sometimes delivered diagnoses without saying anything about the evidence that led them to their conclusion. However, they only did this when such 'evidence' had been brought into view earlier in the interaction by a physical examination or a study of the medical records. For example, a doctor might examine a child's ear and state that there is an infection present. The doctor would not do this without examining the ear, or otherwise eliciting evidence for the conclusion (for example asking about pain or looking at a referral letter from another doctor in a patient's medical notes). But in two deviant cases a diagnosis was given without such conjuring up of evidence. Closer examination established that in fact these deliveries of diagnosis were instances where the delivery was being done for the second time during the consultation, the first time having been accompanied by the relevant evidential basis. Thus the cases were not in fact deviant and did not modify the analysis.

Another example, again from a conversation analytic study, comes from Silverman's (1997b) study of counselling sessions with people who have come for an HIV test. He identifies two general 'formats' for such counselling. On the one hand, there is the 'interview' (IV) format, in which counsellors elicit clients' concerns before delivering advice tailored to those concerns. This format is normally marked by numerous acknowledgements by the client that the advice has been heard, these acknowledgements taking the form of utterances like 'That's right' or 'Yes'. 'Information delivery' (ID) formats, on the other hand, tend not to contain such acknowledgements, being occasions where the counsellor quickly delivers a standard package of information about safe sex practices and other matters, regardless of the client's concerns, which have not been elicited.

Silverman, however, found a case where an ID format, contrary to the norm, did contain many marked acknowledgements. Here, the counsellor had been running through how HIV-positive people ought to look after their health, with plenty of exercise, sleep and healthy foods. The client, in addition to several acknowledgements of the 'yes' and 'right' sort, at one point goes so far as to say: 'Right. Rather than let yourself get run down' (1997b: 129). Silverman explains this as follows:

> The answer seems to lie in the hit-or-miss character of non-recipient-designed advice sequences like these. In most cases . . . [they] elicit a minimal response. In a minority of such advice-givings, however, a counsellor will fortuitously hit upon a topic upon which [the client] has some prior interest and knowledge. This, I suggest, is why [the client] offers his marked acknowledgements . . . However [in ID format] it is *optional* whether patients offer marked acknowledgements . . . When they do so . . . they do not implicate themselves in any future lines of action because they are only responding to what can be heard as information and not necessarily advice. (1997b: 129–30)

Later, Silverman offers another potential explanation:

> An alternative possible explanation is that this patient is simply a personality type that will intervene in this kind of way however [the counsellor] sets up her advice. (1997b: 133)

Clearly, Silverman feels that his original view, that IV formats are successful in gaining genuine acknowledgements of uptake from clients, remains intact. One could argue that his explanations are quite speculative, perhaps themselves being falsifiable, but that is an acceptable part of the fallibilistic approach to social research that I am advocating. Certainty is never possible, and threats to the validity of all arguments are always feasible, including attempts to argue away deviant cases. This is not, as some might claim, an acceptance of relativism, but simply a strategy for pursuing explanations that have greater rather than lesser credibility as good accounts of the social world.

We can now turn to a more specialized use of negative instances, one that is focused on identifying the causal conditions for particular phenomena to occur: analytic induction (AI).

TABLE 6.2   Five steps of analytic induction (AI)

---

1   Roughly define the problem.
2   Construct a hypothetical explanation for the problem.
3   Examine a case to see whether it supports the hypothesis.
4   If the case does not fit, either reformulate the hypothesis or redefine the problem to exclude the negative case. After a few cases like this, a reasonable degree of certainty about the truth of the hypothesis will have built up.
5   Continue this search through several cases until negative instances are no longer found. At this point, early proponents of the method claimed (for example Znaniecki, 1934), a universal generalization will have been established.

Analytic induction

Study of the history of this term locates its origin within a highly positivist enterprise within qualitative research, which focused on a search for deterministic laws governing human social experience. While contemporary sensibilities may disallow this ambition, the logic of analytic induction played out in practice in various research studies is helpful in showing how the approach can be a part of a more fallibilistic research strategy. In this respect, analytic induction is like member validation and triangulation, originally arising from the working through of positivist ambitions, but proving helpful in improving rigour and deepening understanding if applied in non-positivist research contexts.

Description of the method with examples

Analytic induction can be broken down into five steps, shown in Table 6.2.

The classic examples of this method in use are studies by Lindesmith (1947) and Becker (1963) on drug use, Cressey's (1950, 1953) study of the criminal violation of financial trust and Bloor's (1976, 1978) modified usage in his study of surgeons' decision making. I will concentrate on Cressey's work to exemplify the method.

Cressey (1950) set himself the task of explaining why some people in positions of financial trust violated that trust in acts of embezzlement. He rejected explanations that focused on the way the money was spent (for example gambling or drink as the cause of the crime). He interviewed people who had been imprisoned for the crime, establishing a clear definition of the phenomenon (step 1) by excluding people who took on the position of trust knowingly intending the crime; in this part of his work he only wanted to understand people who were initially honest in their positions. His first hypothesis (step 2) was that embezzlement occurred when people persuaded themselves that the action was not really bad or wrong. However, he quickly found people (step 3) who told him that they had always known the act to be wrong. Cressey proceeded to step 4, reformulating his hypothesis to say that embezzlement occurs when the person experiences an emergency requiring funds that are otherwise unavailable. Examples contradicting this were found, however. Some people reported no such emergency, preferring instead to refer to feelings of being abused or exploited by their employers.

Further hypotheses were constructed and modified according to the same cycle between theorizing (or, we might say, 'claims') and evidence. The third hypothesis stated that embezzlement occurs if the activity it funds is regarded as socially unacceptable by the violator. However, examples were found where this did not occur but embezzlement still happened, and where it had occurred earlier but embezzlement was not triggered. The fourth hypothesis came very close to the final one. For the event to occur, the person should have problems that were felt to be socially unacceptable, but should also possess the knowledge that the problem could be solved by the action and have the skill to conduct the crime. Because there were still some negative instances, the final hypothesis was constructed, incorporating all of the conditions present in the fourth hypothesis, but adding that people must retain an image of themselves as trustworthy in spite of committing this crime; they were simply making unorthodox use of entrusted money, that might be refunded at a later date.

Significantly, Cressey states that 'future revision will be necessary if negative cases are found' (1950: 743), suggesting a fallibilistic attitude towards the scope of the generalization he has constructed. Here he is in tune with philosophical discussions of induction, which point out the mistake of assuming that the sun will rise tomorrow just because it has always risen before. Cressey was aware that tomorrow he might meet an embezzler who would force him to rethink his claims, though he knew he had met enough to be reasonably confident about their general applicability. Like Znaniecki (1934), however, he believed that analytic induction had the potential to produce universal rather than probabilistic statements. In saying this, Znaniecki was trying to emphasize the difference between his approach and that of enumerative induction, which is based on probabilistic reasoning, so allowing certain cases to deviate from the proposed law. The sort of generalization made in statistical analysis involves specifying the likelihood that events will occur given certain preconditions, rather than offering certainty.

It will be clear that any discussion of analytic induction merges with discussions of the generalizability of research and with theoretical generalization in particular (see Chapter 8). Additionally, we can see even more clearly that analytic induction is an elaboration of the general principle of searching for deviant cases, though with the specific purpose of constructing causal laws.

Criticisms and limitations

Robinson (1951) and Turner (1953) present the classic criticisms of analytic induction. Robinson takes issue with the attempt to prove analytic induction superior to enumerative induction. He points out that it only describes necessary conditions for a phenomenon to occur, rather than sufficient ones. That is to say, we know what conditions were needed by Cressey's embezzlers for them to commit their crime, but we do not know if these are always sufficient to trigger embezzlement. To discover this, we would have to compare Cressey's people with another group of financial controllers who did not embezzle to see if they too had experienced the conditions. This is a classic control group design from which Znaniecki was concerned to distance himself, since such a design can only produce probabilistic statements of the sort: 'given that A, B and C are present, the phenomenon occurs in X per cent of cases'. Robinson advocates representative sampling as well, to take account of the classic philosophical problems of induction mentioned earlier.

Turner's (1953) critique focuses on the difficulties in making predictions on the basis of the supposed universal laws created by analytic induction. He points out that Cressey's study depends on retrospective reasoning. One cannot say, for example, that a problem is felt by a person to be socially unacceptable (non-shareable) until the phenomenon of embezzlement has occurred. Up until the point at which the crime is committed, it is always possible for the person to change his or her mind and share the problems. Like Robinson, Turner reasserts the value of probabilistic reasoning.

These criticisms have been summarized by later writers (Bloor, 1976; Hammersley and Atkinson, 1983; Hammersley, 1995a), suggesting that the initial claims made for analytic induction were overambitious, being an attempt to propose that qualitative work might compete on the same grounds as quantitative research, claiming a viable alternative to a central enterprise in positivist social science, that of producing universal causal laws determining human behaviour. We can agree with Fontana (1994) that, along with grounded theory (see Chapter 7), the method represented an approach to 'scientizing interactionist fieldwork' (1994: 205) that was politically strategic in its time, but now looks out of place. Nevertheless, as a reminder to be systematic in the search for negative instances and to modify one's theories in the light of new evidence, the spirit of analytic induction seems worth preserving in qualitative work.

Conclusion

In this chapter and the last one I have outlined a variety of techniques which researchers have used to seek out evidence that challenges or extends their arguments, in pursuit of an ideal whereby the quality of a research account is enhanced by supporting key claims with adequate and persuasive evidence. Accounting for negative instances encapsulates the fallibilistic research strategy that I have been advocating in this book. I have given several examples of this from a variety of research reports in furtherance of the argument that the best way to see the value of some general methodological rule or procedure is to see how it works out on the ground, as it were, in the context of particular research projects. I have suggested that the search for negative instances is a concept which to some extent incorporates analytic induction as well as member validation and triangulation, in the sense that all of these involve the researcher in seeking out potential challenges to an emerging account, and modifying that account in the light of this.

Analytic induction, though initially conceived as a watertight method for proving causal statements, in an attempt to replicate in qualitative research the success of the experiment in natural science, can also be used to good effect without subscribing to these positivist ambitions. This is because it involves an active seeking out of evidence to extend the scope and sophistication of theories.

KEY POINTS

- Seeking out and accounting for negative instances (deviant cases) that contradict an emerging account lies at the heart of a fallibilistic research strategy.

- Member validation, triangulation and analytic induction can be understood as different ways of generating and/or accounting for negative instances.

- Although these techniques arose as a part of a somewhat positivist agenda, they also have the potential to enhance the quality of studies done within other guiding philosophies.

7

Grounding Theory

CONTENTS

Theoretical speculation can be a fertile source of ideas for practising researchers seeking original ways of looking at problems that otherwise may seem old and worn. Layder (1998) provides a helpful discussion of the uses of theory in the practice of social research, giving an account that emphasizes its use in stimulating creativity. Some social theory can initially seem detached from its audience's social experience, making it hard to recognize what concepts are seeking to describe. Meanings may appear ambiguous, with a puzzling relationship to practice. Readers of theory may then feel immersed in a self-sustaining literary fantasy. Yet researchers can use this experience as a resource for research purposes, reinterpreting concepts in ways that the original thinker could not have predicted, applying them in novel ways to new areas of the social world so that they are developed and enriched.

Good research work is in some respects a more demanding discipline than pure theorizing, because it demands of writers that they continually specify what they mean by telling readers about things which they have seen, heard or otherwise observed. At the same time, researchers cannot get away with the pretence that observation alone is enough, so they must also become proficient in manipulating theoretical concepts, at times taken from texts whose writers may have taken little care to define the empirical referents for their ideas. Treading the middle road between grand theory and abstracted empiricism is an evocative depiction of the task that faces researchers who wish to do high-quality work. As Mills, who coined these terms, wrote: 'The capacity to shuttle between levels of abstraction, with ease and with clarity, is a signal mark of an imaginative and systematic thinker' (1959: 43).

The grounding of theory in data is an important element in achieving the more general aim of supporting claims with credible evidence. Accounts of grounded theorizing depend on a separation between data and theory which is to an extent artificial if we accept the philosophical point that all observational data depend on some theoretical system. I hope, however, that I have done enough in previous chapters to convince readers that such separation is a necessary part of research activity, even from within a committed constructivism that might perceive distinctions between 'research', 'data' and 'theory' as elements in a language game. I would argue that at the very least it is a game that we must choose whether or not to play. Once chosen, there are rules of play that are fundamental to its successful and satisfying conduct. More in tune with the philosophy of subtle realism, which is my preference, is the point that a key strength of research texts is that their shape has been influenced and constrained by a reality that exists independently of the text. If this is accepted, it becomes inevitable that we must separate statements that report data from statements that explain data. Grounded theorizing represents a particular version of the link between data and theory statements, emphasizing their interdependence and proposing that theory can in fact be generated from close examination of data.

For the moment, however, let us look at things the other way around and consider not the generation of theory from data, but the advantages of exemplifying theory with sufficient instances of data so that theoretical statements become convincing, because they are understood to be linked with life experiences that everyone can recognize. This quality is a by-product of grounded theorizing, but can be understood as desirable in all research texts. This ambition lies behind the idea that research texts ought to be understandable and even validated by members (Glaser and Strauss, 1967; Turner, 1981), although this is an argument which, earlier in this book (Chapter 5), I have shown to lead to some problems if uncritically applied.

Grounding theoretical statements

Put simply, this is achieved by giving plentiful and good examples of general concepts. Classically, it is done by recognizably 'well-chosen' illustrative examples of key concepts, so that readers know what the researcher is referring to, and can see that the concept is indeed referring to a distinct class of objects, rather than overlapping with other things that might be superficially similar. We can note immediately that this principle is very close to the ideal of creating good concept-indicator links that is seen in discussions of measurement validity in quantitative texts (see Chapter 4). The principle that concepts need to be refined and clarified before being operationalized in, for example, questionnaire items is one that is rehearsed in numerous textbooks on quantitative methods. The hypothetico-deductive method, proposing a particular way of linking theory to data, cannot work if statements made in the theoretical realm do not have clear and well-understood linkages with researchers' observations.

Rose (1982) has presented a strong argument drawing out similarities between quantitative and qualitative research in this area, claiming that 'the process of developing concepts and indicators is the core of the analysis of qualitative data' (1982: 118). Rose distinguishes between the concepts used by participants in navigating their way through their social worlds, and theoretical concepts constructed by the researcher, giving the example of Wiener's (1975) study of the experience of rheumatoid arthritis (RA), where she generated the concept of 'normalization' to understand her data, which were based on interviews with people experiencing this condition, as well as observation of their care. This was not a term that the people with RA used, but arose from Wiener's data analysis. Her account of the translation of data into theory captures this moment with unusual clarity:

Analysis of field data was conducted in the following manner: indicators in the data (descriptions by the arthritic, or observations by the researcher, of an action, episode or event) were coded into categories and their properties. For example, all descriptions of behavioral attempts to continue a normal life were initially coded as *normalization* and then broken down into categories of normalization, such as *covering-up, keeping up* and *pacing*. Concepts which have been dictated by the data, and thus coded, can then be interrelated . . . and can be carried forward in the writing . . . one can carry forward a concept such as *covering-up* to demonstrate its relationship to another concept such as *justifying inaction*, but one cannot constantly carry forward a description such as 'When I walk, I walk as normally as possible' and demonstrate its relationship to another description such as 'My husband doesn't really understand' . . . It is intended that conceptually specifying behavior will strengthen its applicability as a guideline for health professionals. (1975: 97)

The advantages of constructing a theoretical language grounded in instances of data are demonstrated in the report, which presents an evocative meta-story about the lives of people with RA that is potentially generalizable because it is able to highlight common experiences:

A successful repertoire for covering-up and keeping-up may at times turn out to be a mixed blessing. Relationships generally remain normal, but when the arthritic cannot get by, it is harder to *justify inaction* to others . . . This problem is increased when others have stakes in the arthritic's remaining active, as was the case with a young mother whose condition worsened when she tried to keep athletic pace with her husband and son: 'My husband really doesn't understand. He is very healthy and he thinks there is some magic formula that I'm not following – if I would just exercise, or have people over.' (Wiener, 1975: 100)

An alternative example can be seen in a passage from Kluckholn (quoted in Pelto and Pelto, 1978), who presents an account of Navajo moral values that at first appears deceptively 'descriptive', not at all containing theory, because it looks initially like an attempt to outline the concepts used by Navajo people themselves rather than building some structure of researcher-generated concepts. Yet closer inspection demonstrates a mixture of the author's unexamined assumptions with Navajo categories, which might have been remedied by a more sustained attempt to illustrate concepts systematically with instances of data:

The Protestant virtue of care of possessions (though not the frequently paired one of cleanliness) is shared by the Navajo: destructiveness, waste, carelessness, and even cleanliness are disapproved of. Gambling is wrong 'if you lost your mother's jewelry . . .' Games must not interfere with work. One must not even attend ceremonials too often lest this become a way of loafing. Knowledge, including ceremonial knowledge and sound judgement, are good because they are conducive to health and long life . . . Sobriety, self control, and adherence to old custom are valued . . . drinking is wrong if it results in loss of superego control, if one becomes 'wild and without sense.' One should talk 'pretty nice' to everyone. (Kluckholn, quoted in Pelto and Pelto 1978: 170)

Pelto and Pelto (1978), in commenting on this passage, point out that these generalizations are not supported by any systematic reporting of data that might illustrate what they mean in practice. For example, Kluckholn could have shown us instances of Navajo talk about people deemed to have attended ceremonials 'too often' so that we could understand what this meant in practice. Instances of what Navajo count as 'pretty nice' talk would also have helped in clarifying the concept's empirical referents, perhaps dispelling concerns that Kluckholn's own definitions of nice talk were involved in this category. Kluckholn's comments on cleanliness raise particular concerns that his own categories for this idea have become mixed up with those of his informants: what do his informants count as 'clean'? All of these categories (cleanliness, attending too often, pretty nice talk) might have been used in variable ways in different contexts in which Navajo found themselves. The example shows that even text with an apparently low level of theoretical abstraction can benefit from sustained attention to providing illustrative instances from a body of data.

The discovery of grounded theory

A scheme for grounded theorizing was famously outlined by Glaser and Strauss (1967), representing an elaboration of the ways in which linkages between data and theory might be maintained. Specifically, this involved an attempt to overthrow the positivist, verificationist paradigm, whereby data were collected in order to test the truth value of theoretical propositions, in favour of an approach that emphasized the inductive generation of theory from data. The scheme has had a revolutionary appeal for a sociological proletariat of qualitative research workers, keen to overthrow the twin domination of their field by 'theoretical capitalists' and big-time, government-funded, quantitative survey research work, represented for Glaser and Strauss in the 1960s by the work of theoreticians such as Talcott Parsons or the quantitative methodologist Paul Lazarsfeld.

Before becoming involved in the research project on the experience of dying that led to the ideas outlined in *The Discovery of Grounded Theory*, Glaser had worked in Columbia University, an institution also associated with Lazarsfeld, who had been an important influence in the development of the 'elaboration paradigm' for the causal analysis of quantitative survey research data, an approach described both by himself (Lazarsfeld and Rosenberg, 1955) and others (Hyman, 1955; Rosenberg, 1968), which exerted great influence on social survey researchers.

It is appropriate here to point out parallels between the underlying ideas of quantitative and qualitative approaches at this stage in the development of qualitative method. Both the elaboration paradigm and grounded theorizing stress the continual cycling back and forth between theory construction and examination of data. The generation of theoretical categories through 'property space' analysis described by Lazarsfeld and Barton (see Barton, 1955; Becker, 1998) is an example of this (I discuss this in more detail later in this chapter). Another parallel is in the stress placed within the elaboration paradigm on seeing data analysis as a matter of generating falsifiable theoretical arguments, whose complexity and scope develop through the discovery of negative evidence. The proposition that A has caused B is continually subject to checks that this appearance of causality is not, for example, spuriously created by some third variable C. Such checks on internal validity might also involve the consideration that C might intervene between A and B, or that the association exists only under certain conditions of C (called 'specification'), or indeed that the absence of an association may be an illusion, as C is suppressing this, so that when C's influence is removed the truth can be revealed. Throughout discussions of the elaboration paradigm one sees this sense of arguments being constructed against threats, a genuinely fallibilistic approach to reasoning with data, involving continual re-examination of data in the light of developing theoretical arguments.

Theoretical sampling and theoretical saturation

This commitment, then, is shared by Glaser and Strauss, whose concept of theoretical sampling modifies the principle (which was at the time well established by Becker and others) of searching for negative instances to show how this could be used in theory construction rather than purely as a test of theory. Here, a difference becomes apparent with the elaboration paradigm whose authors, for practical reasons, could not envisage frequent returns to data collection so that a relatively rapid cycling between fieldwork and data analysis might occur. Large-scale social survey work does not permit very much repetition of expensive data-gathering exercises if a researcher discovers a key question has not been included in an interview schedule, thus limiting the exploratory potential of such work. The qualitative researcher is more fortunate in this regard, however, and Glaser and Strauss were able to exploit this very fully. They advocated that through theoretical sampling, a researcher might extend and broaden the scope of an emerging theory. Such sampling involves choosing cases to study, people to interview, settings to observe, with a view to finding things that might challenge the limitations of the existing theory, forcing the researcher to change it in order to incorporate the new phenomena. Here, they outline this aspect of their method:

> Theoretical sampling is the process of data collection for generating theory whereby the analyst jointly collects, codes, and analyzes his data and decides what data to collect next and where to find them, in order to develop his theory as it emerges. This process of data collection is *controlled* by the emerging theory . . . The basic question in theoretical sampling (in either substantive or formal theory) is: *what* groups or subgroups does one turn to *next* in data collection? And for *what* theoretical purpose? In short, how does the sociologist select multiple comparison groups? The possibility of multiple comparisons are infinite, and so groups must be chosen according to theoretical criteria. (1967: 45, 47)

They illustrate theoretical sampling from their own work on 'awareness contexts' among dying people:

> Visits to the various medical services were scheduled as follows: I wished first to look at services that minimized patient awareness (and so first looked at a premature baby service and then a neurosurgical service where patients were frequently comatose). I wished then to look at dying in a situation

where expectancy of staff and often of patients was great and dying was quick, so I observed on an Intensive Care Unit. Then I wished to observe on a service where staff expectations of terminality were great but where the patient's might or might not be, and where dying tended to be slow. So I looked next at a cancer service. I wished then to look at conditions where death was unexpected and rapid, and so looked at an emergency service. While we were looking at some different types of services, we also observed the above types of service at other types of hospitals. So our scheduling of types of service was directed by a general conceptual scheme – which included hypotheses about awareness, expectedness and rate of dying – as well as by a developing conceptual structure including matters not at first envisioned. Sometimes we returned to services after the initial two or three or four weeks of continuous observation, in order to check upon items which needed checking or had been missed in the initial period. (1967: 59)

This process of theoretical sampling is of course potentially limitless, since it comes up against the general problem of induction, which concerns the ever-present possibility that a further case will exhibit properties that force some further changes in a theory. Undaunted, Glaser and Strauss propose a typically pragmatic solution by describing a state of 'theoretical saturation':

The criterion for judging when to stop sampling the different groups pertinent to a category is the category's *theoretical saturation. Saturation* means that no additional data are being found whereby the sociologist can develop properties of the category. As he sees similar instances over and over again, the researcher becomes empirically confident that a category is saturated. He goes out of his way to look for groups that stretch diversity of data as far as possible, just to make certain that saturation is based on the widest possible range of data on the category . . . The adequate theoretical sampling is judged on the basis of how widely and diversely the analyst chose his groups for saturating categories according to the type of theory he wished to develop. The adequate statistical sample, on the other hand, is judged on the basis of techniques of random and stratified sampling used in relation to the social structure of a group for groups sampled. The inadequate theoretical sample is easily spotted, since the theory associated with it is usually thin and not well integrated, and has too many obvious unexplained exceptions. (1967: 61, 63)

This discussion of when to stop sampling is somehow reminiscent of debates among psychoanalysts about when it is appropriate to finish a particular programme of analysis; in theory further work and exploration of the patient can always occur, as we are all in a form of self-analysis all the time that might be facilitated by some outside help. A view of research as creating provisional truths is consistent with this view, suggesting that researchers operate in the same pragmatic manner as ordinary members, who cease inquiry when this seems unlikely to be fruitful for practical purposes.

Thick description and theoretical saturation The idea of theoretical saturation is also somewhat similar to Geertz's (1993, first published 1973) notion of 'thick description'. Indeed, the same metaphor of thinness and thickness of an analysis is used. Geertz used this idea (borrowed from Ryle) to account for a particular quality of good anthropological writing as revealing and building on many-layered interpretations of social life, so that a rich and detailed understanding of the several meanings available for particular events is made possible. Thin description, on the other hand, fails to engage with cultural meanings, and is both uninspired and uninspiring.

In his own work, for example, Geertz demonstrates what he means by thick description in an account of Balinese cockfights, which he is able to interpret as possessing meaning at many different levels. A 'thin' description of such a fight might interpret it as 'a chicken hacking another mindlessly to bits' (1993: 449) or, indeed, as nothing more than an expression of masculinity. Thus Geertz dismisses Bateson and Mead's (1942) psychological interpretation of the cocks as detachable penises, regarding this as a thin and uninteresting explanation rather than one that is untrue. Indeed, he notes that 'the deep psychological identification of Balinese men with their cocks is unmistakable . . . the fact that they are masculine symbols par excellence is about as indubitable, and to the Balinese about as evident, as the fact that water runs downhill' (1993: 417–18).

Although Geertz does not present himself as following the methods of grounded theorizing in order to generate a 'thicker' description, one can reread his method as doing this, in the sense that his lengthy period spent in the field allowed him to 'sample' a wide variety of events in order to develop his theory. His field observations revealed instances that are hard to explain by a simple sexual metaphor, suggesting, among other things, religious symbolism as well:

> No temple festival should be conducted until [a cockfight] is made. (If it is omitted, someone will inevitably fall into a trance and command with the voice of an angered spirit that the oversight be immediately corrected.) Collective responses to natural evils – illness, crop failure, volcanic eruptions – almost always involve them. And that famous holiday in Bali, 'The Day of Silence' (*Njepi*), when everyone sits silent and immobile all day long in order to avoid contact with a sudden influx of demons chased momentarily out of hell, is preceded the previous day by large-scale cockfights . . . in almost every village on the island. (1993: 420)

From these and other observations, Geertz developed a richly exemplified understanding of the many layers of meaning which Balinese attached to cockfights, presenting a more complex and theoretically saturated account of the phenomenon than the simple response of

Bateson and Mead, being also one that is imbued with considerable
literary power:

> The cockfight is 'really real' only to the cocks – it does not kill anyone,
> castrate anyone, reduce anyone to animal status, alter the hierarchical rela-
> tions among people, or refashion the hierarchy; it does not even redistribute
> income in any significant way. What it does is what, for other people with
> other temperaments and other conventions, *Lear* and *Crime and Punishment*
> do; it catches up these themes – death, masculinity, rage, pride, loss, bene-
> ficence, chance – and, ordering them into an encompassing structure,
> presents them in such a way as to throw into relief a particular view of their
> essential nature. (1993: 443)

The historical context

Let us return to the more scientifically oriented ideas of Glaser and
Strauss, whose tone in general is less committed to literary qualities
than that of Geertz in spite of certain similarities. Grounded theory
must be understood in its institutional and historical context, in which
sociologists felt that they must pay homage to principles of rigour
defined by a scientific community. Anthropology, on the other hand,
was relatively more free of the need to justify itself in these terms.
Glaser, as we saw, had been indirectly associated with Lazarsfeld and
indeed Merton, whose advocacy of 'theories of the middle range' (1968)
was in similar spirit to the views of Mills about the limits of empiricism
reported earlier. Strauss, on the other hand, had worked with Becker, a
leading representative of the postwar Chicago School, in his study of
medical students (Becker et al., 1961). Yet Glaser and Strauss also
sought to distinguish themselves from Chicago School ethnographic
method, saying that this often 'consisted of lengthy, detailed descriptions which resulted in very small amounts of theory, if any' (1967: 15).
Perhaps recognizing that this can hardly be said to characterize
the work of Becker (though it is an accurate depiction of much prewar
work in Chicago), they are critical of his work on other grounds,
claiming that he was overconcerned with verificationism. Support for
this view can be found in Becker's (1970b) article on problems of
inference and proof in participant observation, where there is a continual stress on the need to test theories in data so that conclusions can
be regarded as valid and reliable. He continues to pursue this commitment (Becker, 1998).

 This combination of influences, from mainstream sociological ethnography and from the scientific orientations of positivist quantitative
work, as well as a general commitment to middle-range theorizing,
proved to be a highly potent brew. Glaser and Strauss were able to
address the concerns of these various audiences, as well as to break free
from the constraints which these had hitherto imposed on qualitative

workers. There was massive appeal in the idea that everyone could generate theory, and that this at the same time could be presented as an articulation of a scientific spirit that had been lost by quantitative workers, seen in the claim that grounded theory was based in the inductive method. It provided a generation of qualitative research workers with a set of legitimating ideas, which could be used with audiences in grant-making bodies, supervisors and readers of research reports.

As Bryman (1988) has pointed out, however, this enthusiasm has at times led to some superficial strategies, where writers have claimed that they have done grounded theory when it is clear that they do not understand what the procedure involves. Silverman (1998a) presents similar criticisms in relation to a series of small-scale interview studies whose quality he examines, suggesting that these are over-reliant on an analytic approach that simply reports members' common-sense categories, without developing those of the researcher, in spite of claiming at times to be 'doing' grounded theory. Melia (1996) makes a similar point, claiming that some such studies 'can amount to little more than a nod in the direction of grounded theory and then a progression to a generalized qualitative analysis' (1996: 376).

Constant comparison

In addition to the strategy of theoretical sampling, perhaps the second core idea of grounded theorizing is that of the constant comparative method, which is used as a systematic tool for developing and refining theoretical categories and their properties. If applied rigorously, it can aid in taking researchers beyond common-sense reporting of participants' categories so that a study becomes genuinely relevant at a theoretical level. The method is not a loosely structured free-for-all, in which researchers glance impressionistically through their field notes looking for anecdotes that support their preconceived ideas. Instead, it is a rigorous strategy for producing thoroughly saturated theoretical accounts.

The method of constant comparison proceeds in four stages. First, incidents in data are coded into categories so that the different incidents that have been grouped together by the coding process can be compared. Very quickly, this begins to generate ideas about the properties of the category. An example can be given that is taken (and somewhat modified) from the work of Glaser and Strauss (1964a). As they observed nurses in hospital wards, they noticed that when a patient died nurses commonly would reflect on the death, expressing sentiments such as: 'He was so young', 'He was to be a doctor', 'She had a full life' or 'What will the children do without her?' These moments were coded as *social loss stories* by Glaser and Strauss, indicating that some calculation was being made of the degree to which the death represented a loss. As they looked at these different incidents, they gathered that this category had certain properties. For example age, social class and parental status appeared to influence the calculation of social loss.

The second stage of the constant comparative method involves the integration of categories and their properties, noting, for example, how properties interact. From detailed inspection and comparison of instances, it became clear that age and education interacted, so that educational level was very important in calculating social loss if the person who died was a middle-aged adult; for a very elderly person, however, educational level was of little importance. Additionally, at this second stage the interaction of different categories is noted. Glaser and Strauss found that nurses sometimes lost their composure and wept when certain patients died, but did not do so in other cases. This, again established through constantly comparing different instances, related to whether a social loss story constituted a successful rationale for the death. Death could be understood as a welcome relief in some cases, but a dreadful tragedy with which nurses identified in others.

The third stage is represented by theoretical saturation, discussed earlier, in which no new properties of categories appear and no new interactions occur. Theoretical sampling will appear to have exhausted all such possibilities. The fourth stage, writing the theory, is then relatively straightforward, since categories and their interactions provide chapter headings or titles of papers, properties provide section headings and the coded data provide plentiful illustrative examples, which may even be counted so that the reader may assess the generality of the phenomena described. Theories developed in this way will, in the first instance, be 'substantive', in that they explain the immediate phenomena of interest to the researcher. However, they may be thought to be generalizable to other related settings, in which case their potential scope is considerably broadened. Thus, as a substantive theory, the idea of the social loss rationale may only be applied in the sort of healthcare settings in which the theory was developed. But in a formal extrapolation, it might be applied more generally to the relationships between professionals and their clients. Thus, it can be hypothesized that all professionals involved in the provision of human services (social workers, teachers etc.) may calculate the social value of their clients according to their age, social class, educational background and so on, and vary the quality of their service to suit this perceived social value.

Staying on the ground

Although there is, in Glaser and Strauss, an emphasis on theory generation rather than verification, and this has been appealing to researchers wishing to propose themselves as theoreticians, their approach is not just about this. It is clear that grounded theorizing, by the very fact of its being 'grounded', involves a kind of 'testing' of researchers' ideas in data. In later work, Strauss (1987) was to place emphasis on the theory-testing element of grounded theorizing. Understandably, given the political context in which Glaser and Strauss were working, it was important to emphasize the theory-generating side of the approach, but equally these authors were quick to warn against the production, by mental operations alone, of free-floating concepts. Hammersley and Atkinson (1983), for example, propose that Glaser and Strauss might have extended their well-known typology of 'awareness contexts' by purely logical operations, without seeking out instances in data. Glaser and Strauss (1966) had proposed that the levels of aware-ness by dying people and those around them that death was a likely outcome were variable, so that some people were dying in 'closed awareness', not knowing that they were going to die, but surrounded by people who did know this. On the other hand, others knew that they were dying and openly acknowledged this fact with those around them, so that they existed in an 'open awareness' context. Between these two extremes lay 'pretense' (where both know but pretend not to know) and 'suspicion' (where one suspects but the other knows). Hammersley and Atkinson make the point, and indeed illustrate it with a diagram, that further possibilities logically exist. For example, there are situations where both parties do not know, or both suspect, or one suspects and the other does not know. Indeed, it is not hard to imagine such instances in a hypothetical research study.

In fact, Glaser and Strauss (1967) considered just such an analytic strategy, but the possibility that it might lead to ungrounded theory gave them cause for concern:

> Logical combination of these variables would yield 36 possible types, but to start research with all the logical combinations of these variables would be an unnecessarily complex task, considering that many or most types are empirically non-existent. Therefore, the procedure used to develop awareness context types related to interaction was first, to search data for relevant types; second, to logically substruct the variables involved; and so, on the basis of these variables to judge whether other possible types would be useful or necessary for handling the data. (1967: 103)

The use of the word 'substruct' in the quotation above is a clue to the source of their ideas, which lie in Lazarsfeld and Barton's (Barton, 1955) idea of 'property space analysis' (PSA), developed in the context of quantitative data analysis. Substruction was a term conceived by them to refer to a process conceived as the opposite of 'reduction' in PSA. PSA involves cross-tabulating variables to produce combinations. It is a useful logical 'trick of the trade' (Becker, 1998) for helping data analysts perceive that the things they have not yet found in data may nevertheless logically occur. This may be of assistance in directing further data collection, in the spirit of theoretical sampling. Yet the opposite process of 'reduction' may also be necessary in ruling out fruitless inquiry into situations which are either logically impossible, or are of little relevance to the purpose of the research, so can be ignored. Property space analysis is a good example of the use of theoretical operations as a resource to enhance creative data analysis.

Here, Glaser and Strauss are concerned to preserve an aspect of quality that otherwise they do not emphasize, the need to supply plentiful instances of illustrative examples, taken from things the researcher has seen or heard during fieldwork, rather than engaging in pure speculation, the hallmark of the 'theoretical capitalists' they were concerned to overthrow. Perhaps we may now judge them as over-cautious in this respect, but the ideal of maintaining rigorously explored linkages between theorizing and data is something from which most social research studies would benefit.

Later development of grounded theory

Both Glaser and Strauss have produced further book-length statements about the grounded theory approach (Glaser, 1978, 1992; Strauss, 1987; Strauss and Corbin, 1990). Of these, Strauss and Corbin (1990) is perhaps the best known, being a distillation of years of experience in supervising students and other researchers applying the original grounded theory approach, which in the 1967 book was expressed in language that was at times difficult to apply. The Strauss and Corbin volume has more of the feel of a textbook, focusing on showing researchers how to apply a well-established method by applying some well-tried procedures.

Strauss and Corbin are also significant in introducing three distinctive ways of coding data. In *open coding*, the researcher is involved in:

> naming and categorizing phenomena through close examination of data. Without this first basic analytical step, the rest of the analysis and communication that follows could not take place. During open coding the data are broken down into discrete parts, closely examined, compared for similarities and differences, and questions are asked about the phenomena as reflected in the data. Through this process, one's own and others' assumptions about phenomena are questioned or explored, leading to new discoveries. (Strauss and Corbin, 1990: 62)

Subsequently, *axial coding* becomes relevant, according to Strauss and Corbin. This involves intensive work with a single category, examining how it connects with other categories and seeking to explore its 'conditions, contexts, action/interactional strategies and consequences'

(Strauss and Corbin 1990: 96). The third type of coding activity Strauss and Corbin called *selective*, and this they associate with the point at which a fully fledged theory emerges. Taking a single 'core category' (such as 'awareness contexts', Glaser and Strauss, 1966, or 'dying trajectory', Glaser and Strauss, 1968), all other categories and their properties are regarded as subsidiary to the core. Strauss and Corbin give an example from Corbin's (1987) work on the approach of women with chronic illness towards their pregnancies, in which she found that the women played an active part in managing pregnancy risks. The core category that eventually emerged was that of 'protective governing', in which women were understood to be continually monitoring the risk status of their pregnancies, taking cues from a variety of sources including signs and the reactions of others. A variety of categories of action emanated from protective governing, including at times a trusting and cooperative relationship with healthcare staff, but at others a withdrawal from this relationship in order to 'save their babies' (Strauss and Corbin, 1990: 138).

To call these three activities 'coding' is something of a sleight of hand, as it is clear that only the first constitutes 'coding' as it was conceptualized in the 1967 book. Axial and selective 'coding' are in fact further elaborations of open codes, through a method of constant comparison. The book has a rather programmatic, formulaic feel to it and tends, according to Glaser (1992) in a critical response, to encourage an unwelcome degree of preconception. Glaser also argues that there is too much stress on verification in Strauss and Corbin, thus returning to one of the central issues of the original work on grounded theory. Indeed, a number of critics of grounded theorizing (Hammersley and Atkinson, 1995; Hammersley, 1995a; Rose, 1982) have noted both that theory verification should be regarded as important to qualitative researchers, and that Glaser and Strauss failed to recognize in their own work strong elements of theory testing. Glaser's main point of disagreement, however, concerns the overtechnical, rule-following behaviour that is expected of researchers following the Strauss and Corbin text. He prefers to stress the centrality of the idea of constant comparison as containing the simple central idea of grounded theorizing:

> Strauss' method of labelling and then grouping is totally unnecessary, laborious and is a waste of time. Using constant comparison method gets the analyst to the desired conceptual power, quickly, with ease and joy. Categories emerge upon comparison and properties emerge upon more comparison. And that is all there is to it. (Glaser, 1992: 43)

Quantitative data

Before assessing some criticisms that have been made of the grounded theory approach, it is worth stressing once again the overlaps between this method for analysing qualitative data and quantitative methodology. Traditionally, quantitative method is cast as hypothetico-deductive, with pre-existing theories being tested in data, rather than inductively generated. Yet this view of science is a narrow one, if the experience of natural scientists is examined. Peter Medawar's famous (1991; first published 1963) paper 'Is the scientific paper a fraud?' was in fact premised on the view that the method of induction was widely felt by natural scientists to be at the core of the scientific approach (even though Medawar himself was questioning this). In fact, both characterizations of science are limited, as neither pure induction nor pure deduction can wholly account for what scientists do (Blaikie, 1993).

Glaser and Strauss (1967) contains a chapter on the 'theoretical elaboration of quantitative data', in which they point out that such data are amenable to theory generation as much as qualitative data, even though quantitative data have often been used to verify theories in practice. Drawing on Glaser's experience of the elaboration paradigm, they advocate an exploratory approach to quantitative data analysis that 'breaks' some of the 'rules' erected by those concerned with verification alone. Thus they advocate a relaxed approach towards representative sampling and argue for the use of crude, *ad hoc* indices made during secondary analysis of data sets in order to explore emerging ideas. In a striking contravention of conventional advice about the proper approach to significant testing, they advocate running as many cross-tabulations as possible in order to see which ones look interesting (a 'fishing' approach that is anathema to the conventional quantitative methodologist – Selvin and Stuart, 1966). They also suggest the liberal use of cluster analysis in the pursuit of ideas.

It is remarkable that Glaser and Strauss were able in 1967 to sketch the outlines of this flexible and creative approach to quantitative data analysis which, in their day, would have had to be implemented by laborious hand calculations. The advent of statistical packages and personal computers has made this exploratory use of quantitative data sets feasible, through the provision of rapid feedback on researchers' emerging questions asked of data, enabling a rapid, interactive cycling between data and theorizing that could only be imagined in 1967.

Having said that, it is significant that Durkheim, in the pre-computer age, supplies us with just such an approach, in his study of *Suicide* (1970; first published 1897). Clearly, the measurement validity of the official statistics on which Durkheim relied is now questionable (Douglas, 1967), but we can, nevertheless, see that *Suicide* is a remarkable early example from social research demonstrating the inductive generation of theory from data. Thus Durkheim began by noting raised rates of suicide in certain social groups: Protestants, the old, urban dwellers, the unmarried, the childless, the male sex and the rich. By asking what these apparently diverse groups could have in common, he was able to generate a substantive theory to explain the phenomenon, involving the idea of anomie, whereby the conditions under which certain groups lived distanced them from social regulation, leaving them relatively unintegrated with society. Obviously this was also a formal theory of very broad scope, prompting analysts of many different phenomena to apply this social model of moral regulation and cohesion.

Quantitative as well as qualitative data can thus be incorporated into a grounded theory approach. This is consistent with one important message of this book (for which see Chapter 9), that an insistence on artificial and essentialist divides between data expressed in words and data expressed in numbers damages rather than enhances the quality of social research.

Limitations and criticisms of grounded theory

The point made by Brown (1973) and Rose (1982) that the grounded theory approach fails to recognize that theory can be generated from quantitative data is therefore hardly sustainable if we examine the original text of Glaser and Strauss. It is true, however, that the political appeal of the approach lay in its capacity to defend the claims of qualitative work to rigour, as well as giving it a distinctive new identity to contrast with the quantitative orthodoxy of the day. This may account for the underplaying of quantitative method that Brown and Rose perceive.

More significant, however, is Brown's point that grounded theorizing is an inappropriate methodology for certain types of research problem. Brown, for example, was interested in unconscious processes at work in the connection between social factors and mental disorder, inferring the existence of these by demonstrating causal links that could be explained by no other means. Clearly, such things cannot be observed directly. Brown also notes that certain types of long-term historical process would not be amenable to the grounded theory approach. Thus he argues:

> [Grounded theory] may only be profitable in a fairly limited range of cir-
> cumstances. The type of material best given to the development of grounded
> theory . . . tends to involve relatively short-term processes, sequences of
> behaviour that are directly observed or can be easily reported upon, and
> behaviour which has a repetitive character. Something missed can often be
> observed again. (1973: 8)

In defence of grounded theory, nevertheless, we can say that Brown's points relate not so much to the analytic methods described by Glaser and Strauss – the method of constant comparison, theoretical sampling and so on – but more to the common dependence of grounded theory on observational and interview data. In fact, there is no logical reason why other types of data cannot be included in the approach. Comparative analysis, using historical records that relate to large-scale societal developments, for example, has a distinguished history in social research (Llobera, 1998), though its practitioners will rarely have conceptualized their methods in terms of grounded theory.

Critique from postmodernism   Another strand of criticism is expressed by Coffey et al. (1996) who object to the narrow analytic strategy imposed by a heavy reliance on coding as a first step. This, they feel, is particularly encouraged by computer software for the analysis of qualitative data, based on a code-and-retrieve logic, often explicitly linked by software authors to a grounded theory style of analysis (for example Thomas Muhr's ATLASti programme, or John Seidel's ETHNOGRAPH). These authors worry that this results in the application of 'standardized, often mechanistic procedures' (1996: 7.6). Coffey and Atkinson (1996) describe a variety of analytic strategies that, they feel, do not involve the coding and retrieval approach which, they say, is inevitably linked to grounded theorizing. Thus, they argue that discourse analysis (Potter and Wetherell, 1987) or the analysis of formal narrative structure (for example Riessman, 1993) depend more on the thoughtful teasing out of the subtle and various meanings of particular words, or on a global perception of whole structures within data, that are otherwise fragmented and decontextualized if discrete segments are coded and grouped with others under invented categories. Coffey et al. (1996) propose instead an approach to data analysis and representation that is consistent with postmodern sensibilities. This depends on the use of 'hypertext' links, which preserve data in their original form, allowing the 'reader' or user to leap from one link to another in an exploration of data that is open ended, akin to the experience of the original producers of the data themselves. They equate grounded theorizing with an attempt to impose a single, exclusive interpretation of data, and advocate their hypertext alternative as allowing a much more open-ended presentation, recognizing multiple meanings that both actors and readers may bring to instances of text. In this respect they espouse a similar approach to research writing to those advocated by postmodern ethnographers (for example Tyler, 1986), reviewed in Chapter 11 of this book.

Against this, Kelle (1997) has pointed out that the equation of coding with grounded theorizing and indeed with the imposition of singular interpretations is somewhat forced. He argues instead that two broad possibilities exist for data analysts who wish to identify similarities and differences between particular text passages, and that these had been in existence in various branches of scholarship (including biblical hermeneutics) for hundreds of years, before becoming an issue for social scientists. On the one hand are *indexes*, such as an author or subject index in a book. 'Coding' of the sort described by Glaser and Strauss might equally well be termed 'indexing' in this sense. On the other hand, *cross-references* can be constructed, of the sort that Coffey et al. describe in their advocacy of hyperlinks, whereby textual passages are linked together. A King James bible contains such devices, so that a teaching of Jesus in one of the gospels is linked with the Old Testament passage to which Jesus refers.

Kelle then observes that in biblical scholarship 'techniques for indexing or cross references are used similarly by all interpreters . . . whether they take into account or not the polyvocality and diversity of biblical authors' (1997: 2.4). The distinction between the two, made by Coffey et al., which equates indexing with univocality and cross-references with polyvocality is, Kelle argues, therefore unsustainable. This diversion into the deeper reaches of the scholarly tradition is helpful in addressing some issues raised by postmodern critics of grounded theorizing as being overscientized or, perhaps, simply old-fashioned. We saw this at the start of this book, in Denzin's critique of grounded theorizing, in which he declared it out of touch with the sensibilities of 'fifth-moment' qualitative researchers. Glaser and Strauss are indeed committed to a strong authorial presence, and to the con-struction of a persuasive singular narrative. But this is done within a fallibilistic context that allows for continual revision and development as new evidence, or voices, emerge.

Conclusion

As with many methodological developments that emerged in earlier contexts in which qualitative research flourished, such as analytic induction, triangulation or member validation, I propose that qualitative researchers would benefit by retaining a hold on the underlying prin-ciples of grounded theorizing, rather than dismissing these as incon-sistent with contemporary sensibilities or opting, wholesale, for the postmodern alternative *à la* Denzin. Although grounded theory emerged in an era of scientism, and its more technical explications are sometimes unwelcome reminders of this, the spirit that lies behind the approach can be simply explained, and does not have to be attached to a naively realist epistemology, or indeed to an oppressive urge to force readers to regard its products as true for all time. It demands a rigorous spirit of self-awareness and self-criticism, as well as an openness to new ideas that is often a hallmark of research studies of good quality.

KEY POINTS

- The methods of grounded theory encourage a helpful discipline in researchers, assisting a creative interaction between theory and research practice.

- The grounding of theoretical statements creates clear links between concepts and their indicators, and between claims and the evidence for these.

- Theoretical sampling and constant comparison generate thick, saturated descriptions of considerable scope.

- The method of grounded theorizing should be understood within the predominantly scientific context in which it was created; yet researchers working within more contemporary paradigms can benefit from attention to the methods that it emphasizes.

8

Generalizing from Qualitative Research

CONTENTS

In the discussion of external validity in Chapter 4, I described the perception held by some that social research can be divided into two great camps: the nomothetic and the ideographic. This distinction brings us very close to what many see as the key distinction between quantitative and qualitative methodologies. Ideographic methods elucidate unique aspects of particular phenomena, often seen in studies of historical events as well as other qualitative case studies. Nomothetic approaches, on the other hand, seek to generate law-like statements that apply across many settings and events, some of which may lie in the future and are relatively free of particular contingencies of time and space. The distinction was originally proposed by the neo-Kantian Windelband as a way of separating natural and social science. Weber, however, took issue with this (1949), arguing that it was possible to achieve both in social science. This is consistent with his approach to other oppositions that his predecessors stressed, such as the supposed separation of studies of cause and of meaning. Weber, of course, argued for both as legitimate goals for social scientists (Crotty, 1998).

This synthesizing approach of Weber has in fact been reflected in the experience of many practising social researchers, who have commonly found it helpful to combine qualitative and quantitative, ideographic and nomothetic, the study of the particular with attempts to make this generally relevant. In this chapter I shall discuss a variety of conceptions of the generalizability of qualitative research studies. Some of these, we shall see, depend on the use of numbers, others do not. Although some of these ideas are persuasive, others are less so.

It is worth noting, however, that the goal of generalization is not always an important consideration for research studies. Particular cases may be worth investigating for their own sake. For example, an evaluation study of whether some programme is effective or not may not involve concerns about whether that programme will work elsewhere. A study of the workings of an institution, if it is sufficiently important (say, a government department), may be of great importance to many people without seeking to learn general lessons about the working of equivalent institutions. However, while this is sufficient to justify some research work, obviously any case study of this sort will generate greater benefit if it can be a reliable guide to what happens elsewhere. The goal of generalization therefore seems worth pursuing if at all possible.

Naturalism and thick description

Generalization in quantitative survey research is based on choosing representative samples and using ideas about probability and chance to estimate the likelihood of events occurring in similar cases outside the sample. An essential part of this strategy is the study of fairly large numbers of cases, something which qualitative researchers have found difficult, since they have commonly thought of themselves as studying individual cases in depth, sometimes just a single one. Generalizing from a case of one on the basis of the statistical probability of its being representative of some population has led many to say that external validity is very difficult to achieve for qualitative researchers. Against this view is the argument that qualitative studies of individual cases are strong on 'naturalism' or 'ecological validity'. Pursuing this kind of argument, Lincoln and Guba (1985) suggest that naturalistic inquiry can therefore be effective in achieving 'transferability', especially if full details of the context in which events occur within a case are given in a research report. Yet on its own this is not enough, as the following quote suggests:

> Whether [working hypotheses] hold in some other context, or even in the same context at some other time, is an empirical issue, the resolution of which depends upon the degree of similarity between sending and receiving (or earlier and later) contexts. Thus the naturalist cannot specify the external

validity of an inquiry; he or she can provide only the thick description necessary to enable someone interested in making a transfer to reach a conclusion about whether the transfer can be contemplated as a possibility. (Lincoln and Guba, 1985: 316)

Note that it is not just the 'sending' context but also the 'receiving' context about which details are needed, according to Lincoln and Guba. Logically, this would require study of at least two cases. These authors in fact use this to argue against the adequacy of quantitative researchers' ideas about external validity, claiming that one cannot generalize from a sample to a population unless one makes unwarranted assumptions about the characteristics of the population. This is a rather extreme position, going beyond, for example, LeCompte and Goetz's (1982) rather similar ideas about transferability. In practice, both qualitative and quantitative researchers rely on the common sense of readers to establish whether the proposed receiving context (or 'population') is similar to the cases studied. Indeed, it is hard to imagine any other basis on which research could proceed. Just as quantitative researchers often study samples because they cannot afford to do a complete population census, so qualitative researchers cannot study every context to which readers might wish to generalize results. Put simply, this means that readers must always make their own judgements about the relevance of findings for their own situations. Threats to such transferability are dealt with most adequately if details, or 'thick' descriptions of the 'sending' context (or the 'sample'), are provided.

This is precisely the conclusion reached by Brown and Harris (1978), whose mixing of qualitative and quantitative work is discussed in Chapter 9. Classically, thick description is achieved in participant observation, where long periods of fieldwork and the resultant 'immersion' of the researcher in the setting are likely to provide an adequate level of detail. Geertz (1988) describes a variety of textual strategies used by anthropologists to persuade readers that they have, in his terms, 'been there'. These give the reader a vicarious experience of having 'been there' with the researcher:

> Ethnographers need to convince us . . . not merely that they themselves have truly 'been there,' but . . . that had we been there we should have seen what they saw, felt what they felt, concluded what they concluded. (Geertz, 1988: 16)

Although Geertz does not relate this to the issue of transferability, it is clear that if research texts can give readers this experience, transferability of the type described by Lincoln and Guba is likely to be enhanced. Readers, like travellers returning home, can use their human judgement to establish whether the conditions they have encountered 'abroad' have any relevance for their present circumstances.

Theoretical generalization

Theoretical generalization is a second rationale for generalizing from qualitative research studies (Mitchell, 1983). This concept deserves some attention, if only because it is widely cited by authors seeking to dispense with statistical or 'empirical' generalization (for example Silverman, 1993; Yin, 1989; Bryman, 1988; Dingwall, 1992). As I shall show, however, all generalization from research is in some sense 'empirical' and depends on assumptions that are, in the last analysis, only thoroughly testable by further information about 'receiving' contexts.

Mitchell's (1983) account of generalization from case study is an influential piece outlining the rationale for theoretical generalization. He argues that after the 1950s, interest in generalizing from case studies declined as surveys and the logic of statistical inference dominated. Case studies could nevertheless be useful in leading to general theoretical principles, a rationale very different from that of statistical sampling. The basis of theoretical generalization lies in logic rather than probability: 'We infer that the features present in a case study will be related in a wider population not because the case is representative but because our analysis is unassailable.' (Mitchell, 1983: 200). He points out that Znaniecki's (1934) distinction between enumerative and analytic induction follows the same reasoning. Enumerative induction involves studying cases belonging to some class of phenomenon to see if they all share a characteristic. In analytic induction, the cases are not taken to be examples of a class beforehand; the analyst proceeds by selecting cases that illuminate aspects of a general theory. Although one case might be enough to get complete knowledge, in practice cases may not have all elements present that can support a theory, so often extra cases must be studied.

Mitchell advocates choosing the case for its power to explain rather than for its typicality, arguing that idiosyncratic cases can throw general principles into sharp relief. Here, he gives the example of Pasteur and the discovery of penicillin. A case, then, is only significant in the context of a theory. Mitchell speaks of logical inference replacing statistical inference, where the researcher can be confident that a theoretically necessary or logical connection can be generalized from a case study to some other population of cases. The validity of the extrapolation depends not on the typicality of the case, but on the strength of the theoretical reasoning.

One can see continuities between this argument and the ideas of Glaser and Strauss (1967) concerning theoretical sampling (see Chapter 7). The original article by Mitchell is strikingly short on examples of theoretical generalization; it is therefore interesting that two later authors who advocate this approach rely on examples from Glaser and Strauss's study of dying in hospitals. Thus Silverman (1993: 160) uses the following quote from Bryman's (1988) discussion of this:

> The issue of whether the particular hospital studied is 'typical' is not the critical issue; what is important is whether the experiences of dying patients are typical of the broad class of phenomena . . . to which the theory refers. Subsequent research would then focus on the validity of the proposition in other milieux (e.g. doctors' surgeries). (Bryman, 1988: 91)

This, of course, follows the classic distinction made by Glaser and Strauss between substantive theory and formal theory (described in Chapter 7). As we saw, they illustrated this with the example of 'social loss stories', whereby nurses calculated the social value of patients who had died. Glaser and Strauss argued that similar processes might occur between any professionals and their clients, suggesting that this represented the move from substantive to formal theory. Dingwall (1992) follows the same thinking, explaining theoretical generalization by using the example of Goffman (1961) on asylums and his generalization from this type of institution to the theoretical class of 'total institutions' (prisons, the army, public schools), which he understood to share certain core characteristics. But perhaps the most telling example of theoretical generalization is contained in a study written long before the term was coined; it both illustrates the concept and points us towards its key deficiency, so is worth quoting at length. It arises in a case study of a particular religion, whose core features were taken to be shared by all religions:

> At the beginning of this work, we announced that the religion whose study we were taking up contained within it the most characteristic elements of the religious life. The exactness of this proposition may now be verified. Howsoever simple the system that we have studied may be, we have found within it all the great ideas and the principal ritual attitudes which are at the basis of even the most advanced religions: the division of things into sacred and profane, the notions of the soul, of spirits, of mythical personalities, and of a national and even international divinity [etc.] . . . nothing essential is lacking. We are thus in a position to hope that the results at which we have arrived are not peculiar to totemism alone, but can aid us in an understanding of what religion in general is.
>
> It may be objected that one single religion, whatever its field of extension may be, is too narrow a base for such an induction. We have not dreamed for a moment of ignoring the fact that an extended verification may add to the authority of a theory, but it is equally true that when a law has been proven by one well-made experiment, this proof is valid universally. If in one single case a scientist succeeded in finding out the secret of the life of even the most protoplasmic creature that can be imagined, the truths thus obtained would be applicable to all living beings, even the most advanced. Then if, in our studies of these very humble societies, we have really succeeded in discovering some of the elements out of which the most fundamental religious notions are made up, there is no reason for not extending the most general results of our researches to other religions. In fact, it is inconceivable that the same effect may be due now to one cause, now to another, according to the

circumstances, unless the two causes are at bottom only one. A single idea cannot express one reality here and another one there, unless the duality is only apparent. If among certain peoples the ideas of sacredness, the soul and God are to be explained sociologically, it should be presumed scientifically that, in principle, the same explanation is valid for all the peoples among whom these same ideas are found with the same essential characteristics. Therefore, supposing that we have not been deceived, certain at least of our conclusions can be legitimately generalized. (Durkheim, 1976: 415–16; first published 1915)

This comes from Durkheim's *The Elementary Forms of the Religious Life*, which reflected his underlying assumption that societies could be arranged along an evolutionary spectrum, from the simplest to the most complex. Simple societies exhibited structures that were also fundamental to more complex societies, just as protoplasmic organisms contained structures shared by more advanced organisms. These are positivist and essentialist assumptions which are in general no longer shared by qualitative social researchers. Apart from any philosophical objections that one might have, it seems factually wrong to imagine that human social organization is structured hierarchically, in the manner of biological organisms. Durkheim's evolutionism now seems little more than an imaginative, but misleading metaphor.

Having said this, we can note that some qualitative researchers still wish to discover a set of building blocks forming the universal basis for human social interaction across cultures. This is particularly evident in conversation analytic studies which, as we have seen, involve some surprisingly positivistic ambitions. Peräkylä (1997) expresses this well when he says:

In studies of ordinary conversation, the baseline assumption is that the results are or should be generalizable to the whole domain of ordinary conversations, and to a certain extent even across linguistic and cultural boundaries. Even though it may be that the most primordial conversational practices and structures – such as turn-taking or adjacency pairs – are almost universal, there are others, such as openings of telephone calls . . . which show considerable variation in different cultures. (1997: 214)

The metaphors from evolutionary biology in both Durkheim and Peräkylä ('protoplasmic' and 'primordial') show the similarity of thought. Conversation analysts, however, are unusual in their ambitions, compared with most qualitative researchers who are in general highly sensitive to the context-bounded character of the phenomena that they study. That this sensitivity has a political edge is reflected in a later sentence from Peräkylä, where he discusses the generalizability of one of his own studies: 'there is no reason to think that they could not be made possible by any competent member of (at least any Western) society' (1997: 215). The phrase in brackets alerts us to the anxieties of many social researchers faced with the potential charge of ethnocentrism should generalizing ambitions reach too far.

Clearly, Durkheim generated a theory from his study of a single religion; Glaser and Strauss generated a theory from their study of dying; Goffman did the same from his study of an asylum. Theoretical concepts arising from these case studies attest to this: the sacred/ profane distinction; the calculation of social loss; the notion of the total institution. Conversation analysis also generates theoretical categories (for example adjacency pairs, turn taking). One can call this 'generalizing to a theory' if one likes, but I believe it is less misleading to say, along with Glaser and Strauss, that this constitutes the generation of theory, whose general relevance has to be established by further empirical study. In the absence of such study, readers must rely on the personal knowledge of the 'receiving contexts' to which they wish to apply the lessons learned in the 'sending' case. Otherwise, they fall prey to precisely the weakness of some quantitative work identified by those advocating qualitative research as a better alternative: unwarranted assumptions are made about the characteristics of the population of cases not yet studied, and the attempt to generalize is, at least potentially, an act of violation.

There is another way of putting this objection to theoretical generalization that some readers may find persuasive. The similarities between arguments for theoretical generalization and analytic induction have already been noted. Hammersley (1992b), who also points to this, observes that one of Znaniecki's (1934) arguments in favour of analytic induction was that the researcher must try to determine the essential characteristics of a case, excluding incidental or atypical characteristics. In this way, the problem of rival interpretations of a single case might be solved, so that its essential core is revealed. As Hammersley (1992b) points out, however, such operations are less secure in social research compared, say, with natural science, since confident assumptions in the stability and universality of social phenomena cannot be made. The identification of 'essential features' of a case will always be somewhat speculative and refutable by further examples. Many will claim the right to see different features as essential. Resolution of differences will be a subtle mixture of careful observation and persuasive argument in the context of existing assumptions within the research literature.

Theoretical generalization, then, is an idea that potentially misleads qualitative social researchers concerned to improve the generalizability of their studies. Thick and detailed description of individual 'sending' cases, chosen on the basis of evidence about the similarities with proposed 'receiving' cases, preferably bolstered by a study of several cases rather than just one, is a more secure basis for good work. Theories generated from single cases should always be seen as fallible propositions that might be modified in the light of further experience, however impeccable the logic that ties them to the single setting in which they were created. Additionally, as I shall show in the next section, the desire to generalize (which is a legitimate goal for social researchers) is enhanced by exploiting the potential of numbers, recognizing the importance of enumerative induction.

Using numbers to generalize

Bryman's (1988) work is helpful in outlining several ways in which the use of numbers can help qualitative researchers establish the generalizability of their results. In particular, he cites several studies that combine a quantitative social survey approach with a qualitative in-depth case study of particular cases. The distribution of variables revealed by the social survey is used to indicate the degree to which the cases chosen for qualitative study are typical. Bryman describes examples from educational research. Smith and Robbins (1982) surveyed over 1000 schools and school districts to establish the degree to which parents were involved in the running of schools. Using the results of this survey, a small number of schools were selected to represent different degrees of involvement (as well as other variables), which were then studied in depth. A similar approach was followed by Huberman and Crandall (1982), who used a survey of some 4000 people in 145 school districts to select just 12 sites for more detailed ethnographic study. Readers of these reports were then able to judge the degree to which case study material was representative of the variety to be found within these populations.

Combining survey with case study: an example

In my own study of equal opportunities policies in secondary schools (Pratt et al., 1982) I and my colleagues used a similar approach. Our aim in this study was to establish the degree to which secondary schools conformed to the letter and spirit of the 1975 Sex Discrimination Act. Our first step in doing this was to write to every local education authority (LEA) in England and Wales asking the chief education officer to nominate two schools that he or she believed to be following good practice in this policy area. In addition to this *nominated* sample, a second *cluster* sample of all the schools in six randomly chosen LEAs was drawn. The schools in these two samples were sent postal questionnaires asking about key features of their practice relating to equality of opportunity between the sexes. For example, they were asked whether all clubs and societies were open to both sexes, whether careers education included analysis of gender issues, whether special provision was made for pupils doing subjects that were not traditional for their sex.

Additionally, we asked schools to send us a variety of written materials which most schools routinely produce: a school prospectus; a booklet describing the subject options available to pupils at age 13; a copy of the choice form on which pupils recorded their hoped-for subject choices. We devised standard tests for these materials, with quantifiable results. Thus we recorded whether school prospectuses contained a statement saying that all subjects were equally open to boys and girls. We recorded whether options booklets contained statements that particular subjects were for one sex only. We tested, for each choice form, whether particular combinations of subjects that mixed traditionally gendered subjects (for example needlework or technical drawing) were possible, or whether this led to a timetable clash.

With the questionnaire results and the results of the standard tests, we were able to rank all the schools in our two samples according to whether they scored highly on particular aspects of good practice. Thus a crude scale was built up, meaning that schools with many features of 'good practice' could score up to nine points. An alternative ranking was a 'bad school' score, which added together features of 'bad practice'. Our statistical analysis revealed that schools in areas with a relatively high level of financial provision for educational services were likely to score highly on 'good practice'.

With this information, as well as standard information about the size of schools, their type (grammar, comprehensive, single sex etc.) and other matters of record in official statistics, we were able to select 14 schools for detailed case studies, involving extended visits to these schools by the research team in which lessons were observed and interviews with pupils and teachers were carried out. In these case studies we were able to follow up new lines of inquiry, uncover practices that did not appear in the survey results, and in general gain a holistic picture of the life of the institution as it related to the equal opportunities issue. Schools were sent reports summarizing our impressions of their practices for comments and, in some cases, correction.

An extract from the appendix to our research report shows how we were able to select a variety of schools when the survey information was used. This consists of brief summaries of core characteristics of five of the selected schools:

'*Midland Comprehensive*' 11–18 comprehensive; 720 pupils; Midlands; city centre catchment; Labour LEA; amalgamation of two single-sex schools; poor situation and catchment; 50 per cent of pupils non-European background; positive discrimination policy towards non-traditional choice, pioneered by headteacher.

'*Inner City Comprehensive*' 11–18 comprehensive; 850 pupils; London city centre catchment; Labour LEA; popular school with active equal opportunities policy promoted by dynamic headteacher and widely supported by staff.

'*Northern Modern*' 11–16 secondary modern; 760 pupils; mainly council estate catchment; northern region; Conservative LEA; head least sympathetic to equal opportunities of all we visited.

'*Smallchange Secondary*' 12–18 secondary modern; 720 pupils; in southern rural catchment; Conservative LEA; passive view of equal opportunities.

'*Oldboys Grammar*' 11–18 grammar school in prosperous London suburb; 700 pupils; Conservative LEA; highly traditional atmosphere and emphasis on academic excellence; little concern with equal opportunities. (1982: 240–1)

An extract from a report on one of these schools shows how practices hidden to the survey researcher could sometimes be revealed:

> An . . . example of modification of [commitment to equal opportunities] because of opposition was encountered in 'Northern Modern'. In the first year all pupils experience an 'intermediate' form of all crafts in co-educational groups. In years 2 and 3, single-sex classes are introduced and boys and girls follow craft courses traditional for their sex. This arrangement is said to comply with the Act while compromising with the staff in the craft departments, who opposed it . . . the female home economics teacher . . . said she resented the loss of time to boys who opted for the subject and emphasized the 'inescapable biological fact that girls have a more natural aptitude for needlework'. (1982: 144–5)

In another school ('Smallchange Secondary'), a choice form that had apparently 'passed' all our tests of non-discrimination possessed some mysterious boxes next to each subject description. A home economics teacher told us that these were used to indicate whether each subject teacher felt that particular pupils should be excluded from certain subjects. Thus pupils judged to be of lower ability might, for example, be excluded from the 'difficult' subjects of physics or chemistry. The teacher added that these were often used, in practice, to exclude the non-traditional sex if teachers did not wish to have mixed classes. To test this, we asked to see the completed forms for a previous year group of pupils; sure enough, several teachers of craft subjects had systematically crossed the boxes of pupils of the 'wrong' sex.

The important point to note is that our survey results had also shown both of these schools to rate low on the 'good practice' score. Such hidden practices were less likely to be found in our high-scoring case study schools, giving us a basis on which to claim that they probably occurred only in a small minority of schools, however dramatic the individual anecdotes might appear. Thus a sense of proportion about the likely prevalence of these events was gained, tempered by the many examples of good practice reported and observed in other schools. Had we simply studied the 14 case study schools in depth, this judgement would not have been possible.

Sampling within the case

As well as assessment of the external representativeness of case studies, attention to sampling issues *within* cases can be enhanced by counting.

Typically, field workers proceed by infiltrating social networks, seeking out individuals who seem likely to be cooperative or interesting, or choosing settings to enter according to opportunistic criteria. Interactions and access negotiations are heavily influenced by the researcher's characteristics, by the relatively fixed ones like gender, age or ethnic appearance, or by characteristics that are culturally ascribed by actors. Such snowball or volunteer sampling can lead to an unrepresentative account, stressing the views of an exclusive group of informants for example. The essence of the Mead/Freeman dispute (see Chapter 10) appears to rest, at least in part, on this problem. Mead's informants were largely teenage girls; Freeman's were male heads of family. Small wonder that Mead recorded sexual liberation and Freeman recorded an oppressive morality about sex. The only surprising aspect is that one study could be conceived as a refutation of the other, given that each researcher was effectively studying a different group of people.

Attention to sampling within a case guards against assuming that the view gained from one vantage point is representative of the whole. The use of numbers makes it possible to estimate such bias, aided by a willingness to imagine one's own results as fallible. Sieber (1979) gives an example from his study of schools, where he was particularly concerned that he might have overestimated the job satisfaction of rank-and-file teachers, due to his having interacted disproportionately with their superiors in the hierarchy of the educational system:

> our own fieldwork . . . developed into a study of school boards, superintendents, and the leaders of the high school teachers. After conducting a survey, however, I was able to correct certain impressions that emerged from my elite bias. This can be shown quite simply. Prior to looking at the results of the survey, I predicted the proportion of teachers who would respond in particular ways to the survey questions. I then compared my predictions with the actual responses. It became obvious when observing these comparisons that I had unwittingly adopted the elites' version of reality. For example, I overestimated the extent to which teachers felt that the administration accepted criticism. Here are the relevant questions and the statistics: 'Do you think that teachers who are interested in administrative openings jeopardize their opportunities in this district by voicing criticism of present school policies and practices?' (% responding 'definitely' and 'possibly'):

	Predicted	Observed
System A	40	60
System B	40	65

> Similarly, I had assumed that the teachers were more satisfied with evaluative procedures than was in fact the case: 'All in all, how well do you think the evaluation of teachers is done in your school?' (% responding 'as well as possible' and 'fairly well'):

	Predicted	Observed
System A		
Elementary	80	65
Secondary	50	36
System B		
Elementary	80	74
Secondary	75	56

Although to a lesser extent, I also overestimated the rank-and-file support for the leaders of the teachers' association, with whom I had spent a good deal of time. In short, I had fallen prey to the elite bias, despite recent training in the dangers of giving greater weight to prestigious figures as informants. (1979: 1353)

Sieber suggests that qualitative field research benefits most from this sort of information if it is gathered before the end of fieldwork, so that such obvious biases can be remedied by seeking out people or settings insufficiently represented up to that point. It is important to note that this does not require the researcher to extend depth investigations to all elements within cases. In-depth fieldwork can still be restricted to a few key informants or settings, with the elements in the wider-ranging counting procedure being studied superficially if at all, perhaps only requiring that a few simple facts be recorded about each case (for example age, gender and occupational level). These are not impossible requirements, but can be invaluable in persuading readers of the objectivity with which a study has been conducted.

Additionally, we can note that certain other features of good qualitative work depend on ideas that are inextricable from the sort of reasoning that numbers encourage. The desirability of theoretical sampling and the search for negative instances in the pursuit of a fallibilistic research strategy have been stressed earlier in this book. These procedures depend on implicit reasoning about the universe of cases (or elements within cases) available for study. Glaser and Strauss, in deciding to extend their study of awareness contexts to include, first, settings where dying trajectories were brief, then lengthy, or where awareness was absent or present, had some sense that dying people could be ranked on these variables that at the time of their ground-breaking fieldwork they were only beginning to conceptualize. Aware that they had only studied one end of a variable's distribution, they sought out cases that existed at the other end in acts which they called theoretical sampling. This was done without the aid of explicit counting; they did not know the exact statistical distributions of awareness levels or dying trajectories, but their sampling decisions depended on the notion that these could exist. In fact, later work has been done to establish such distributions in representative statistical samples of dying people (Seale et al., 1997). There is clearly potential for incorporating such counting operations in exploratory qualitative work largely devoted to the generation of theory.

Conclusion

I have argued in this chapter that generalization is a desirable goal for qualitative social researchers. Thick, detailed case study description can give readers a vicarious experience of 'being there' with the researcher, so that they can use their human judgement to assess the likelihood of the same processes applying to other settings which they know. While the generation of theory in qualitative work may be desirable for other purposes, I have argued that theoretical generalization is a flawed rationale, as it depends on the assumption of universal structures or laws; in the last analysis, all attempts at generalization are 'empirical'. Finally, I turned to the uses of numbers in supporting generalization to defined populations, pursuing a rationale similar to that applied by quantitative survey researchers. In the chapter that follows, I shall expand considerably the discussion of the uses of numbers by qualitative researchers, to the point of claiming that it may be time finally to abandon the distinction between 'qualitative' and quantitative' social research.

KEY POINTS

- Although some case studies are of intrinsic interest, in most cases it is an advantage to try to generalize the relevance of qualitative research studies.

- Transferability to other settings is enhanced by a rich, detailed account of the 'sending' context, and may be helped by analysis of the extent to which similar conditions apply in the 'receiving' context.

- The success of theoretical generalization is, in the last analysis, dependent on empirical confirmation.

- Statistical surveys can help researchers establish the typicality of cases and of the representativeness of elements studied within cases.

9

Using Numbers

CONTENTS

The simplest way in which qualitative social research can be defined is in terms of a negative: it is research that does not use numbers. Although a little familiarity with the products of qualitative research soon reveals that this is not exclusively the case, and reflection of any depth about qualitative methodology soon leads us to question the division between qualitative and quantitative, this nevertheless remains an underlying sentiment for many qualitative research practitioners. In part, this is because of the critique of numbers within the creation myth of qualitative research (see Chapter 4) which works away at a sub-conscious level, supporting researchers at moments of uncertainty by giving a firm, if crude, bedrock on which to build a secure sense of purpose.

Classically, one sees the turn away from numbers and towards words in the famous deconstructions of quantitative methodology that preceded the very widespread shift towards the interpretive alternatives that really gathered pace in the 1970s. Cicourel's (1964) devastating and (to my eyes) somewhat ironic critique of measurement strategies was one such deconstruction. He argued, convincingly, that 'measurement by fiat' occurred commonly in quantitative work at the data-analysis stage. Correlations between variables, once found, had to be explained, and this was done by the power of imagination rather than on the basis of evidence. Quantitative researchers decided that a measurement result 'meant' a certain thing rather than another, thus fixing meanings in ways that suited their preconceptions. Additionally, attitude measurement in particular, especially if done through fixed-choice questions, depended on (and itself constructed) an essentialist vision of personality, as if people carried with them a set of fixed, relatively inflexible (indeed 'frozen') views which they applied to all their interactions. The qualitative alternative stressed instead the study of the local production of meaning in specific contexts.

The critique of official statistics (for example Hindess, 1973) continued this theme, demonstrating the myriad ways in which crude quantification placed unlike things together, so that particular stories might be told by those in power about suicide, crime, disease, immigration, race, sexuality and other matters of official concern. More recently, and less overtly linked to the issuing of methodological advice, we have scholarly analyses of the role that numbers have played in generating a mentality of government. Hacking (1990) has shown how the avalanche of statistics that occurred in the nineteenth century enacted a new approach to social regulation, defining normal behaviour in terms of statistical averages. Numbers defined new classes of person and initiated a general public sense that social affairs were subject to the laws of probability, themselves calculable and therefore perhaps controllable. The subtext to this is to identify numbers as governmental tools, penetrating everyday thought in an all-pervasive surveillance operation that both watches and subtly constructs behaviour. Although Hacking's Foucauldian analysis is not itself explicitly linked to the advocacy of an alternative methodological project of qualitative research, such analyses help to continue the suspicion of numbers already widespread among practising qualitative researchers. Postmodern assaults on science and reason, regarding any attempts to generalize across social settings as oppressive, preferring instead to 'activate the differences' (Lyotard, 1993: 46), are readily incorporated into this analysis, which then becomes a value-laden critique.

Yet, as I showed in the last chapter, numbers have a place within qualitative research, assisting, for example, in sensitive attempts to learn lessons in one place that have relevance for actions and understanding in another place. There is a variety of other uses of numbers which can enhance the quality of qualitative research, which will be illustrated in this chapter. A short example is relevant here, before a scheme for understanding this variety is outlined, together with examples of the fruitful usage of numbers by practising qualitative researchers.

Counting the countable: an example

Fox (1992) reports an observation that he made on hospital wards, where he perceived differences in the wearing of surgical masks by different categories of staff:

> Nurses speak of surgeons as seeing themselves as 'above infection'. An infection control nurse commented: 'You very seldom find both surgeon and anaesthetist with masks adjusted properly.' Student nurses, on the other hand, look as if they practise in front of the mirror, so perfectly straight are their masks. Nurses are told to wear them whenever in theatre . . . So perhaps it is simply an issue of status, and the degree of compliance with masking routine is inversely related to the position in the hierarchy . . . as has been seen in the above extracts, nurses are aware of the doubtful value of masks, yet it is the doctors who flout the rules, yet are silent over this matter. [Fox then quotes a doctor saying:] 'Nurses are very conservative and fairly rigid in their outlook. They are by far the best people for maintaining surgical sterility.' (Fox, 1992: 26)

Note that his attempted generalization from these events is quite tentative ('So perhaps it is . . .'). His observation about student nurses in the third sentence records his own impressions rather than reporting actual incidents that enable the reader to exercise judgement about whether this is the correct impression. Otherwise, he relies on a few quotations from conversations he has had, relying on the speakers to have made accurately the observations they report. We are left feeling that although Fox's story is plausible, he may simply be reporting a folk myth that is current among staff. Compare this with Roth's (1957) study of a similar phenomenon in a tuberculosis hospital where, using the method of participant observation, he observed inconsistencies in the sterilization procedures designed, at least nominally, to control the possible spread of contagion. Unlike Fox, he supports his observations with counts of events, though initially he reports qualitative anecdotes in detail, in a manner similar to Fox:

> Books are sometimes sterilized before being sent out, sometimes not. Other articles mailed by patients may or may not be sterilized depending largely upon whether or not patients request it. Letters are never sterilized. The inconsistency of these procedures is not lost on the workers. One volunteer worker held up a package she was mailing for a patient and said: 'Now, I can mail this without sterilizing it, but if someone wants to send home some OT work, I have to sterilize it before I can mail it for him. It doesn't make any sense.' (1957: 310)

TABLE 9.1   Wearing of protective clothing by doctors and nursing personnel in hospital

	Times entered room	Percentages wearing		
		Cap	Gown	Mask
Doctors	47	5	0	5
Professional nurses	100	24	18	14
Practical nurses*	121	86	45	46
Aides	142	94	80	72
Students	97	100	100	100

Note: * Practical nurses were of a lower grade than professional nurses
Source: Roth, 1957: 312, Table 2

TABLE 9.2   Wearing of protective clothing by practical nurses when carrying out duties and when 'socializing' with patients

	Times entered room	Percentages wearing		
		Cap	Gown	Mask
Carrying out duties	39	97	75	80
Socializing	23	91	17	9

Source: Roth, 1957: 314, Table 4

After reporting a series of such anecdotes, Roth then informs us that he counted a particular phenomenon: the wearing of protective clothing by various categories of staff in the hospital. The results of this counting exercise are shown in Tables 9.1 and 9.2.

Commenting on these results, Roth remarks: '[This] suggests that the tubercle bacillus works only during business hours' (Roth, 1957: 314). The important point to note is that Roth was counting events which were, in Silverman's terms, 'countable' (1985: 140; 1993: 165). That is, he enumerated a phenomenon whose possible meanings and contexts had already been thoroughly explored, so that the theoretical generalizations enabled by the counts (for example, that high social status within an occupational hierarchy enabled the bearer to break rules which others had to follow) were thoroughly grounded in observational, qualitative work of the particular context. Measurement by fiat was thus avoided. Study of the meanings of individual instances of a phenomenon made possible a more general comparison across cases, so that a generalization (itself containing a causal proposition: that differential social status causes differential rule-following behaviour) could be made.

Because of Roth's study we can have considerable confidence that Fox is right, but Fox's report on its own would be less convincing. He asks us to trust that he has performed the sort of count that Roth carried out, reporting only impressions, with supporting anecdotes from interviews.

Without counts of actual observations these could be unrepresentative; Fox's claims therefore carry less weight.

Other uses of numbers

In fact, there is a variety of ways in which attention to quantification can enhance qualitative work, in addition to the goal of generalization discussed in Chapter 8. Bryman (1988) presents a helpful list of ways in which the two can be combined, based on a comprehensive survey of social research studies in which both approaches were used. Some of the more important items are given in Table 9.3. I shall illustrate and extend many of these and add some more categories during the course of this chapter.

We have discussed triangulation in Chapter 5. The second two suggestions, that the two forms of research can 'facilitate' each other, are illustrated by Bryman with a number of examples from research practice. Item 2 is the classical position of survey researchers, that exploratory qualitative work can be a useful preliminary step in constructing questionnaire items, or suggesting hypotheses for quantitative work to test, or in helping to elucidate causal processes. Rossman and Wilson (1994) provide examples of this fairly common strategy. In their study of the introduction of minimum competency tests in schools, they first spent some days in each school district talking to staff responsible for these tests:

> The guiding principle in the interviews was to get informants to talk about what was important to them when implementing statewide testing programs. These findings provided the outline for the development of the survey instrument. The interview data revealed five themes around which a series of questions were developed. The themes included: the contexts in which the districts operated, the responses the districts made to tests, the strategies they employed to carry out those responses, the uses to which the tests were put, and the effects of the tests. In addition to the major themes around which the questions were organized, the interview data also offered specific information for the wording of survey questions. Thus, the qualitative data in phase one of the study were designed to inform the development of the survey in phase two. (1994: 322–3)

Quantitative research facilitates qualitative research

Bryman's third item, however, is of more interest for present purposes. It was in fact illustrated by the examples given earlier in this chapter which showed survey results being used to select cases for qualitative depth study, in the interests of improving generalization. Yet there is more to it than this. Bryman gives some similar examples, but also mentions

TABLE 9.3 Ways of using numbers to enhance qualitative research

---

1 The logic of triangulation.
2 Qualitative research facilitates quantitative research.
3 Quantitative research facilitates qualitative research.
4 Quantitative and qualitative research are combined in order to produce a general picture.
5 Structure and process.
6 Researchers' and subjects' perspectives.
7 The problem of generality.
8 Qualitative research may facilitate the interpretation of relations between variables.

Source: adapted from Bryman, 1988: 131–51

Whyte's (1976) study of Peruvian villages, which goes somewhat beyond the simple use of survey results to select cases and touches on the possibilities for theory development by combining the two approaches. Whyte was familiar with the dispute between Lewis and Redfield (discussed in Chapter 10), where one had found that consensus and the other had found that conflict characterized relationships between villagers in a single village. One of his researchers found, in contrast, that in one village there were low levels of both conflict *and* cooperation: it occurred to Whyte that far from being opposite ends of a single spectrum, the two could be thought of as separate dimensions. This is much like my own study of equal opportunities in schools, where it was possible for some schools to score highly on both 'good school' and 'bad school' measures. Whyte's first step, then, was an example of moving from qualitative to quantitative (Bryman's item 2): his case study led him to analyse survey data that he had collected across villages, confirming that both conflict and consensus could co-exist in a setting. Yet his survey data also revealed one village which had shifted over the period of years from a situation of high cooperation and low conflict to a later situation where this was reversed (low cooperation, high conflict). His subsequent step was to study this village in depth, using the survey results to select a case on the grounds of theoretical interest. The second and third items on Bryman's list can therefore interact so that the issues addressed move beyond the ones of the simple generalizability of cases, to involve a creative mix of the two forms of data and the generation and testing of theory.

Combination of the two to produce a general picture

Bryman illustrates his fourth item with studies showing ethnographers using surveys to fill in gaps in knowledge that could not have been done with participant observation or depth interviewing alone. He discusses Gans' (1967) community study of Levittown, Barker's (1984) study of Moonies and Jenkins' (1983) study of Belfast youths, pointing out that:

The qualitative research in each case provides rich data about the world-views and interpretations of Levittowners, Moonies and Belfast youth but additional information is deemed to be necessary to provide a complete picture. In much the same way that Gans (1967, table 7) documents the changes in Levittowners' attitudes, Barker (1984, tables 12–15) portrays various shifts in Moonies' perceptions of how they, their lives, and their ideals have changed, while Jenkins (1983, tables 6.6 and 6.7) details such 'unobservables' as the methods of obtaining jobs used by each of the three groups of boys and their reasons for leaving jobs. In each case the researcher has judged the establishment of various patterns to be inaccessible through qualitative research and has made a technical decision to augment the investigation with quantitative methods in order to gain access to the areas and issues that cannot otherwise be reached so that a complete account can be provided. (1988: 140)

Again, it is possible to go somewhat beyond this conceptualization to point out that such *ad hoc* resort to quantitative methods by ethno-graphers can help develop and test theories. McKeganey et al. (1995, 1996) demonstrated this in their ethnographic study of needle sharing among drug injectors. McKeganey (1996) reports that five different types of needle sharing were identified in the study: it could happen accidentally; due to necessity where, for example, no other means of injection were available; due to intense needs in withdrawal; when an injector believes another person to be 'clean'; or in settings where a social norm of reciprocal favours was strong. Rich descriptions of each type of situation were provided in observational data. The researchers also did a rough count in their fieldwork observations to see how men and women differed in their sharing behaviour, suggesting that women shared with their sexual partners more than men, for example. Social distance also seemed to make a difference, as did the length of time a person had been involved in injecting drugs. Yet McKeganey (1996) felt the need for a more precise estimate of the influence of these factors on needle-sharing behaviour than accounts of ethnographic observations provided. His research report (McKeganey et al., 1995) explains that the systematic use of 'vignettes' enabled estimates to be made of the relative strengths of the parts played by social distance, gender and length of time injecting.

Vignettes drew on actual descriptions of sharing situations provided by informants during qualitative work and were refined by presenting them to drug users to comment on whether the situations they described 'seemed real' (1995: 1254). Two of the vignettes are shown in Table 9.4.

Other vignettes represented systematic variations on these themes to give different gradations of social distance or other factors. For example, 'Lending vignette 1' is repeated in other vignettes with the variation that the person involved is 'your best friend whom you have known for years' or 'your steady partner'. They were given to 505 injectors and the

TABLE 9.4   Vignettes of needle-sharing incidents

Borrowing Vignette 1
I want you to imagine that you are with your steady partner. You have both just scored and you both have your own tools (needle and syringe). The two of you are in a stairwell of a block of flats preparing to inject but your needle has just blocked. Would you:

1   Go away and try and get a new set of works (needle and syringe).
2   Ask your partner if you could use his/hers saying that you can wash them out with the bottle of water in your pocket . . .

Lending Vignette 1
I want you to imagine that you are standing on a street corner. In your pocket you have a set of works that you used earlier the same day. Someone that you don't know very well comes up and says that he/she is strung out, that he/she's got drugs to hit up but no tools. He/she asks if you have a set on you. Would you:

1   Tell him/her to get lost.
2   Say that you can't let him/her have the works in your pocket.
3   Give him/her a set of tools but tell him/her that they are your only set and you want them back.
4   Tell him/her that he/she can use the works in your pocket but that you don't want them back.

Source: McKeganey et al., 1995: 1254–5

results were subjected to conventional statistical analysis. Tables 9.5 and 9.6 show some of the results, indicating that a high proportion of people were willing to borrow and lend equipment, and that in the case of borrowing (Table 9.5) this is highly influenced by social distance. Social distance was somewhat less important in influencing lending (Table 9.6). Other analysis enabled the influence of gender and length of injecting experience to be assessed. Clearly, in terms of Bryman's fourth item, these researchers found that quantitative methods had enabled a 'more general picture' to emerge, in this case one that enabled the confirmation of a theory about social distance and sharing behaviour.

Structure and process

Bryman's fifth item is illustrated by an evocative example from his own study of schooling. It is his view that the regularities of social life can be established by quantitative work; these may be somewhat static in appearance, but qualitative data can reveal underlying processes that lead to these regularized structures. In Blease and Bryman (1986), he was able to find out how teachers ranked the children in their class in terms of general ability. This was done by applying standardized quantitative procedure to establish teachers' personal constructs. The result was a score for each child which, in combination with observational data, proved revealing. Teachers sometimes made public comparisons of pupils which served to reinforce their 'rankings'. One could say that such events, in fact, socially constructed a pupil's public

TABLE 9.5 Borrowing vignettes (n = 505)

	Partner	Very good friend	Acquaintance	Total*
Yes (%)	331 (65.6)	193 (38.2)	64 (12.7)	346 (68.5)
No (%)	148 (29.3)	308 (61.0)	436 (86.3)	141 (27.9)
Other (%)	26 (5.1)	4 (0.8)	5 (1.0)	18 (3.6)

Note: * Total: yes = number prepared to borrow on at least one of the
vignettes; no = number not prepared to borrow on any of the vignettes.
Source: McKeganey et al., 1995: Table 1

TABLE 9.6 Lending vignettes (n = 505)

	Partner	Very good friend	Acquaintance	Total*
Yes (%)	370 (73.3)	398 (78.8)	331 (65.6)	435 (86.1)
No (%)	99 (19.6)	104 (20.6)	172 (34.0)	63 (12.5)
Other (%)	36 (7.1)	3 (0.6)	2 (0.4)	7 (1.4)

Note: * Total: yes = number prepared to lend on at least one of the vignettes;
no = number not prepared to lend on any of the vignettes.
Source: McKeganey et al., 1995: Table 2

reputation. Here John Perry, who was ranked low, is compared with
Dean Berwick, who is second from top, in a physical education lesson in
which John has been asked to count on his fingers the number of times
the teacher bounces a ball:

> *Miss Shiels*: now there's no fingers there (*bounce*). (*Giggles from class who are
> sitting around watching.*) There's still five fingers there, (*bounce*) still five
> (*bounce*). There's four (*bounce*), still four (*bounce*), three, yes good (*bounce*)
> two, yes good, (*bounce*) one. (*She laughs.*) Is he always like this?
> *The class in chorus*: Yes (*laughter*).
> *Miss Shiels*: Remind me to pick Dean Berwick next time, he usually manages
> to do what I ask! (Blease and Bryman, 1986: 165)

The relative ranking of John and Dean is a social fact, regularly reinforced
by events like this, which are qualitatively unique which together produce a fixed, fairly static identity for the pupils in the social setting of the
school.

Researchers' and subjects' perspectives

While Bryman's fifth item is readily illustrated, the sixth is more problematic. It depends on the idea that '[quantitative research] is orientated
to the specific concerns of the investigator and [qualitative research] to

subjects' perspectives' (1988: 42), so that combinations of the two will provide a bit of both. I hope to have persuaded readers in earlier chapters that this dichotomy is a false one. First, the view that the two are separate is itself contentious if one takes the view that all observation is driven by theory. Even if one modifies an extreme commitment to this position, there are many examples of qualitative work which are largely informed by the desire to answer researcher-generated questions. Indeed, it is sometimes argued that such an approach is an important component of qualitative research, which should avoid being driven by a romantic or humanistic impulse to discover how things look or feel from the point of view of the experiencing subject (Silverman, 1993; Dingwall, 1997a).

Simple counts

Bryman's seventh item, however, is of greater importance in arguing the case for enhancing qualitative work through the use of numbers, although it is named by Bryman in a somewhat misleading way as being related to 'generality'. Far from being concerned with the external validity of case study work (a topic covered in Chapter 8), Bryman is in fact concerned with the enumeration of phenomena within case studies and his example here comes from Silverman's (1984) work, in which Silverman demonstrates the value of what he has called 'simple counting techniques' (Silverman, 1993: 163) in avoiding anecdotalism. Thus the 'generality' of phenomena within a case is established, rather than some statistical estimate of the extent to which phenomena are likely to occur outside the case.

   Such counting is an important way of showing data to the reader as fully as possible, enabling readers to judge whether the writer has relied excessively on rare events, to the exclusion of more common ones that might contradict the general line of argument. This can help readers gain a sense of how representative and widespread particular instances are. This was shown in my study of 163 elderly people living alone in their last year of life, where relatives and others were interviewed after the deaths of the people concerned (Seale, 1996). Here is an extract from the report of this study:

> It was very common for the people living on their own to be described either as not seeking help for problems that they had (65 instances covering 48 people), or refusing help when offered (144 instances in 83 people). Accounts of this often stressed that this reflected on the character of the person involved, although other associations were also made. In particular, 33 speakers gave 44 instances where they stressed the independence which this indicated: '(She) never really talked about her problems, was very independent . . .'; '(She) was just one of those independent people who would

struggle on. She wouldn't ask on her own'; 'She used to shout at me because I was doing things for her. She didn't like to be helped. She was very independent.' Being 'self sufficient', 'would not be beaten', and being said to 'hate to give in' were associated with resisting help. (1996: 84)

Reading through all of the interviews and marking each instance of talk about help was the first step towards generating this report. Using a computer programme (ETHNOGRAPH) to select all these segments then made a further coding exercise possible, in which instances of talk about not seeking help were distinguised from talk about refusing help when offered. A variety of reasons for these two events were also coded, distinguishing the 33 people who understood independence to be indicated by this behaviour. The report then goes on to show how other meanings were conferred on these events by speakers (for example, that the elderly person was 'being difficult' rather than being independent) but that these were less common sentiments.

I also used this approach in analysing the content of booklets about subject choice produced by secondary schools, where I was searching for messages about gender:

In domestic science subjects, 12 per cent of booklets assumed or stated that the subjects were open to either sex; 10 per cent assumed or requested one sex . . . Sexist bias was highest in child care, where 15 per cent assumed or requested girls only; and lowest in home economics, where nine schools assumed girls only, but four requested boys. Similarly, home economics had the highest proportion (16 per cent) of statements assuming or stating that the subject was open to both sexes.

Two statements about domestic science courses used 'boys and girls' to describe pupils taking child care. Two schools included child care or parent-craft in their compulsory courses. A number of schools called their course 'parentcraft' rather than 'child care' and . . . it may be that this reflects a willingness to consider boys. On the other hand, one school called its course 'mother and child', another 'mothercare'. One stated that 'mother's help' might be a career that the subject led to, another proclaimed that 'Today's girls will be tomorrow's mothers' and that the National Association for Maternal and Child Welfare offered certificates to those completing one course. Another suggested that if those taking the child care course did not marry, a certificate in the subject might lead to a variety of careers. One school in the cluster sample ran a course in 'typewriting and childcare', another in 'good grooming', involving makeup and manicure. (Pratt et al., 1982: 136)

Here, the combination of qualitative anecdotes and counts of the frequency of phenomena give a more balanced picture than selected anecdotes alone could provide. Studies that rely solely on anecdotes, especially if they report contentious findings, tend to be less persuasive.

Counting to mislead   Furthermore, counts may be presented in a selective way to give a misleading impression. For example, Graham and Oakley (1981) studied relationships between mothers and doctors in antenatal clinics in which they took the view that 'Mothers view themselves as knowledgeable about pregnancy and birth' (1981: 55), and assert the existence of a 'holistic way in which women view childbearing' (1981: 54). Doctors, on the other hand, treat pregnancies as episodes of abnormality or illness. The researchers' report consists of a series of atrocity stories about insensitive behaviour by doctors, supported by counts of the number of times these incidents occurred. In their article quantitative words like 'usually', 'some' or 'many' are used on several occasions, but on 12 occasions the authors present actual counts of events. These are as follows:

1   The proportion of women saying that they would prefer to see the same doctor on each occasion.
2   The proportion of women feeling that they had learned nothing from their antenatal checkup, or that they could not ask questions.
3   The proportion expressing anxiety about antenatal checkups.
4   The average time of doctor–patient encounters.
5   The proportion of encounters involving an internal examination.
6   The proportion of interactions that involved reference to medical technology.
7   The proportion of consultations involving questions from women.
8   The proportion of questions concerning the condition of the baby, physiological aspects of pregnancy, birth and related medical procedures.
9   The percentage of questions and statements that concerned dates of delivery.
10   The percentage of statements by women about their own feelings or social circumstances related to birth.
11   The percentage of women's statements involving reports of pain or discomfort that are dismissed by the doctor.
12   The proportion of statements reflecting worry or anxiety.

The first three counts are taken from interviews with a sample of women in York. The authors do not say how large this sample was, or how it was chosen, nor do they give information about how interviews were done, yet we learn that '40 per cent felt they couldn't ask questions' (1981: 64) in consultations, or that 'two-thirds of women expressed anxiety about antenatal checkups' (1981: 58). The rest are counts of events observed in a London hospital. Counts 4 and 5 look value neutral, but are in fact presented to reflect badly on the quality of care: for example, the researchers say that clinic encounters are too brief before presenting count 4. The sixth count is similarly designed to support a view that is critical of the medicalization of childbirth. We are told that in an unspecified number of 'antenatal clinic encounters' (1981: 60) 677 statements were made by patients. Counts 7–12 are clearly based on an analysis of these. Although, as we have seen, 40 per cent of the York sample felt that they could not ask questions, in the London hospital 'questions asked by patients averaged slightly more than 1 per encounter' (1981: 64; count 7), although we are not told the proportion of consultations that did not involve such questions in order to test the view that the York 40 per cent can be supported in the London observations. Count 8 is given and then followed by the statement that 'These are serious requests but often casually treated by doctors' (1981: 61). The other four counts, if not in themselves obviously damning of doctors' behaviour, are presented in contexts that make them so.

Additionally, 8 quotations from interviews and 13 from recordings of doctor–patient interaction occur. All but one of the interview quotes involve direct criticisms of doctors or medical services. For example:

> The nurse says 'now do you want to ask the doctor anything?' And more invariably than not you say 'no' because you just don't feel you can. The way they ask you, 'Right, do you want to ask the doctor anything?' You think, no. All you want to do is get up and get out. (1981: 64)

The quote that did not involve such criticism was an extract where a woman expressed fears and anxieties about having an internal examination. This occurred in a context where the authors expressed their view that the number of internal examinations was too high. All of the 13 extracts involving doctor–patient interaction demonstrated insensitive behaviour by doctors, who were either patronizing, did not take women's concerns into account, or were coercive in some way. For example:

> *Patient*: I've got a pain in my shoulder.
> *Doctor*: Well, that's your shopping bag hand, isn't it? (1981: 59)

Clearly, this is a classic case of 'lies, damn lies and statistics', with selective presentation of numbers (as well as qualitative anecdotes) to support a pre-existing view. I may have considerable sympathy for the view that childbirth at that time was overmedicalized, but a research report like this would not have convinced me were I sceptical of this fact. Counting on its own is not enough; it must be supported by a genuinely self-critical, fallibilistic mindset, involving a commitment to examine negative instances. For example, the authors might have presented the proportion of women who *did* feel that they had learned something from checkups (count 2), or the proportion of statements involving pain or discomfort that were *not* dismissed by doctors (count 11). It is very likely that these proportions would have been low, perhaps helping the authors feel safer in presenting the occasional qualitative anecdote showing a good quality of care. Such a report would have been far more persuasive for readers sceptical about the authors' case.

Counting interactions Silverman's illustrations of the value of simple counting in qualitative research come from his studies of medical consultations. He argues (Silverman, 1993) that:

> Simple counting techniques can offer a means to survey the whole corpus of data ordinarily lost in intensive, qualitative research. Instead of taking the researcher's word for it, the reader has a chance to gain a sense of the flavour of the data as a whole. In turn, researchers are able to test and to revise their generalisations, removing nagging doubts about the accuracy of their impressions about the data. (1993: 163)

In his comparative study of private and public oncology clinics, he gained the impression that a more 'personalized' service was made available in the private setting and to see if he could support this he counted phenomena that had led him to sense this difference. Thus private consultations lasted longer; private patients were more likely to ask questions and make unsolicited statements. Additionally, appointments for future treatments or consultations were more likely to be fixed at patients' convenience and 'social elicitation', where there was polite small talk, was more likely in the private setting. These counts, supported by extensive illustrative examples, succeed in presenting a persuasive case for Silverman's general thesis of a more personalized service in the private setting.

Yet one may say that these examples of my own and Silverman's work are no more than simple content analysis. They reflect a commitment to counting well-defined phenomena, so that like things are placed with like, and there is no attempt at measurement by fiat, but they hardly make use of the full power of advanced statistical techniques. Silverman does no more than present simple cross-tabulations with chi-squared based tests of significance. In this respect, his work is like that of McKeganey et al. (1995, 1996) discussed earlier in this chapter, who presented a series of two-way cross-tabulations between his three independent variables (gender, social distance, length of experience) and his dependent variable (preparedness to share). Why stop there? To assess the *relative* strength of influence of independent variables, multivariate analysis is necessary, involving fuller commitment to causal reasoning and statistical sophistication than most qualitative researchers appear willing to use. But before we turn to these matters more fully, let us examine Bryman's eighth item.

Facilitating the interpretation of relations between variables

This issue gets to the heart of Cicourel's (1964) critique of 'measurement by fiat', and indeed a whole set of objections to the type of social survey work that relies on unwarranted assumptions about the meanings of questions and answers. Bryman (1988) illustrates this item on his list with three examples, two of which show researchers explaining some puzzling findings from questionnaire surveys by recourse to depth interviews, in which respondents revealed deeper complexities of meaning than the surveys had been able to identify. His third example is from a study of classroom interaction, involving analysis of lesson transcripts and interviews with pupils which together 'explained' quantitative differences between teachers in the verbal moves they made. He is critical of Marsh (1982), who also seeks a marriage between quantitative and qualitative, cause and meaning, in the context of an impassioned defence of the social survey. Bryman dislikes her apparent emphasis on the 'survey alone' (1988: 147) for combining qualitative and quantitative, appearing to believe that the approaches he has illustrated are better ones:

> while Marsh seeks to develop a framework within which findings which are adequate at the levels of both cause and meaning can be generated by the survey alone, the research reported in this section points to the advantages of conjoining quantitative and qualitative research in order to achieve much the same end. (1988: 147)

This is a very odd thing to say, since two of his three examples are from survey research, and Marsh does not in fact rule out the advantages of other methods. The aim is to overcome the prejudice that equates the social survey approach with quantitative work. This, she recognizes, is exemplified in the work of Brown and Harris (1978), who demonstrate that the social survey is founded on qualitative method, though it also can involve counting. It is worth spending a little time, once again, in expounding the essence of their work, as Marsh's book is now difficult to obtain and Brown and Harris's work is a complex edifice whose major methodological features are at times hard to distinguish.

Measuring meaning Brown and Harris, like Cicourel, are very much aware of the problem of measurement by fiat, criticizing Durkheim as well as many survey researchers for doing this:

> For Durkheim, men and women responded differently to experiences such as marriage, widowhood, divorce, and childlessness because, according to his commonsense judgement, they *meant* different things to the two sexes; but he never established this by interviewing individual men and women . . . such

speculation about the meaning of experience to others is essentially what has been done in . . . hundreds of studies . . . that have followed Durkheim's. (1978: 89–90)

Later, they continue their criticism of superficial social survey work:

one of (the survey's) greatest failures is where, at first acquaintance, it might appear to be strongest: in measurement – the placing of like with like . . . research workers have almost entirely relied on administrating to large numbers of people some form of the standardized questionnaire, with its dispiriting pretensions to measure almost anything by means of a few, often fixed-choice, questions . . . there must be the gravest doubt about the ability of such questionnaires to collect accurate and unbiased accounts of anything complex or of emotional depth . . . because such questionnaires cannot be trusted to have placed like with like . . . the survey . . . has great potential but, with some notable exceptions, its promise has not been fulfilled. (1978: 9–13)

They start instead from the position of the phenomenologist Schutz, who argued (1970; first published 1953) that social scientists should seek to understand actors' constructs by investigating the subjective meanings typically bestowed on the actions of everyday life. Schutz's work, of course, inspired a generation of qualitative researchers to reject the use of numbers and social survey work for their supposed 'positivism'. Brown and Harris illustrate a more constructive use of these ideas. In their study of the social origins of depressive illness in women they began by doing depth interviews with women, generating the sort of material used in countless grounded theory analyses. Rather than go down this analytic route, however, they quantify the meaning of 'life events' in order to explain the social causes of depression. While fundamentally driven by a desire to identify the causes of a phenomenon, this is done within an approach that acknowledges the influence of individual variability and biographical context on meaning.

Brown and Harris are critical of what they call a 'dictionary approach' to quantifying the impact of life events, illustrated by 'checklist' devices such as that promoted by Holmes and Rahe (1967). These researchers proposed to allocate weights to particular events, according to a scale of severity. For example, the death of a spouse attracts a 'score' of 100; divorce counts for 73 points; dismissal from work is 47; birth of a child is 39. Adding events together produces an overall score indicating the level of stress that a person has experienced in a defined time period. The problem with this approach is its lack of contextual sensitivity to variability in meaning. Dismissal from work for an actor, used to having several jobs in a year, will be experienced very differently from the response of a middle-aged factory worker who has only ever had that job and now faces a lifetime of unemployment. The birth of a first child is different from the birth of a third, in terms of the disruption to family life that this causes.

TABLE 9.7 Severity of life events in terms of long-term threat

---

(a) Severe
Woman's father died aged 81. She was married and he had lived with her for 7 years.

Woman had a car crash, her car was 'written off'. She was badly hurt, lost seven teeth, had a broken arm and ribs. She said it was her fault; she had been drunk.

Woman's husband was sent to prison for two years; woman was pregnant.

(b) Non-severe
Woman had to tell her husband that his sister had died.

Woman was in a car accident. In a rainstorm a woman 'walked into the car'; her husband was driving. The woman left hospital the same evening as the accident. There were no police charges.

Woman's friend moved to North London; she still sees her occasionally but has only a fraction of their previous rate of contact.

Source: Adapted from Brown and Harris, 1978: 307–14

Panels of raters examined the transcripts of the qualitative interviews produced by Brown and Harris and, using their own judgement and knowledge of each woman's life circumstances, seeking consistency through continual discussion and the use of precedent from previous interviews, gave quantitative scores to different aspects of the events experienced by each woman. These included, for example, whether the event was associated with different degrees of immediate anxiety, whether changes in routine were involved, whether there was any emotional preparation for the event, whether positive support from others was experienced, and whether the life event involved a long-term threat. Table 9.7 shows some examples of events categorized at opposite ends of this last dimension of long-term threat.

Since raters did this without knowing whether the interview was with someone diagnosed with depressive illness or not, associations between these scores and depression could plausibly be argued to be causal. Events posing a severe long-term threat, especially if they occurred to women with no close confidantes or who were also looking after very young children, were found to be predictive of depression.

Although this study arises from within a quantitative survey research tradition, it is clear that it is fundamentally a qualitative method that incorporates the use of numbers and an interest in causal processes. Because of the sensitivity to meanings and context display, the meanings of associations between variables were well understood. The example of Brown and Harris is also useful in showing that qualitative researchers need not be shy of going beyond 'simple counts' once the meaning of numbers is well understood. Multivariate analysis, on the life events project, proved useful in showing the influence of several factors on depression, some of which needed to interact to produce their effect.

Advanced statistics and qualitative method

There are other examples of qualitative researchers moving beyond simple univariate counts and bivariate cross-tabulations in order to achieve more sophisticated understandings of phenomena. This is particularly evident in work using computer-assisted qualitative data analysis (CAQDAS) packages, use of which appears to be an indicator of willingness to get past the negative feelings that some people have about advanced number work. I have written more extensively about the advantages and limitations of CAQDAS elsewhere (Seale, 1999), so I will confine this discussion to showing examples taken from a work (Kelle, 1995) in which a number of qualitative researchers describe how CAQDAS has supported statistical aspects of their work.

In that volume Kuckharz (1995) describes a study of girls and computers, in which qualitative interviews with a non-random sample of girls were coded, focusing on girls' statements about their self-image, as well as their parents' responses to computer use. On this study, statistical analysis was helpful in exploring the data to look for suggestive patterns for further qualitative analysis. Kuckharz correctly points out that statistical inference (the basis of generalizing from a sample to a population) is inappropriate with data from a non-random sample such as this. Yet statistics like chi squared, strictly speaking an aid to statistical inference, were found useful in identifying bivariate relationships that were of interest, to be explored by looking at the quotations associated with particular interactions of variables. Cluster analysis, a multivariate technique that shows how particular phenomena tend to occur together, is particularly suited to such exploratory analysis of patterns in data, and was used by Kuckharz to identify ideal-typical clusters of statements about self-image, which could then be illustrated with qualitative case histories.

Roller et al. (1995) in the same volume report their content analysis of interviews, eliciting their attitudes towards welfare state provision in Germany. Having coded the statements made by interviewees, quantitative analysis found that 45 per cent of all statements made about financial problems co-occurred with the mention of particular objects of the welfare state – pensions, unemployment benefit and so on. Selection of the text associated with these co-occurrences and close examination of the sentiments being expressed was then possible, revealing in the end a lack of fundamental criticism of state welfare provisions by respondents.

Truth tables and Qualitative Comparison Analysis (QCA) Ragin (1995), in Kelle's volume, takes a rather different and more ambitious approach, which he has outlined more fully in book form (Ragin, 1987). His work is similar to that of Brown and Harris in proposing a fundamental rethinking of the relationship between qualitative and quantitative method. He

TABLE 9.8   Ragin's 'truth table'

A	B	C	S	No. of cases
0	0	0	0	4
0	0	1	0	6
0	1	0	1	8
0	1	1	0	3
1	0	0	0	10
1	0	1	1	9
1	1	0	1	2
1	1	1	1	7

Source: Adapted from Ragin, 1995

begins from a critique of the assumptions about causality contained in conventional statistical analysis, which he sees as particularly inappropriate if (as is the case in many qualitative research studies) only a small number of cases can be studied, albeit in considerable depth. Conventional statistical analysis (such as multivariate analysis – multiple regression, path analysis), which generally requires large numbers of cases, expresses its conclusions in terms of the contribution made to a particular phenomenon by each causal variable (or combination of these) in an equation. This, argues Ragin, overlooks the fact that in particular contexts in which a phenomenon occurs the part played by a particular variable may differ. Conventional statistical analysis averages this out, positing by implication some ideal average 'case' which in reality may not exist. What is needed instead is an approach which explains variability between contexts. To this end, Ragin incorporates Boolean logic to conceptualize causal relationships in multiple case studies.

This is easier to appreciate through an example, which I take from Ragin (1995), also discussed in Becker's (1998) excellent explanation of Ragin's method. Imagine that a researcher with access to historical data is concerned to discover the causes of successful strikes. These might be due to three factors: the presence of a high level of demand for an industry's product (A); threats of sympathy strikes by other unions (B); and a large union strike fund (C).

The results of a study of 49 strikes might be presented as a 'truth table', shown in Table 9.8, where a '0' indicates the absence of a characteristic and a '1' indicates its presence. This shows, for example, that the researcher discovered eight cases where a strike (S) was successful, with only the factor of sympathy strikes (B) having been threatened to account for this.

In fact, only four possible combinations lead to successful strikes: AC, B, AB and ABC. From this it is possible to derive the statement that the minimum conditions for successful strikes involve either a large strike fund and high demand for the product, or a threat of sympathy strikes.

Additionally, the conditions that lead to failure can be specified by a similar logic. Once analysed, case study material can be presented to the reader to illustrate the processes involved. The approach preserves an in-depth understanding of the complexities of individual cases while still being able to deal with medium to large numbers of cases.

The approach shares with analytic induction (see Chapter 6) the requirement to explain *all* of the cases studied. Unlike conventional statistical analysis, which accepts that a proportion of cases will deviate from the general trend specified by a probabilistic causal rule, the use of the truth table means that rules that cover all cases can be specified. The discovery of a deviant case simply leads to a rethinking of the conditions necessary to produce an effect, involving the insertion of a new column in a truth table. In fact, initial data collection for the sort of analysis that Ragin proposes is likely to involve a conscious search for cases demonstrating diversity, provisional truth tables serving to inform episodes of theoretically driven sampling, which in turn lead to revisions of truth tables as ideas develop.

Conclusion

This chapter has covered a broad range of issues concerning the use of numbers by qualitative researchers. Through numerous examples I hope that I have shown that it is possible to maintain a commitment to qualitative work and to use numbers to improve its quality. As shown in Chapter 8, numbers can help to generalize from case studies and can increase the persuasiveness of qualitative data presentations that are otherwise open to the charge of anecdotalism. A variety of examples of productive interchange between the two traditions has been illustrated, using and extending Bryman's framework. In the final section I have pointed to the possibilities which some qualitative researchers have seen in using more advanced statistical techniques to enhance qualitative analysis. Here, we begin to see a breakdown of the divide between the traditions, as it becomes clear that survey research is based in qualitative method, and that qualitative researchers can legitimately be interested in hypothesis testing and causal analysis. Ragin's work is particularly interesting in conceptualizing causal analysis in a novel form.

To exploit fully the potential of numbers in qualitative research, I believe that we need to dispense with the view that researchers can be divided into these two great camps. This is by no means an original conclusion, having been stated by various methodologists for a number of years (for example Bryman, 1988; Hammersley, 1992b). We are beginning to see this realized in practice, as social researchers who – and this is the essential point – possess the relevant technical and methodological skills to integrate the two increasingly show us through their example what is possible.

KEY POINTS

- Counting events that are well defined and illustrated can increase the credibility of claims made by qualitative researchers, by guarding against the charge of anecdotalism.

- In addition to the uses of numbers in assisting generalization, there is a variety of other uses that can enhance the quality of research.

- Simple counting is often all that is needed, but more complex multivariate and Boolean statistical methods have a potential place in 'qualitative' work. This depends on researchers developing skills in both qualitative and quantitative methods.

10

Reliability and Replicability

CONTENTS

Alternative ways of thinking about reliability and replicability have been suggested by qualitative methodologists. LeCompte and Goetz (1982), for example, make a useful distinction between 'internal' and 'external' reliability. The first of these refers to concerns that are rather similar to those traditionally placed under the heading of 'inter-rater reliability' in quantitative research. It concerns the degree to which other researchers applying similar constructs would match these to data in the same way as original researchers. Internal reliability of this sort was the focus of concern in the Armstrong et al. (1997) exercise discussed in Chapter 3. External reliability, on the other hand, concerns the replicability of entire studies: would other researchers studying the same or similar settings generate the same findings? (This is also a form of triangulation (of investigators), for which see Chapter 5.) In general, LeCompte and Goetz argue, establishing reliability in replication studies – especially of the external sort – is a 'herculean' (1982: 35) task for qualitative researchers, requiring (in theory at least) knowledge of the sort of apprenticeship that the original researcher has served, and requiring a complete specification of background assumptions and field procedures, information which many researchers, in practice, do not provide.

External reliability

Nevertheless, LeCompte and Goetz argue, it is possible to take steps to improve both internal and external reliability. External reliability can be improved, they say, by addressing five issues. First, a research report should identify the particular status position taken by the researcher in the field. Partly because of fixed attributes, such as gender and age, but also due to the adoption of particular identities (for example the researcher as part of the hierarchy; the researcher identifying with an 'underdog' group), researchers can see some things but not others. Full details of this, argue LeCompte and Goetz, should be given in a report if replication is to be attempted. Secondly, researchers should say as much as possible about who offered data and, thirdly, the social situations in which this was done. In this way, any attempt at replication might follow up similar contacts. Fourthly, LeCompte and Goetz advocate that a full account is given of the theories and ideas that informed the research, including those which were involved in any coding schemes. The fifth point involves attention to methodological reporting, with a detailed account of all aspects of methods used.

All of these things are, of course, components of reflexivity, likely to help readers of reports to assess the credibility of findings regardless of whether some attempt at replication is going to be made. In the terms used by Lincoln and Guba (1985), who also propose alternative concepts to encompass qualitative researchers' concerns with reliability (see Chapter 4), they are likely to enhance both the dependability and the credibility of a study. An elaborate and somewhat exhaustive procedure of 'auditing' is proposed by Lincoln and Guba, being a less time consuming but somewhat more realistic approach than getting teams of researchers to repeat entire studies. The creation of an 'audit trail' is a systematized approach to reflexive methodological accounting, incorporating peers in quite tightly specified roles during and after the research process, to provide a critique of the procedures used and a check on their clarity and consistency. For example, peer auditors would be brought in at various stages to examine the 'transcripts . . . category cards (index cards) with referent index; lists of units of information . . . tally sheets; computer analyses' (1985: 382) produced during the course of a project. These are the physical 'evidence' that such auditors can use to assess the adequacy with which raw data have been reduced and analysed. Auditors would also examine closely the results of any triangulation or member validation checks, as well as seeking out daily entries in a research journal that might document the 'daily activities . . . decision-making rules and procedures . . . sampling techniques . . . descriptions of emerging design . . . analytic strategy [and] . . . instrument development' (1985: 383) that a project might have involved. Auditing would proceed as a series of negotiated steps, in which auditors visit the project at various stages to assess its adequacy, agreeing procedures to resolve differences between auditors and researchers, and feeding the results of auditing into methodological decisions that might yet need to be made. In all, the scheme is one of methodological consultancy, of a type similar to that which one might expect from a good PhD supervisor, though there is perhaps somewhat more emphasis on using evidence of auditing to place a stamp of approval on the end product.

While auditing may appear to be an elaborate way of establishing reliability, it is considerably less time consuming than mounting full-scale replications of qualitative studies. The history of such replications has been a disappointing one, in part because of the practical difficulties involved in creating true replications, but also because replications have generally revealed discrepancies between the first and second study, leading to some quite well-publicized and painful disputes between researchers, and damaging confidence in qualitative social research. This has not been helped when the second researcher has given the impression of being antagonistic to the reputation of the first. Additionally, these awkward moments in the history of qualitative research have become tied to epistemological debates about realism as an adequate philosophical basis for research practice.

Replication

Mead and Freeman on Samoa

The most famous restudy of this sort is Freeman's (1983) study of Samoa, purporting to be a replication (and refutation) of Margaret Mead's *Coming of Age in Samoa* (1943, first published in 1928), a book that exerted a profound influence in anthropology and on a Western general public fascinated by its portrayal of adolescence as a time for free, easy and apparently healthy sexual experimentation. Mead's fieldwork was influenced by having ready access to the lives of adolescent girls, in whose company she clearly delighted, understandable in view of her own age at the time (mid-20s), gender and the more restricted adolescent culture of middle-class America from which she came:

> I concentrated upon the girls of the community. I spent the greater part of my time with them. I studied most closely the households in which adolescent girls lived. I spent more time in the games of children than in the councils of

their elders. Speaking their language, eating their food, sitting barefoot and cross-legged upon the pebbly floor, I did my best to minimize the differences between us and to learn to know and understand all the girls of three little villages on the coast of the little island of Tau, in the Manu'a Archipelago. (1943: 16)

She argued that these girls' lives showed that adolescence did not have to be a time of strife and conflict as it had become in the USA; in Samoa adolescence was relatively conflict free. Sexual permissiveness was an aspect of this; adolescents led untroubled lives, superficial in the sense that no strong, conflicting passions or difficulties troubled them. Because caretaking of children occurred in extended families, attachments between children and biological parents were weak, meaning that harsh or oppressive parental discipline was not feasible, even if desired. In all, Samoa appeared to be something of a pleasurable idyll if Mead's informants were representative.

Freeman, however, who carried out fieldwork in Samoa in the early 1940s, and again in the mid-1960s, argued that Mead was wrong on almost every point. His work (Freeman, 1983), published after Mead's death, suggested that Samoan society was in fact replete with evidence of aggression, rape and authoritarian control and he supported this with a considerable body of evidence, presented somewhat more carefully than Mead's more impressionistic style. Children commonly suffered harsh punishments at the hands of their parents. Virginity was a fiercely guarded state and parental monitoring of this was closer than represented by Mead. Freeman argued that Mead had been overinfluenced by her mentor, Franz Boas, whose personal campaign against the eugenics movement led him to encourage Mead to regard many matters which might be thought of as biologically determined (such as sexual development, or parent–child relationships) as being in fact the product of culture. Mead was therefore overconcerned to prove cultural variation through a Samoan case study.

The publicity that ensued was enormous, to a degree that disputes between academics rarely reach. This reflected Mead's status as the only anthropologist whose name most educated Americans knew, and one of the few whose ideas had entered general public debates. The reputation of anthropology as an objective science appeared to be at stake. In a special section of the *American Anthropologist* (Brady, 1983), a number of anthropologists were able to reflect on this dispute. Some of these authors had worked with Mead; one had himself described Samoan life in a less publicized 1954 restudy of the village in which Mead had stayed (Holmes, 1983). The picture that emerges from these commentaries, which are not all sympathetic to Mead, is that Freeman's study is not in fact a true replication. With time, things change. Westernization can make people ashamed of their past. Freeman not only studied Samoans many years after Mead, he studied a different island and mixed with different people. Because of his gender, he found that access to the households of chiefs and other important members of the community was feasible. These individuals promoted an image of respectability, involving strict control over their children, for example, as well as an 'official' cult of virginity. One can imagine that if a researcher had compared American teenage culture in the 1950s with the views of parents a discrepancy similar to that between Mead and Freeman might have emerged.

What both researchers failed to do was to provide the sort of exhaustive accounting and evidence-checking procedures advocated by Lincoln and Guba and others concerned to promote a culture of self-criticism and fallibilism, which also incorporates an active search for negative instances. Mead may have been guilty of generalizing about Samoan culture as a whole from an unrepresentative group, but Freeman compounds this error by doing the same with another group and adding a measure of vindictiveness against the original investigator.

Other replications

One can see quite similar processes at work in other failed 'replication' efforts in ethnography, although none matches the Mead/Freeman dispute for levels of publicity and bad feeling. Lewis's (1951) restudy of a Mexican village found individualism, conflict, fear, envy and distrust where Redfield (1930) had previously found cooperation, contentment and mutual support. As LeCompte and Goetz (1982) state:

> Redfield and Lewis addressed different issues, used different methods and time periods, and elicited responses from different segments of the population. Their studies were conducted from different, unexplicated world views and scientific assumptions. The problem was aggravated by presenting their results as representative of the belief system and social structure of the village as a whole rather than as derived from the discrete units actually investigated. (1982: 37)

Geertz (1988), commenting on the Lewis/Redfield dispute and on replication efforts in anthropology generally, observes that 'the tendency, when both scholars are reputable, is to regard the problem as stemming from different sorts of minds taking hold of different parts of the elephant' (1988: 6), although he admits that this is because reporting practices in anthropology are such that readers are 'Unable to recover the immediacies of field work for empirical reinspection' (1988: 6). Geertz is no naive realist, but this comment suggests potential sympathy for procedures such as peer auditing in order to generate a more comprehensive view of the 'elephant'.

These conclusions made by LeCompte, Goetz and Geertz about these restudies thus involve accepting a view that replication and convergence on a single true version are feasible – at least in theory. All that has gone wrong in these cases is that the replicators have not followed the same procedures as the originators. In part this is due to the lack of specification of these by original researchers working in less methodologically aware times. In part it is due to practical contingencies, such as time having passed so that the setting has changed, or the difficulty of access imposed by researchers' fixed attributes, such as gender.

The constructivist critique: Street Corner Society

To explore the implications of an epistemologically more radical view, which questions the viability of attempts to replicate studies, we can turn to the debates that followed Boelen's (1992) revisit to the setting studied by Whyte (1981; first published in 1943) in *Street Corner Society*, in which she proposes that he misrepresented the facts about Cornerville through, for example, being unable to speak Italian and therefore failing to penetrate Italian family life. Her own interviews with Whyte's original informants, she claims, suggest a rather different picture to that which Whyte paints. Whyte (1996a) presents a classic realist defence against these charges. He did speak some Italian, in fact, but he did not need to as his informants always used English. Boelen accuses him of exaggerating the poverty of a family by saying that they had no bathtub. When Boelen interviewed members of the family they said that the apartments in which they lived in fact did have bathtubs. Whyte retorts that he lived in the building at the time and had to be hospitalized when his polio-weakened legs gave up the struggle to get to a toilet on another floor, where the only washing facility was a sink. Unlike Mead, Whyte says, who was dead at the time of Freeman's assault on her reputation, he is alive, able and willing to answer back. Thus far, then, we see a dispute about the 'facts' along classic realist and empiricist lines.

But for Whyte, the most difficult cross to bear must be that which has been imposed on him by his postmodern interpreters, Richardson (1996) and Denzin (1996), who first damn him with faint praise ('Whyte teaches us a great deal', Denzin, 1996: 230) and then imply that he has, unfashionably, missed the boat of ethnography's 'sixth moment' (Denzin, 1996: 230) by defending his book, which is in fact an 'ethnographic museum' (1996: 231). (Note that Denzin now discovers a previously unannounced moment to add to the five that he and Lincoln (1994) had earlier discovered.) His defence of his reputation against Boelen's supposed 'charge', they imply, is simply misguided, as both Boelen and Whyte are working within an outdated realist illusion. Denzin, for example, uses the opportunity simply to move off the subject of the study's verifiability, to present some reflections on another topic, that of the 'new journalism' of the 1960s and 1970s, in which authors created text that blurred distinctions between fact and fiction.

Before doing this, however, Denzin presents us with a few samples of his position. He notes that Whyte's realism is based on a distinction between facts (such as the existence of bathtubs) and interpretations of these, but states: 'How facts are produced is not clear nor is it clear how the description of a fact can avoid an interpretation' (1996: 231). Denzin also objects to the idea that moral issues can be separated from issues of fact. He argues that because both 'fiction' and social research use rhetoric to express their 'truths', there is no point in trying to draw a line between them. There 'can be no single truth' (1996: 237) and the project of the researcher ought to be that of deconstruction. In response, Whyte (1996b) observes that Denzin is writing about topics that do not concern him, that 'deconstruction is a fad' that 'leads nowhere' (1996b: 242).

Further debate at the philosophical level about the possibility of gathering facts, separate from the theories or values that designate them as facts, seems unnecessary at this stage. We might, instead, 'answer' Denzin's point by asking the more pragmatic question of whether Whyte could have persuaded readers to believe his story had he adopted Denzin's approach to social research. The main point made by *Street Corner Society* is summarized by Whyte, in that book, as follows:

> The middle-class person looks upon the slum district as a formidable mass of confusion, a social chaos. The insider finds in Cornerville a highly organized and integrated social system. (1981: xvi).

Let us imagine how things might have looked had Whyte been writing on Cornerville from within Denzin's 'sixth moment'. He might have proceeded by 'deconstructing' the middle-class assumptions of texts (such as those written by journalists) to show, perhaps, that they were self-contradictory when they represented Cornerville as chaotic, or simply that they did portray 'slum' life in this way. This might have made an interesting discourse analytic project, but would not have presented an alternative account, beyond implying that one was possible. Perhaps Whyte, believing for some reason that street corner life was organized rather than chaotic, could have abandoned the project of persuading readers that he was reporting facts about that life and gone for a quasi-fictional version along the lines of the 'new journalists' for whom Denzin reserves his praise. Indeed, this is a textual strategy adopted by Richardson, Denzin's like-minded critic of the Whyte/Boelen dispute, in her work where she has presented poems based on the words of interviewees, designed to evoke their typical perspective, rather than reporting things said on particular occasions (her work is discussed in Chapter 11). Denzin writes admiringly of the new journalists (for example Tom Wolfe, 1973) who blur the line between fact and fiction, creating characters that are composites of 'real' people, events that are composites of 'real' events, and in general pursuing an agenda as moral witnesses to radical changes in American society.

Yet as Denzin himself points out, this journalistic genre was criticized by its readers precisely on the grounds that it was fiction rather than fact. People wanted to feel that the writer had seen the things referred to in the text (Geertz's (1988) 'being there'), and that writers had done their best to reflect these events accurately, before acceding credibility to them. If Whyte had presented 'faction' of this sort people would have said he was making it up, and he would have been. It is precisely his commitment to realism and fact, rather than fiction, that has given his text its authority over the years, albeit modified by some critics who are basically realist, who point out various omissions, such as the perspective of the women of Cornerville (Morgan, 1981). Whyte's text is refutable not by some alternative fictional text, or by some new reading of his rhetorical strategies, but by an alternative presentation of facts witnessed by another observer. It is precisely Whyte's point that Boelen in various respects fails to do a convincing job of this, giving credibility to the view that his text does indeed represent truth about the way things were in Cornerville at that time, rather than being a free-floating body of signs.

Attempts to make qualitative studies replicable, though the full-scale actual replication of studies may be difficult and therefore disappointing, are worthwhile. Replicability is enhanced by showing readers as much detail as possible of the procedures used to generate the story being told. Reflexive methodological accounting in this spirit, based on a qualified commitment to a broadly realist position, enhances credibility and can improve the quality of qualitative research.

In this section I have largely focused on proving the case for being concerned with replicability and reliability. The studies discussed are classics in their fields, but they arose at a time of lesser sensitivity to methodological critique than is now the case, and are not always good examples of reflexive methodological accounting. An exception, of course, is Whyte, whose methodological appendix on how the research was done remains an important early example of such reflexivity. In the rest of this chapter, in contrast, I will show a variety of procedures that researchers have adopted that serve as examples of good practice in this area, additionally changing focus somewhat to concentrate on internal reliability.

Internal reliability

LeCompte and Goetz (1982) define internal reliability as the degree to which other researchers would match given constructs to data in the same way as original researchers. This is a considerably less ambitious goal than that contained in external reliability, but if demonstrated can aid confidence in the logical consistency with which data analysis has been done. LeCompte and Goetz list five features that enhance this:

1   Use low-inference descriptors.
2   Use multiple researchers.
3   Use participant researchers.
4   Peer examination.
5   Record data mechanically.

The first of these involves recording observations in terms that are as concrete as possible, including verbatim accounts of what people say, for example, rather than researchers' reconstructions of the general sense of what a person said, which would allow researchers' personal perspectives to influence the reporting. The second item refers to the argument that the presence of multiple researchers who continually communicate about methodological decisions is likely to enhance internal reliability. We see this, for example, in the inter-rater reliability exercise reported by Armstrong et al. (1997; see also Chapter 3), or the procedures for gaining agreement between panel members in the study by Brown and Harris (1978; see also Chapter 9). LeCompte and Goetz's third method, that of recruiting 'participant researchers' as informants who can check on whether things are seen similarly by the researcher and by members in the field, is a procedure very similar to that described under member validation (see Chapter 5). Peer examination is listed as the fourth procedure, since LeCompte and Goetz argue that peer review, for example in the form of referees' reports on the apparent adequacy of research procedures, constitutes a check on internal reliability. Clearly, the auditing procedures outlined by Lincoln and Guba (1985), as described earlier in this chapter, can be enlisted for this purpose. Finally, these authors advocate the use of audio and videotapes to record data mechanically, as this preserves data in 'raw' form, removing the selective effect of researchers' perceptual skills. This is, in fact, an extension of the idea contained in the first item (low-inference descriptors), since mechanical recording is another means for describing data while inferring as little as possible about its potential meanings.

I propose to concentrate here on two topics from this list, as others are covered elsewhere in this book under a variety of headings. I shall discuss inter-rater reliability exercises a little further, pointing out the connections of this topic with that of coding and stressing in particular the uses of computer-aided data analysis packages for this purpose. First, however, I shall discuss arguments for the use of low-inference descriptors, giving examples that show the usefulness of this concept but remaining aware of the limits to excluding inference from basic observational acts.

Low-inference descriptors

No act of observation can be free from the underlying assumptions that guide it. Whyte's reporting of whether bathtubs existed in the tenement building in which he lodged may have been accurate, and it may have been possible to prove it so beyond all reasonable doubt. But the reporting of this fact rather than another one, and the placing of facts about bathtubs at a particular point in his research report in order to achieve a particular effect (the family was poor because no bathtub was in the house; the neighbourhood was a 'slum' because it contained houses and families like this), is not a neutral matter. Yet researchers can maintain an awareness of the role of mind in constructing observations and still proceed with their business with some justification, a point best demonstrated through examples.

'Recording' fieldnotes   Most standard accounts of ethnography contain advice about the recording of fieldnotes so that observations are kept separate from interpretations of these, and observations themselves are as detailed and exact as possible. Hammersley and Atkinson (1995), for example, present the following extract as an example of bad practice in this respect:

> The teacher told his colleagues in the staffroom about the wonders of a progressive school he had been to visit the day before. He was attacked from all sides. As I walked up with him to his classroom he continued talking of how the behaviour of the pupils at X had been marvellous. We reached his room. I waited outside, having decided to watch what happened in the hall in the build-up to the morning assembly. He went into his classroom and immediately began shouting at his class. He was taking it out on them for not being like the pupils at X. (1995: 181)

Clearly, we are asked to rely on the researcher's interpretation of unreported speech in the first and second sentences. What appears to one person to be an 'attack' may be a friendly jibe to another. The final sentence presents the writer's interpretation of the teacher's motives as fact. Hammersley and Atkinson contrast this with a more concrete and precise fieldnote, containing attempts at reporting verbatim exchanges such as the following, in support of the view that the teacher (called Walker) was 'attacked from all sides':

> *Greaves*: Projects are not education, just cutting out things.
> *Walker*: Oh no, they don't allow that, there's a strict check on progress.
> *Holton*: The more I hear of this the more wishy washy it sounds . . .
> *Holton*: How can an immature child of that age do a project?
> *Walker*: Those children were self-controlled and well-behaved. (1995: 181–2)

Additionally, the separation of observational reports from interpretations is made more clear in the following extract, where the first and second sentences observations. The third is the interpretation.

> When we reach his room I wait outside to watch the hall as the build-up for the morning assembly begins. He enters his room and immediately begins shouting. The thought crosses my mind that the contrast between the pupils at X he has been describing and defending to his colleagues and the 'behaviour' of his own pupils may be a reason for his shouting at the class, but, of course, I don't know what was going on in the classroom. (1995: 182)

Clearly, the point made in the third sentence allows for the possibility of different interpretations: the researcher does not know what provoked the teacher's shouts, especially since he or she was standing outside the classroom at the time. This is a much more provisional account of the events, showing readers the basis on which interpretations were made, and allowing for their fallibility.

'Constructing' fieldnotes Practical advice on recording data of the sort supplied by Hammersley and Atkinson is, as I say, common in textbook accounts (see for example Kirk and Miller, 1986; Fielding, 1993; Schatzman and Strauss, 1973). At the same time, the keen interest in language and rhetoric evidenced in the ethnographic critique of ethnography (Clifford and Marcus, 1986; see also Chapters 2 and 11) has led to an interest in the constructed nature of ethnographic fieldnotes. Atkinson (1992) provides a good account of the literature on this topic, pointing out that innocence about the literary aspects of ethnographic data records can no longer be sustained. He argues that all fieldnotes are authored; the fieldnote 'enjoys relationships of "intertextuality"' (1992: 20) and this is unavoidable. Rereading fieldnotes evokes memories of things that were not written down at the time, showing that selection must have occurred. He rejects the empiricist position of writers such as those involved in grounded theory methodology since fieldnotes 'are not the inert accumulation of unconnected sense data and recordings. They are already encoded with interpretative qualities' (1992: 18). He argues, indeed, that their form is often influenced by the writers' knowledge of how they might look when included in a final text, confessing to having sustained himself during the 'drudgery' of fieldnote writing with such consoling fantasies. Such observational records are certainly influenced by acquaintance with ethnographic literature, for it is here that researchers learn the conventions of writing, and this includes conventions for the recording of data. At the same time, Atkinson warns against taking these revelations as a sign that researchers should abandon method since, he believes, it is important to retain the project of producing disciplined and coherent research accounts that maintain some sense that language can refer more or less accurately to other events.

Atkinson (1992), then, dabbles with the postmodern analysis of conventional ethnography, but pulls back from the edge of the abyss as far as realism is concerned, retaining the possibility that some fieldnotes might be more reliably recorded than others, though advice on this is not a primary concern of his text. He is less sound on the topic of transcription, largely because he fails to appreciate the progress made in conversation analysis (CA) towards reliable conventions for such records (Silverman, 1998b). Before we turn to an examination of what can be done for reliability if CA conventions are used, let us look briefly at Atkinson's critique of transcription based, as I say, on ethnographers' usage rather than ethnomethodologically informed transcription practices.

Like fieldnotes, Atkinson argues, transcriptions of talk from audio or videotape depend on textual representations. Pointing out that liberal quotations from 'verbatim' records are often used to add authenticity to an ethnographic account, he also points out that even texts that wholly consist of such transcripts, with no apparent authorial voice from the researcher, are highly edited and therefore selective. Oscar Lewis's use of this format is thus critiqued:

> The characters who speak for themselves in Lewis's texts, do so in voices and in narratives that are highly contrived and reconstructed by Lewis himself. The narratives are edited into coherent, extended texts . . . His narrators do not stumble and falter; they do not lose the thread; they do not break off to change the subject . . . The narratives are clearly reconstructed . . . too 'smooth': everyday speech is less fluent, less grammatical, and less readable. (1992: 24–5)

Crapanzano's (1980) use of similar textual devices (which is discussed in Chapter 11) lauded by some (for example Clifford, 1986) as an example of writing that preserves the ideals of postmodern ethnographers to decentre research texts from a reliance on the researcher's authority and supply the possibility of 'multivocality', is also criticized by Atkinson. Yet Atkinson is aware of attempts to create special textual devices that preserve the characteristics of spontaneous speech as far as possible. Even these he nevertheless says are flawed: punctuation and spelling conventions mean that a considerable amount of tidying up goes on, so that accent, for example, is difficult to represent. Use of non-conventional spellings, such as *sez* or *wuz* instead of *says* or *was* in order to convey a non-standard accent, runs the risk of denigrating the speaker's character. Punctuation can artificially enhance the cogency of speakers' arguments.

Transcription in conversation analysis While accepting that these things can occur, and recognizing that critiques such as Atkinson's are helpful in alerting us to the ideological distortions that 'tidying up' can produce, this analysis underemphasizes the extent to which rigorous transcription conventions can overcome these effects. This can be shown by turning to examples from conversation analysis (CA). Consider the following extract, which does not use CA conventions, but represents a 'tidied-up' version of a speech exchange that an ethnographer might consider to be 'verbatim'. It involves the delivery of information by a doctor to a man with cancer:

Version 1
(D, Doctor; P, Patient; W, Wife)
D: It's very hard to be absolutely dogmatic about any predictions with these things. But despite all of those things, in the majority of people the disease does come back, even from the beginning.
P: Yes.
D: And if it does come back, we can try other drugs which may control it for a little while, but generally all that you can try and do is control the symptoms.
P: Yes mm.
D: Uhm, the first time gives us the best chance for a longer survival, hopefully long term, but the odds are generally against that. But *if* [our emphasis] we do nothing for these sorts of diseases, it kills you within a couple of months.
W: The breakdown could be that quick could it?
P: Mmm.
D: Well actually it's quite spectacularly fast. (Seale and Silverman, 1997: 381)

Silverman reports that two out of three coders believed that in this extract the patient had not been told that his condition was incurable, as the word 'incurable' was not used by the doctor. Additionally, a coder felt that the doctor's third statement meant that the message about incurability was ambiguous, allowing the interpretation that if 'something' were to be done, death might not result.

A CA transcription of part of this speech looks very different. It is more laborious to create, but it enables resolution of the reliability issue:

Version 2
1 D: But er despite all of those things, in the majority
2   of people the disease does come *back*
3   (0.8)
4 D: even from the beginning.
5 P: Yes
6 D: And: (0.4) if it does come back we can try
7   other drugs which may control it for a little while
8 P: mm um
9 D: but generally all that you can try and do is control
10   the symptoms.
11 P: Yes mm.
12 D: Uhm, the first time gives us the best chance
13   for a *longer* (0.5) survival hopefully long term
14 P: hhm
15 D: but the odds are generally against that.
16 P: Yes um (0.4)

17 D: But if we do nothing for these sorts of diseases it
18   kills you within a couple of months.
19 P: Yes (Seale and Silverman, 1997: 382)

In version 2, pauses are indicated in fractions of a second by the numbers in brackets. Silverman comments that the 0.8 second pause at line 3 is not used by the patient to indicate his receipt of the bad news, for example by saying 'Yes'. The doctor therefore upgrades the news at line 4, which the patient then 'receives' with the 'Yes' at line 5. Further acknowledgements of the news by the patient occur at lines 11, 16 and 19, suggesting that the patient does indeed take in the news that his disease is incurable. Significantly, some of these interjections by the patient and none of the pregnant pauses were represented in version 1, leading to the appearance of ambiguity. This serves to emphasize the point that low-inference descriptors, such as are provided in version 2, provide a better basis on which to interpret the meaning of data. Additionally, readers of such data extracts are more informed about the basis of researchers' interpretations, so are better equipped to evaluate their adequacy.

An ethnographer might legitimately feel that the microscopic analysis of tiny moments of interaction in which conversation analysts tend to deal would fail to address the broader questions and larger moments with which conventional ethnography is generally concerned. This, of course, is not a reliability issue, but it may explain the reluctance of some to become involved with CA, which is notoriously technical – even technicist – and has too often failed to deliver results that address social problems or even relate to issues in more general social theory. There are signs that this is changing, however. Silverman has himself produced work of considerable relevance for healthcare practitioners (Silverman 1997b); Peräkylä (1997) offers a number of helpful suggestions on combining ethnography with CA; Scheff's account of 'part-whole morphology' (Scheff, 1997) offers an enticing prospect for understanding large-scale historical and social processes through detailed study of micro-interactions at the CA level.

Without going into the detail of these arguments, for they are not within the scope of this book, it is important to note that internal reliability, even with the sort of detail provided by CA, is never finally proven beyond doubt. There is always the possibility that other interpretations are possible; Silverman's interpretation of version 2 may be open to dispute, yet it is a more robust argument than would have been the case had he simply relied on version 1. The degree to which readers should be asked to rely on researchers' inferences is a relative matter, not an absolute one. The level of detail required in describing data must remain a matter of judgement, taking account of the degree to which claims are central to an overall argument in a particular research study.

Reliability of coding

Coding (or 'indexing') is by far the most common initial procedure in qualitative data analysis, representing the researcher's thoughts about how data might be interpreted, given a particular set of concerns. As we have seen, observation and the recording of data can themselves never be wholly free from the values, assumptions and theoretical perspectives of researchers, though a great deal can be done to show readers what these assumptions are, so that judgements of credibility are well informed. Use of low-inference descriptors clearly helps with this. Once data are described, however, it becomes relevant to make inferences about their meaning, and the reliability with which consistent coding decisions are made is a common concern for qualitative researchers.

Coding is, of course, an attempt to fix meaning, constructing a particular vision of the world that excludes other possible viewpoints. I have argued throughout this book that this is a desirable quality for research texts, albeit done within a fallibilistic framework. Without such exclusiveness, research signifies very little in the minds of audiences, except perhaps to represent lack of confidence, or an excess of guilt about the temporary occupancy of a (moderately) authoritative platform. However, coding that fixes meanings too early in the analytic process may stultify creative thought, blocking the analyst's capacity for seeing new things. The early stages of coding are therefore more appropriately called 'indexing', acting as signposts to interesting bits of data, rather than representing some final argument about meaning.

This distinction is similar to one made by Kelle and Laurie (1995), who suggest that indexing is a heuristic device to aid developmental thinking. If used, for example, with computer programs that can retrieve segments of data thus signposted, more intensive and precise work may be done, at which point index words increasingly come to describe phenomena that the researcher believes to have a certain stability or regularity in the way in which they occur across different contexts. At this point we are seeing a gradual transition from indexing to coding. Conceptual clarity, in which phenomena are exposed to more rigorous and exclusive definitions so that they are distinguished clearly from other phenomena, becomes more important. At this point, too, it becomes relevant to ask whether other minds would see things in the same way. In a sense, an inter-rater reliability exercise can be understood as a test of the potential readership of a research report, to examine the degree to which this is likely to convey shared meanings consistently. This, of course, is at variance with the postmodern view that claims a unique meaning to every reading of a text, a position that runs the risk of undermining the value of research texts in creating communities of shared meaning within a broadly scientific enterprise.

Using computers Team working on research projects, as they move from indexing to coding, from brainstorming to the confirmation of shared meanings, can make use of inter-rater reliability exercises at this point. Lee and Fielding (1995), in their survey of computer-assisted qualitative data analysis software (CAQDAS) packages, found that these were often used to facilitate the sharing and comparison of coding decisions between researchers. Team research often involved conflicts about coding decisions, the resolution of which generally led to a stronger sense of confidence about the consistency with which coding had been applied. Such exercises are further opportunities for fallibilistic research practice.

Durkin (1997) is one such user of CAQDAS, who reports a project involving collaboration between British and American researchers to examine how actors in the legal systems of both countries dealt with asbestosis-related litigation. Durkin describes the project:

> First the ABF [American Bar Foundation] project was a team effort. As in much qualitative research these days, team members brought different training (law and sociology) and experiences to the project. We often focused on different issues. As we were often in different time zones and interviewing different people, we needed a way to keep current on our data. A [CAQDAS package] allowed us to code and compare the interviews as they were completed, keeping us informed about each researcher's interviews and preliminary findings. (1997: 94–5)

The initial stages of the project were exploratory, involving open-ended interviews and 'a very simple [analysis] that indexed the data' (1997: 95). Once retrieved and inspected, more precise ideas began to emerge, so that the researchers began to see systematic differences between the two countries in the meanings associated with asbestosis litigation. In the US media, for example, such cases were framed as a part of a growing legal crisis; in the UK, the problem was more likely to be seen as a medical issue. At this point a 'coding system' (1997: 96) rather than an indexing system was constructed. Durkin takes up the story:

> We all discussed the structure and contents of [each] code, making sure coding rules were clear, inclusive and exclusive. We talked about the theoretical approaches that would be most appropriate to describe these realities, and made sure that the appropriate data could be clearly coded . . . intercoder reliability checks are easily accomplished [with CAQDAS]. While we scored very high on inter-coder reliability, [CAQDAS reports] would quickly identify coding problems. If coding rules were unclear, or redundant, the [CAQDAS program] would uncover these problems. (1997: 96)

If exercises like this are carried out by qualitative researchers, and research reports contain accounts of coding schemes with illustrative examples of typical instances coded under each heading, readers are more likely to be persuaded that care has been taken to analyse data in ways that are, at least, logically consistent. This aspect of internal reliability is not, of course, a guarantee of truth or validity. It does, however, help to guard against the errors associated with sole researchers who, free from the checks and balances imposed by the need to demonstrate consistency to others, present readers with categories poorly connected with field observations.

Showing data

A final aspect of internal reliability concerns the issue of 'showing' data to the reader. If readers can see the entire corpus of data on which coding schemes, concepts and conclusions are based, so the argument goes, the adequacy with which (for example) coding decisions were made can be evaluated by the reader. In a way, this is like inviting the reader to participate in an inter-rater reliability exercise. One can see the attractions of this for the methodologist concerned about credibility and dependability, since it would enable this aspect of the research process to be fully exposed to readers' critical gaze. This spirit lies behind Coffey and Atkinson's (1996) advocacy of electronic forms of research reporting, so that readers can use CD-Roms and other high-capacity storage media to conduct their own investigations of data, and to test their level of agreement with the meta-narrative of interpretation presented by the original author.

However, there are problems with showing large amounts of data to readers within conventional print formats. It is often claimed that qualitative researchers face particular difficulties in fitting what they have to say into journals with strict rulings on maximum word lengths. Compared with quantitative researchers, so this story goes, qualitative data cannot be summarized economically. Quantitative researchers can use tables of numbers based on standardized measurement devices described in other articles elsewhere in the literature to summarize vast tracts of data in a small space. For qualitative researchers, in contrast, quotations must be shown, and these take up space; readers do not like wading through large numbers of pages, often preferring executive summaries of main points or abstracts when surveying a field. It seems quite unrealistic to expect most readers to examine qualitative data records closely in order to assess researchers' conclusions (see Hammersley (1997) for an extended discussion of such reluctance). This amounts to researchers asking readers to do their work for them; surely it is possible for researchers to devise shorthand procedures that will alleviate this workload for readers, while at the same time preserving quality.

Conversation analysts and, sometimes, discourse analysts are fortunate in this respect, as they deal for the most part in small data extracts, which can indeed be shown to readers. Peräkylä (1997) makes much of this advantage, arguing that the public accessibility of conversation analytic data means that CA is 'free of many shortcomings in reliability characteristic of other forms of qualitative research, especially ethnography' (1997: 203).

For other types of qualitative research – conventional depth inter-viewing, for example, or ethnography based on extended periods of participant observation – the corpus of data generated is very large, sometimes famously so, consisting of mounds of paper transcripts or gigabytes of hard disk space, gradually accumulated over months of fieldwork or tape transcription sessions. The requirement that all of this is shown to the reader is not only impractical but, I believe, misguided. Coding is in fact a method for 'showing' such bodies of data. Informing readers that a large mass of data like this has been reduced by categ-orizing every element within a scheme of organizing concepts, showing readers counts of the number of times a segment associated with a code occurs, and giving a few typical, illustrative examples (as well as ones which are less typical) exposes data to the reader adequately for most practical purposes. However, for this to work well readers must have confidence in the consistency with which codes have been applied, and the comprehensiveness of the search through data. If the reader senses that some interviews have been missed, or that concepts have been applied to data in an idiosyncratic fashion, data is immediately 'hidden' again. We are returned, therefore, to the practice of inter-rater reliability exercises, and reminded of the importance of systematic, fallibilistic approaches to coding in avoiding these errors.

Conclusion

I have argued in this chapter that concerns about reliability and replicability are relevant to qualitative research. The constructivist or postmodernist critique of this, based on the idealist conception that multiple realities are possible or that adjudication between accounts is politically unacceptable, has only limited appeal, leading to texts that are indistinguishable from fiction, offering no distinctive role for social research. The attempt to use language to refer to, describe or explain aspects of the social world (even if these aspects are the uses made of language in certain contexts) is a basic commitment for qualitative researchers and must ultimately depend on some modified form of realism. However subtle this gets, though, the concerns raised by quantitative researchers under the headings of reliability and replicability are relevant.

We have seen that external reliability, involving the replication of entire studies, has been difficult to achieve in practice, due to the par-ticular difficulties of qualitative work, which often involves the study of unique settings that change over time, making revisits problematic if done in the hope that nothing has changed or that the exact viewpoint of the original researcher can be adopted. A more realistic alternative is the provision of a fully reflexive account of procedures and methods, showing to readers in as much detail as possible the lines of inquiry that have led to particular conclusions. This enables readers imaginatively to 'replicate' studies, and also helps to ensure that claims are supported by adequate evidence.

Internal reliability is a more practical proposition and is enhanced by a variety of procedures, including exercises in inter-rater reliability and the use of low-inference descriptors in recording data. The transcription conventions of conversation analysis were shown to have considerable advantages in giving full details of data, relatively free from the interpretive 'tidying up' that so often occurs in other forms of transcription or indeed ethnographic fieldnotes. These advantages have to be balanced, nevertheless, against the narrowness of scope imposed by CA methods. Inter-rater reliability exercises, especially facilitated by CAQDAS packages, are a viable way of reassuring readers that coding schemes are clear, unambiguous and supported by a good level of intersubjective agreement.

Good practice in relation to replicability and reliability is a further aspect of reflexivity, showing the audience of research studies as much as is possible of the procedures that have led to a particular set of conclusions. In more elaborate conceptions of reflexivity, this is taken to involve an account of the researcher's personal story during the life of the project, exposing assumptions, values and theoretical perspectives for the benefit of the reader, again in the interests of enabling a critical evaluation of conclusions. This consciousness of self has been developed in a variety of ways by qualitative researchers, and the chapter that follows considers a variety of these forms of reflexive writing practice before, in the final chapter, I turn to some other matters concerning the aesthetics of research writing.

KEY POINTS

- Replication of qualitative research studies has been, in practice, extremely difficult, forcing modifications to crude realist assumptions.

- Peer auditing and reflexive methodological accounting are more practical ways of enhancing the credibility of qualitative research studies.

- The use of low inference descriptors in fieldnotes and transcriptions are desirable ways of enhancing reliability.

- Systematic coding schemes, in which several researchers participate and seek to resolve differences of interpretation, can help researchers display to readers the interpretive work done in data analysis.

11

Reflexivity and Writing

CONTENTS

Confessional accounts of field research experiences became a common genre in the 1970s (for example Freilich, 1970; Bell and Newby, 1977) as methodological self-consciousness began to overtake earlier concerns of qualitative researchers to prove their scientific credentials. Geertz (1993; first published 1973) captured this mood among ethnographers when he commented, in his seminal essay on 'thick description':

> In finished anthropological writings [the fact] that what we call our data are really our own constructions of other people's constructions of what they and their compatriots are up to – is obscured, because most of what we need to comprehend a particular event, ritual, custom, idea or whatever is insinuated as background information before the thing itself is directly examined . . . There is nothing particularly wrong with this, and it is in any case inevitable. But it does lead to a view of anthropological research as rather more of an observational and rather less of an interpretive activity than it really is. (1993: 9)

This now seems a rather mild and polite way of prefiguring the storm of deconstructionism that, 10 years later, gathered pace as the ethnographic critique of ethnography (Clifford and Marcus, 1986) led qualitative researchers into what amounted to a new paradigm, placing the discovery of reflexivity at the centre of methodological thinking and, in particular, informing new writing practices. Geertz himself (1988) was later to signal his distaste for the more developed forms of ethnographic self-consciousness that his own sensibilities had helped to create. In this chapter I shall review the thinking behind the advocacy of reflexive or confessional writing in qualitative research, and assess some of the research writing that has been produced under this influence. In the chapter that follows I shall turn to the role of clarity and aesthetic values in the writing of research reports. Some exposure to debates and examples in these areas may help us to think about ways of enhancing the quality of research writing.

Confession versus reflexive accounting

Telling the story of how a research project was done can serve many purposes. It is a mistake to assume that this must always involve a fallibilistic attitude on the part of the researcher. Such an account can equally serve the opposite purpose, of apparently placing the research account beyond criticism, for as any Catholic knows, confession can mask differing degrees of repentance. On the other hand, tales of fieldwork can at times develop into an excruciating degree of self-consciousness, so that the research itself becomes well-nigh impossible. We can see this variation by reviewing some examples.

In his outline of ethnographic writing genres, Van Maanen (1988) distinguishes what he calls 'confessional tales' from an earlier realist genre. Realist tales were to be found in the standardized form of ethnographic reporting for many years, written almost to a routine within anthropology, whereby certain categories were always covered, such as the family life, work life, religious beliefs, authority and kinship systems, material culture and other standard aspects of the life of a 'people' studied. Many of the classics of anthropology (for example Malinowski, 1922; Evans-Pritchard, 1940) are written as realist tales, a style also adopted by sociologists (Whyte, 1981; Becker et al., 1961). In realist tales authors seek to make themselves invisible in order to deal with worries about personal subjectivity biasing the account. The realist ethnographer possessed interpretive omnipotence, having the final say over the meanings signified by the culture described (although this characteristic is not confined to realist tales alone).

Confessional tales, by contrast, often consist of a 'natural history' of the project, with a major emphasis on describing fieldwork experiences. The fieldworker is portrayed, quite commonly, as infiltrating a group in

spite of a series of blunders, leading to a more sophisticated performance as honorary 'insider' after a period of (sometimes painful) learning
of the ways of the group. These have, eventually, the quality of persuading the reader that the researcher has indeed 'been there', seeing
and understanding the way of life thus penetrated in a manner that can
give unique authority to report on it truthfully, so that the reader can
rely on the writer's hard-won objectivity. Treated in this way, the 'confession' is a strategy for gaining authority rather than giving it away,
and involves no departure from realist assumptions. Indeed, it constitutes a claim to authenticity.

A non-fallibilistic example

Such an account is presented by Buckingham in his study (Buckingham
et al., 1976) of wards for terminally ill patients. Here, the striking story
of Buckingham's entrée into the setting serves to emphasize his claims
to authenticity, rather than deconstructing his authority. His reported
tribulations are markers of exceptional experience, which is presented
as giving him a unique right to have his version heard:

> To gain admission to the hospital and establish M's assumed identity, certain
> preparations were required . . . To simulate features of his assumed medical
> history M submitted to supraclavicular incision, indicative of cervical lymph
> node biopsy, and ultraviolet radiation to produce eryhtema over the
> epigastrum and spine, suggestive of radiation therapy to the pancreas. M
> reviewed medical charts and maintained close contact with patients dying
> with carcinoma of the pancreas. He was thus able to observe and imitate
> suitable behaviour. (1976: 1211).

Having lost weight by dieting over six months, and in possession of fake
medical documents, he presented himself at the hospital emergency
department for admission. Once admitted, he found that he actually
experienced symptoms, due to the extent to which he had taken on the
role of dying patient. His back hurt and he felt weak. When transferred
to a palliative care unit:

> he identified closely with these sick people and became weaker and more
> exhausted. He was anorexic and routinely refused food. He felt ill. It took all
> his energy to take a shower. He sat exhausted in a chair. He experienced
> increasing pain, a constant ache in his left leg together with numbness and
> restless nights during which family members of other patients commented
> sympathetically on his 'moaning and groaning'. M himself was unaware of
> this nocturnal behaviour. (1976: 1212)

He was then able to report on the differing regimes of care obtaining in
the hospital and palliative care wards, concluding that the latter was
more humane, through a series of qualitative anecdotes and some

quantitative counts of interactions between staff and patients. Such an account enhances the writer's authority, as it 'proves' the authenticity of his or her witnessing experience, though in fact it does little to expose the claims made in the report to critical scrutiny.

Explaining methods

A slightly more fallibilistic version of reflexive methodological accounting is a type long advocated in both quantitative and qualitative methodological literature, which is easily wedded to conventional scientific projects in qualitative research and is, indeed, often an adjunct to realist tales (seen, classically, in Whyte's (1981) methodological appendix to *Street Corner Society*). Reflexivity interpreted in this way is no more or less than the conventional scientific virtue of giving a full explanation of the methodological procedures used to generate a set of findings, done in the interests of potential replications (see Chapter 10), and for the benefit of readers wishing to assess credibility. In this spirit, one of Howard Becker's solutions to 'problems of inference and proof in participant observation' was to recommend that researchers give 'a description of a natural history of our conclusions, presenting the evidence as it came to the attention of the observer during the successive stages of his conceptualization of the problem' (1970b: 37). Elsewhere, discussing the human judgements that are involved in research, he argues that we must 'try to make the bases of these judgements as explicit as possible so that others may arrive at their own conclusions' (1970d: 5).

A similar spirit informs Coffey and Atkinson's (1996) text in which they argue:

> At every stage of the [research] process . . . transactions and the ideas that emerge from them should be documented. The construction of analytic or methodological memoranda and working papers, and the consequent explication of working hypotheses, are of vital importance. It is important that the processes of exploration and abduction be documented and retrievable. Their documentation is part of the transformation of data from personal experience and intuition to public and accountable knowledge. (1996: 191)

This sort of advice is close to Lincoln and Guba's (1985) specification of what should be recorded in an audit trail (see Chapter 10), created for the purpose of peer review in the interests of accountability and therefore credibility. It concords with the position of subtle realism, whereby authors seek to make strong statements about the social world while remaining sensitive to issues of what, in positivism, was known as bias and is now understood as a 'crisis' of representation.

Lists of what should be included in such exercises in reflexivity are commonly made. Thus Altheide and Johnson (1994) feel that researchers should report how they gained access to the research setting, how they presented themselves within it, including details of the roles taken, the degree to which researchers believe that trust and rapport were achieved and an account of any 'mistakes, misconceptions, surprises' (1994: 494). Ways in which data were collected and recorded should also be included, as well as lists of the various types of data available to researchers and coding and other analytic procedures.

Making theories explicit   More ambitiously, but linked to such lists of the contents of reflexive methodological accounting, are calls to make plain the theoretical orientations and preconceptions of the researcher, seen for example in Kirk and Miller (1986). The lead taken by feminist researchers in advocating reflexivity at this level is shown by Maynard (1994), who argues that 'rigour involves being clear about one's theoretical assumptions' (1994: 25). This is, of course, far more demanding than simply placing an interview schedule or a coding scheme in a methodological appendix. For Kirk and Miller, this exhortation arises in a discussion of the standard philosophical objection to empiricism, that no observation can be free of theory. The best that can be done is to make explicit whatever theory has been used. This 'discovery' of the limits of empiricism is at the root of the interpretive critique of positivism, and for many years represented a key claim by interpretivists to know something that positivists did not, figuring very large in the stories told by qualitative creation mythologists (see Chapter 4).

Yet it is clear that the word 'theory' is here standing for many things, such as the values, prejudices or subconscious desires of the researcher, many of which are by definition not available for explanation by the person who has been influenced by them. Indeed, intensive psychoanalytic study may be needed in order to expose these, as is done by Clough (1992) in relation to the work of the symbolic interactionist Herbert Blumer. She presents an extract from Blumer's methodological writing, pointing out its (unconscious) use of erotic terminology. Blumer writes:

> The metaphor that I like is that of lifting the veils that obscure or hide what is going on. The task of scientific study is to lift the veils that cover the area of group life that one proposes to study . . . The veils are lifted by getting close to the area and by digging deep into it through careful study . . . This is not a simple matter of just approaching a given area and looking at it. It is a tough job requiring a high order of careful and honest probing . . . It is not a 'soft' study. (Blumer, 1969: 40)

With the aid of Clough's vision, it is not hard to see the sexual imagery here. One can easily understand the difficulty that women researchers might have in identifying themselves with the tough, hard probing that digs deep after lifting the metaphoric veil. Generations of hard-headed (mostly male) interpretivist researchers took inspiration from such writing, apparently unaware of the connotations that now seem so obviously to inform their strategies for data production. The prioritization of 'private accounts' (Cornwell, 1984), informed by an urge to seek authenticity by stripping away 'false' public fronts and the consequent devaluing of public accounts as data by some ethnographers, is perhaps one consequence of this. Clough also observes possible connections between exhortations not to 'go native' and castration anxieties, claiming that fear of immersion and absorption underlies the determination to hold on to firmly realist modes of accounting.

If research is informed by such deeply rooted subconscious structures of the mind, how can it be possible for a researcher to become aware of them all so that such 'theories' can be shown to the reader at the same time as they inform the research narrative? The very description of these as 'assumptions' (as in Maynard, above) seems to suggest that this will be a problem: once 'assumptions' are clear to those who hold them, they are presumably no longer 'assumed', since they have been brought to consciousness and acquire the status of belief, if they are held to at all any longer. There seem to be inevitable limits to the possibilities for reflexive accounting. Some of the motives and preconceptions that drive researchers are as yet not exposed to analysis by later writers, in the way that Blumer's approach has now been exposed by Clough's feminist deconstruction. To the contemporary mind it seems likely, indeed inevitable, that we shall see in 20 years' time numerous deconstructions of present-day forms of research practice. We shall perhaps see deconstructions of deconstructionism (indeed, one might interpret the present text as containing this). We cannot predict these possibilities, and this inability to predict what might happen can seem to lie at the heart of our methodological anxieties in this area. Abandoning research, or the equally blind alternative, pursuing a relentlessly non-reflexive empiricism, may seem attractive escapes from these irresolvable dilemmas.

The dilemmas experienced by researchers on this point are reflections of more widespread issues of trust and truth in the conditions of late modernity. Giddens' (1990, 1991) analysis of these is relevant here. He points out (1990) that uncertainty about the future and about truth are endemic in a situation where sources of traditional authority are no longer automatically respected, and individuals are exposed (through global media, for example) to a multitude of conflicting perspectives and expertise on every subject imaginable. In these conditions people are thrown back on themselves, managing their lives by collecting information as far as possible, and occasionally engaging in leaps of faith where difficult situations ('fateful moments') appear to require this. This mode of life is accompanied by some chronic anxieties for those whose security is undermined by the lack of authoritative answers, as well as creative opportunities for those who are freed from the dead weight of past traditions.

Giddens' analysis of the roots of trust, particularly that between representatives of expert systems and their clients, is particularly relevant
for our purpose, which is to understand the relationship between
research writers and their readers. For example, in describing the
consequences of late modernity for the conduct of intimate relationships, where trust may be an issue, he makes a compelling case for the
role of confession in generating such trust (1991). Psychotherapeutic
expertise helps people confess to each other details of their emotional
lives, so that partners can see things from the point of view of the other,
thus generating warmth and trust. In the context of professional–client
relationships, trust is generated by confessional practices on both sides,
so that professionals now feel obliged to explain the thinking behind
their pronouncements to critical consumers, as well as eliciting clients'
stories.

Similar problems of trust arise in the relations between authors of
research reports and their readers. Confessional accounts, in which
readers are empowered to a critical scrutiny of conclusions, can be
understood as attempts to deal with problems of trust, subsumed under
headings such as validity or credibility. If only the writer were able to
confess all, so the argument goes, sufficient information and empathy
will be generated to believe his or her story.

Once again, however, as has been argued consistently throughout this
book, we should evaluate these general arguments by considering
examples of research practice, for it is at this level that we can judge in a
more context-related way the adequacy of a variety of attempts at
reflexive methodological accounting. We can begin by examining a
fairly standard example of a confessional tale, before moving on to more
radical varieties of this genre.

Deciphering a confessional tale: investigating health beliefs Jocelyn
Cornwell (1988) presents a chapter-length account subtitled 'Reconsidering the research process' (1988: 219) in which she records her
experience of doing her PhD. This was published as *Hard Earned Lives* in
1984, being an investigation of the health beliefs of members of a small
number of families in the East End of London, based on repeated depth
interviews. The original study stressed the disjunction between what
Cornwell called 'public accounts' in which people spoke about health
and illness in ways that they felt would be acceptable to relative
strangers, and 'private accounts' where more personal thoughts were
revealed, not all of which were felt to be publicly acceptable. Cornwell
(1984: 16) observed that her initial interviews with people were
generally taken up with public accounts, whereas once trust between
researcher and researched had built up, private accounts began to be
revealed. Without using the sexual metaphors of Blumer (see earlier), it
is clear that Cornwell subscribes to the view that researchers can get
past public fronts given sufficient trust. In this respect, she adopts a

position similar to Oakley's (1981) feminist account of depth interviewing (though in other respects she records differences with Oakley).

In the later confessional chapter, in which she expands on a brief
methodological account given in the original book report, Cornwell
gives every impression that she will be providing her own 'private
account' of the research project. She complains that:

> The accounts researchers give of their work in academic papers are much like
> other accounts: they reconstruct the past to make it fit with and seem to have
> logically led to the present. As a result, certain aspects of the research process
> tend to go unmentioned . . . it is perhaps worth asking why they very rarely
> choose to describe periods of relatively little headway or ideas which led up
> blind alleys. (1988: 219)

The implication is that such conventional reporting is covering something up. Clearly, Cornwell is inviting us to regard her account as
unusually frank, using a rhetorical turn that is similar to that of many
ethnographers who present their credentials to readers as honest
reporters who will 'tell it like it is', except that in this case the 'field' is
her own research practice. The account proceeds in three parts. First, we
learn about the way in which the research problem was formulated. She
illustrates the fact that she sometimes followed false leads with an
anecdote derived from a diary which she kept at the time: two women
had discussed the phenomenon of illegal abortion with Cornwell, and
so the idea had arisen of investigating this topic, abandoned when a key
informant on this decided not to cooperate with her and when no
subsequent respondents mentioned the topic. She also describes how
time was 'wasted' (1988: 222) as she was 'ambushed' (1988: 223) by
quantitative methods, finding herself trying to find 'objective' (1988:
222) measures of health needs because she was doing the work within a
department of social administration that valued such an approach,
finally shaking this off in favour of qualitative interviews that sought to
elucidate 'commonsense' meanings (1988: 223). Additionally, she presents some reflections on the intellectual limitations of conceptualiza-
tions of health beliefs within the medical sociology literature, with
which she became dissatisfied, seeing her project as a way of righting
this wrong.

Secondly, she describes some 'choices and difficulties' (1988: 223)
concerning methods that she had to make during the study. Thus she
says that she rejected standardized interviews due to the need to
explore things with respondents. Observational methods were desirable,
but impractical, so interviews were chosen. At first, the interviews were
too long, so they had to be shortened. A standardized checklist included
in the early interviews had to be abandoned as it spoiled the relaxed
atmosphere of unstructured interviewing. This was, on reflection, a last
remainder of the attempt to integrate quantitative methods. Although

Cornwell initially planned to interview people belonging to a few 'social networks' (1988: 225), she found that the literature on networks over-emphasized the cohesiveness of these; in practice, relationships between respondents were often less close than implied in the literature, meaning that neatly defined 'networks' were hard to identify. Additionally, she found it much easier to meet women in this way, and had to break out of this cosy method of introduction to new respondents in order to include some men in her sample.

The third part of the account presents some reflections on her analysis and interpretation of data. She describes how the distinction between public and private accounts arose, initially from a perception that in early interviews people presented responses to questions that were very predictable, designed for public consumption, which were at variance to replies to the same questions much later in a sequence of interviews. She reflects that in retrospect this distinction may have been applied a little too rigidly. She was working on another study in Oxford, she reports, where the 'repertoire of public accounts has been much less striking' (1988: 229). She has found that a more complex scheme of analysis, derived from readings in social theory, is potentially more attractive.

Cornwell concludes that she has reported her experiences in ways that highlight the time that can be wasted on problems and difficulties in a research project, and that show how her gender led to greater ease in eliciting accounts from women. She says that her study is fairly typical of qualitative research studies, in that 'all studies are shaped by social relations which can pose theoretical and practical difficulties or obstacles to the work, and that researchers should make this explicit in their accounts of the research process?' (1988: 230). This is because 'the difficulties and obstacles are in themselves rich sources of data' (1988: 231).

Having presented as full and fair a summary as I can, let us now evaluate this report as a fairly standard piece of reflexive methodological accounting. What does it tell us about the preconceptions that Cornwell brought to her field; how can it help us in assessing the credibility of her findings?

First, it is clear that her subsequent research experience in Oxford has led her to question the simplicity of her public/private finding, suggesting that it may be a local phenomenon. We are also alerted to the tendency to have over-represented women's views in her observations, due to the relationships that her own gender imposed on her, although she does not speculate on how her findings might have looked had she been able to generate more trusting relations with men. The brief account of the limitations of medical sociology in describing health beliefs gives a little insight into her background reading, though it is somewhat unclear as to how this affected the analysis. In these limited ways, then, the account may help in assessing the eventual research report, containing some of the elements recommended for inclusion in such pieces (see earlier).

More negatively, it is evident that large tracts of the piece are devoted to repeating qualitative creation mythology by exposing (or sometimes just claiming) limitations of quantitative methods. Additionally, although the account of false leads followed (the illegal abortions) is within the terms of the remit that Cornwell sets herself (to show how researchers can sometimes waste time on false leads), this has no obvious implication for the credibility of her eventual findings. Finally, the claim that an account of her difficulties and obstacles itself constitutes a 'rich source . . . of data' (1988: 231) seems overblown. It is mildly interesting to see how it felt to do a research project, perhaps being of use to novice researchers in particular, but it is hard to see what new theoretical, methodological or policy issues are illuminated by these experiences.

I have deliberately chosen an example of reflexive methodological accounting that is not well known, nor particularly distinguished in the level of insight that it provides. It is possible to learn how to do good-quality work from better-quality examples, but I believe that it is also illuminative to consider more modest efforts, in the hope that this will spur people to do better. Cornwell could have attempted a feminist deconstruction of her public/private distinction, along the lines of Clough's account of Blumer; she could have explored the assumptions contained in the somewhat static notion of 'beliefs' in the term 'lay health beliefs', she might have questioned her reliance on interview data rather than observational data more rigorously. In other words, she might have presented a considerably more self-critical account if she had wanted to help readers to assess her findings. At the same time, it is clear that even had she generated such self-criticisms, readers would still have needed to evaluate the plausibility of these, so that the problem of trust and truth would never finally be 'solved'.

Nevertheless, she does more than most to help to generate a critical reading of her original report. Her account also reflects the degree to which expectations of fully reflexive methodological accounting may be unrealistic. Imagine that Cornwell possessed such a level of self-awareness and self-criticism as is implied in exhortations to make *all* theoretical 'assumptions' explicit. Such superhuman self-consciousness is likely to have led her to pursue a different research project, or indeed to retire from the business of research due to the pressure of its contradictions.

Cornwell's account, as we have interpreted its purpose here, can be located within modernist aspirations to produce a trustworthy single narrative from research. Clearly, if this is the goal, a degree of methodological confession is appropriate. Other writers, however, have gone considerably further than this, reponding to the conditions of late modernity by discarding the project of generating a single defensible account.

Postmodern reflexivity

We can now examine other ways in which researchers have dealt with the intense level of reflexivity engendered in postmodern sensibility, a topic also reviewed briefly in Chapter 2. A more detailed analysis of contemporary research writing practices can help us see the strengths and limitations of radically reflexive self-awareness. Here, of course, the project of credibility is (at least in theory) abandoned in favour of a decentring of writers' authority in order to allow voices that are otherwise suppressed or contradictory to emerge. The attempt to construct a defensible, rationally consistent meta-narrative is abandoned. Such writing does not so much constitute an explicit confession by the researcher, but reflects a de-emphasizing of claims to authorial presence. Readers are encouraged to have differing interpretations of the stories told, rather than a single story being imposed.

First, let us review some of the ideas that have led to these forms of research writing. Lincoln and Denzin (1994) convey the spirit behind much textual experimentation, saying that it reflects a move:

> toward pluralism, and many social scientists now recognize that no picture is ever complete, that what is needed is many perspectives, many voices, before we can achieve deeper understandings of social phenomena, and before we can assert that a narrative is complete.
>
> The modernist dream of a grand or master narrative is now a dead project; the recognition of the futility and the oppression of such a project is the postmodern condition. The postmodern project challenges the modernist belief (and desire) that it is possible to develop a progressive program for incorporating all the cultures of the world under a single umbrella. The postmodern era is defined, in part, by the belief that there is no single umbrella in the history of the world that might incorporate and represent fairly the dreams, aspirations, and experiences of all peoples. (1994: 580)

Later, discussing the future of qualitative research, they observe that:

> there may not be one future, one 'moment,' but rather many; not one 'voice,' but polyvocality; not one story but many tales, dramas, pieces of fiction, fables, memories, histories, autobiographies, poems, and other texts to inform our sense of lifeways, to extend our understanding of the Other . . . The modernist project has bent and is breaking under the weight of postmodern resistance to its narratives. (1994: 584).

Tyler (1986) perhaps represents one of the more radical statements of this position in relation to ethnography, in his contribution to Clifford and Marcus's (1986) volume. He claims that science is now an archaic mode of consciousness that has not led to successful universal laws. Postmodern ethnography involves cooperatively evolved text, a pastiche of fragments of discourse allowing both reader and writer a fantasy of possible worlds, in the manner of some poetry. The experience of reading such texts, claims Tyler, should transport people into a sacred world, allowing them to return to the everyday world with refreshed visions. Polyphony and dialogue are the ideals, with problematic status accorded to the voice of the author. Ethnographic discourse evokes rather than represents. The old scientific rhetoric, using words like 'objects', 'facts', 'descriptions', 'inductions', 'generalization', 'verification', 'experimentation' and 'truth', can now be substituted by a vision of writing as a magical act, where there is no consensus, only fragmentation.

Lincoln and Denzin (1994), though broadly supportive of such sentiments, warn against the excesses to which they might lead, arguing that a great deal can be learned from the classic texts of past research genres. Elements of the methods used by writers within a 'given "passé" perspective' (1994: 577), such as grounded theorizing, can be preserved in research practice, even though the claims to universality based on these can no longer legitimately be made. Additionally, these authors observe, in line with the argument of the present book, that methodological 'criticisms and exchanges can operate at a level of abstraction that does little to help the people who just go out and do research' (1994: 577).

Similar expressions of caution are evident in Atkinson (1992), who criticizes Tyler for presenting an 'extreme logical conclusion' (1992: 50), noting also that there exist:

> a series of problems and paradoxes, limitations and liabilities inherent in the extreme 'postmodern' position. There is danger that in rejecting the naive adherence to representation . . . as problematic, the texts lose all sense of reference to a social world, but become overwhelmingly *self*-referential. The problems arise if a particular insight or innovation is taken to extremes. Indeed, if it is not too much of an oxymoron, some authors take this understanding of the non-literal character of language far too literally! (1992: 50)

There thus exist a variety of positions on the desirability of textual radicalism which are, once again, best assessed with the aid of some examples.

Examples of textual radicalism

Methodological angst In the early phases of the growth in postmodern sensibilities, it became common for researchers simply to remind readers of their doubts about the canons of traditional research practice at regular intervals in the text, periodically presenting the reader with episodes of acute methodological self-consciousness. Compare this extract from Margaret Mead, writing in a previous moment in the history of anthropology, with that of a later anthropologist:

> This account is the result of six months' concentrated and uninterrupted field work. From a thatched house on piles, built in the centre of the Manus village of Peri, I learned the native language, the children's games, the intricacies of social organization, economic custom, and religious belief and practice which formed the social framework within which the child grows up. In my large living-room, on the wide verandas, on the tiny islet adjoining the houses, in the surrounding lagoon, the children played all day and I watched them, now from the midst of a play group, now from behind the concealment of the thatched walls. I rode in their canoes, attended their feasts, watched in the house of mourning and sat severely still while the mediums conversed with the spirits of the dead. I observed the children when no grown-up people were present, and I watched their behaviour towards their parents. Within a social setting which I learned to know intimately enough not to offend against the hundreds of name taboos, I watched the Manus baby, the Manus child, the Manus adolescent, in an attempt to understand the way in which each of these was becoming a Manus adult. (Mead, 1942, first published in 1930: 15–16)

Here, there are no doubts that the observer could, in expeditions away from her wide veranda and generous living room, watch objectively the things she says she saw, learn the things she learned, and report these to us as they were. Indeed, her credentials to do so, by learning the language and rules 'intimately enough not to offend', are displayed. There is very little self-doubt in her writing. Compare this with an extract from Danforth's study of death rituals in rural Greece:

> Anthropology inevitably involves an encounter with the Other. All too often, however, the ethnographic distance that separates the reader of anthropological texts and the anthropologist himself from the Other is rigidly maintained and at times even artificially exaggerated. In many cases this distancing leads to an exclusive focus on the Other as primitive, bizarre, and exotic. The gap between a familiar 'we' and an exotic 'they' is a major obstacle to a meaningful understanding of the Other, an obstacle that can only be overcome through some form of participation in the world of the Other.
> . . .
> Whenever I observed death rituals in rural Greece, I was acutely aware of a paradoxical sense of simultaneous closeness, otherness and oneness . . . I was conscious at all times that it is not just Others who die. I was aware that my friends and relatives will die, that I will die, that death comes to all, Self and Other alike.
> . . .
> As I sat by the body of a man who had died several hours earlier and listened to his wife, his sisters, and his daughters lament his death, I imagined these rites being performed and these laments being sung at the death of my relatives, at my own death . . . I thought of my own brother and cried. The

distance between Self and Other had grown small indeed. (Danforth, quoted in Geertz, 1988: 14–15)

Danforth here expresses his reservations about the emotional distance that he feels might be imposed by the sort of traditional approaches to fieldwork represented by Mead, instead using his emotional responses as a way of understanding the perspective of the people he was studying. In so doing, he questions critically the appearance of exoticism conveyed by such writing, since an essential similarity between himself and the people he studied, in terms of basic existential problems of life and death, is asserted.

In a similar piece, Renato Rosaldo (1993) used his personal experience of bereavement (the accidental death of his wife) as a resource for understanding the rage that sometimes impelled the people whom he was studying to headhunt, a practice which hitherto he had found impossible to explain with the elaborate theorizations of Western social science (see also Chapter 5 for a discussion of this account). Personal emotional experience is celebrated by both Danforth and Rosaldo as a means to understanding people in the study settings, at the same time linked to a methodological critique of overdistancing.

Such texts nevertheless remain conventional to the extent that a single authorial presence is assumed, indeed celebrated as the author's personal experiences are presented as an important resource underlying the general interpretations. Thus Rosaldo uses his experience to make some general statements about ritual, which he says is overemphasized as meaningful in the anthropological literature. By contrast, his experience has shown him that formal rituals are not the only means for channelling the strong emotions associated with loss, which circulate unpredictably in 'the informal settings of everyday life' (1993: 14) as well, so that formal rituals may be experienced as platitudinous and empty by comparison with these more informal channels for rage and sorrow. Danforth, too, presents an analysis of meaning making through funeral laments that departs considerably from the traditional anthropological analysis of mortuary ritual. We are not yet in the experimental territory of textual radicalism, though these are its precursors.

Removing the author's voice: examples from Moroccan ethnography - Somewhat further down the line are polyvocal or collaborative texts, which seek deliberately to place the author well away from centre stage. Crapanzano (1980) provides an early example of this, being a collection of edited transcripts from discussions held with Tuhami, a Moroccan man. Crapanzano also presents comments about what might have been going on, psychologically, between himself and Tuhami, including his discomfort at his feeling of being cast in the role of healer of the Moroccan's psychic pain. He writes short passages of commentary in more conventional anthropological mode, but in the majority of the book seeks to be only marginally present in the text. As Atkinson (1992: 43) points out, however, Crapanzano's editing is itself highly selective, an artifice which tends to hide the context in which the speech was produced. The thinking that went into selecting the quotes being shown is hidden from readers rather than being absent from the research. Fontana (1994) observes: 'When all is said and done, what we learn about the subject, Tuhami, is still a product of Crapanzano's under-standing, interpretations and selection of his data' (1994: 212). Clearly, had the original speech been in the language of the research report, more might have been done on this with more rigorous transcription conventions to reduce the level of inference by the author (see Chapter 10), though this would not have made for an easy read and would have involved greater selectivity of data extracts.

Dwyer (1982) notes that Crapanzano's text goes a long way towards 'creating an anthropological work in which the Self is exposed as it searches for the Other' (1982: 280), but he believes 'not far enough' (1982: 280), since Crapanzano's psychoanalytic understanding of the encounter colours the text to a considerable extent. He is also critical of Crapanzano's omission of sections of the interviews which he considers irrelevant, the weaving together of speech taken from different inter-views, and Crapanzano's attempts to summarize large tracts of the speech in his own words. In an effort to go beyond this, Dwyer (1982), who also presents an account of Moroccan fieldwork with a single male informant, represents his field by a transcribed dialogue, in which his own questions and comments are given as well as that of the Moroccan whom he interviews. The book is almost entirely an interview transcript, with no commentary from Dwyer to elucidate his own interpretation of the meaning of his informant's words, beyond some methodological reflections on what the text represents in classic constructivist mode:

> [The text] illustrates the interdependence of Self and Other. In the dialogues we see a complex process of adjustment and readjustment: false beginnings, hesitation and redirection, streaks of continuity and moments of rupture. In the confrontation between anthropologist and informant, each changes and develops while interacting with the other; during their actual encounter and in response to the other, each creates himself in part as a reaction to the other. The anthropologist who encounters people from other societies is not merely observing them . . . [but] engaging each other *creatively*, producing the *new* phenomenon of Self and Other becoming interdependent. (1982: xviii)

One might say, as Dwyer does, that this is an advance on the more severe editing of Crapanzano, in that more context is given for the words of the 'informant'. Yet we are still left with unanswered questions about context, including wider aspects of the informant's life and circum-stances, and indeed the nagging suspicion (if we recall the standards of transcription in conversation analysis) that a considerable amount of interpretive 'tidying up' will have obscured subtleties of meaning of which the author is unaware. Indeed, the transcript in both cases required translation from one language to another, a process notoriously open to distortions of original meaning. We can, in fact, question the radicalism which these authors claim that these forms of writing signify. Clearly, these presentations are different from conventional realist reporting, seeking to exclude from the text any grand interpretations of the meaning of the 'data' (though Dwyer excludes these more than Crapanzano), but in various ways selection has entered the reporting.

We saw in Chapter 2 that Geertz (1988), in his commentary on these and other such texts, noted that the earnest and serious self-consciousness that they display eventually becomes painful to contemplate. Geertz argues that we should try to get used to the idea that ethnographic texts are rhetorical, neither staying blind to the issues this raises nor getting carried away with this insight. One must accept that research writing contains a strong element of art, and also that the author must always be a central figure. Saying that informants are 'authors', as might be suggested by the practice of writers such as Crapanzano and Dwyer, can become an attempt to avoid this burden of personal responsibility for the text. I would add to this that postmodern critique of authorial presence too often makes assumptions about readers' critical faculties: readers are not, on the whole, cultural dopes, unable to evaluate texts on the basis of an understanding of where authors might be coming from.

Poetic and fictional forms   As a further reaction against the perceived limitations of realism, some experimental research writing has turned to poetic and fictional forms in order to convey experiences. Such authors feel that perhaps, somehow, the adoption of forms normally thought of as opposed to factual reporting will lead to the discovery of a style that avoids narrowly scientific assumptions. This is an experimental approach derived from similar principles to that which led to texts like Crapanzano's and Dwyer's, yet here no very clear attempt is made to decentre the author; instead, the author exercises quite a powerful influence over the presentation. Here, then, is Richardson's (1994) poetic evocation of what it is like to be single:

Being Single Is

drying a wishbone
by the kitchen window
'til the bone is chipped

to bits by trinkets
placed beside it,
or it rots, because
there is no one

to take one end
you the other

pulling, wishing
each against each
until the bone
breaks

Richardson (who, it will be recalled from Chapter 10, participated with Denzin in outlining postmodern alternatives to realism in the wake of the Whyte/Boelen dispute) explains that she has sometimes used poetry to place herself as a sociological author to one side in conveying the perspectives of the people she studies:

> I transcribed the tape [of an interview with an informant, Louisa May] into 36 pages of text and then fashioned that text into a three-page poem, using only her words, her tone, and her diction . . . For sociological readers, the poem may seem to omit 'data' that they want to know. But this is Louisa May's narrative, not the sociologist's. She does not choose, for example, to talk about her educational level or her employment. (Richardson, 1992: 126–7)

Elsewhere, authors have experimented with dramatic dialogue in order to convey the sense of things they have witnessed in particular settings. Thus Paget (1995) reports how she abandoned written forms of reporting in favour of a spoken dialogue, which consisted of cast members on stage speaking words taken from Paget's research paper on communicating bad news about cancer diagnoses. They also took on roles that allowed them to comment on the events reported, which concerned some difficulties over communication between doctor and patient. The cast involved a character called 'cancer' who narrated, wearing a long white dress, behaving flirtatiously: 'She would cosy up to anybody in the cast' (1995: 227). Paget continues:

> In keeping with the aversion to talking about cancer so common in this culture and in keeping with its censorship in the original dialogue between the physician and patient, the entire cast always whispered 'cancer,' with urgency and fear, when I used it in my report. Not the character Cancer. She would say her name with great enthusiasm and glee, throwing up her hands as if she was taking a well-deserved bow. The panel, by contrast, would huddle together, worrisomely. The patient was never able to say cancer. When she tried to speak it, she would swallow the word instead.
>   The physician and patient not only appeared and produced a lively and antagonistic dialogue about her medical problems, they danced together. They tangoed. At one point he twirled her around so fast and so long she became dizzy and lost her balance. Sometimes, as she sat on a small table, he examined and asked her questions. Once she left her seat, trying to hide behind a panelist, and he beckoned her back to the table. His mere gesture of patting the table authoritatively brought her resigned return. Thus he expressed his power over her. (1995: 227)

These reporting forms used by Richardson and Paget, like poetry and drama in general, are evocative of particular moods, perspectives and interpretations. Their audience, no doubt, will find that aspects of what is said strike a chord with their own experience or imagination. In this sense, they may be powerful ways of getting a particular message across, more striking than conventional reports of what informants say.

While in this respect there are advantages, it is important to use such reporting forms within a fallibilistic framework. The power of drama runs the risk of obscuring alternative interpretations, and may not afford the opportunity of showing to audiences the methodological procedures that have led to the 'conclusions' conveyed in the dramatic reporting form. This flaw can be seen on closer consideration of the example from Paget. The dramatic presentation does not tell the audience who in the population has had these feelings or experiences, or in what social or psychological context. Specifically, we have no sense of how widespread they are, or of the extent to which variation occurs. In fact, a strong case can be made for disputing the core assumption that runs through her dramatic presentation, that there is 'an aversion to talking about cancer' in American culture.

Better evidence than that which Paget had available (for example Novack et al., 1979; Walter, 1994) suggests that US-led professional ethics and practices with regard to communication issues in terminal care had transformed matters in the direction of openness, rather than the 'silence' of which Paget complains by the time she was writing. Indeed, this openness and associated eagerness to incorporate the subjective and emotional lives of patients within the medical remit have for some time been a topic of sociological commentary (Arney and Bergen, 1984; Armstrong, 1987; Seale, 1995, 1998b). American professional norms towards openness are so extreme that they are even experienced as an oppressive ideology in some cultures more used to seeing value in paternalistic doctor–patient relationships in which silence about cancer and death is thought preferable (for example Long and Long, 1982; Surbone, 1992). Additionally, the stereotype offered for the depiction of medical power is seriously at fault, given evidence from numerous conventional research studies about the huge variability in consultations and the subtleties of any power relationships where they occur, which are far more complex than Paget's table-tapping doctor-actor can represent (see for example Strong, 1979).

If the core assumptions behind Paget's fictional reporting form are so dubious at a factual level, how are we to place credibility in this type of reporting? Although powerful in their ability to convey particular meanings, fictional and dramatic forms should be used with caution by researchers in case they discourage authors from making clear presentations of the evidence that has led to particular conclusions. The propaganda that can result is the antithesis of what is valuable in the research enterprise.

Conclusion

Confession can serve many purposes and is not always done in a fallibilistic spirit. The example from Buckingham showed that confession can act as a rhetorical claim to authenticity. The example from Cornwell, although to some extent assisting an evaluation of the quality of the original report, also demonstrated that confession for its own sake can be of dubious methodological relevance. Yet the attempt to make methodological decisions available to readers of research reports is one way of enhancing the quality of research, even if the requirement to demonstrate an awareness of all the implicit theoretical assumptions made in the course of a research project seems impossibly demanding.

Angst about assuming too much, or imposing too much in the way of a strong narrative or a confident authorial presence, has led to some tortuously expressed research accounts as well as some interesting textual experiments. These have included transcriptions of informants' accounts as well as fictional, poetic and dramatic forms of reporting. While these often present themselves as ways of dealing with the 'problem' of authorial presence, opening text up to multiple interpretations, I have argued by contrast that they may also mask considerable authorial presence. There is no substitute for presenting the evidence that has led to particular conclusions, giving the fullest possible details about the contexts in which research accounts arise. In the last analysis, writers must then trust in their readers' capacity to make their own judgements.

KEY POINTS

- Telling the story of how a research project was done can serve many purposes, not all of which assist judgements about the credibility of findings or the quality of a study.

- Relevant methodological accounting, however, can assist readers in evaluating the quality of conclusions.

- Experimental textual forms reflecting postmodern anxiety about authorial presence can in fact mask a strong authorial presence.

- Fictional, dramatic and other reporting forms nevertheless have value in creating evocative presentations of researchers' conclusions and the perspectives of the 'researched'.

12

Reinstating the Author

CONTENTS

Attempts to delete the author from the text, although required by the logical demands of certain strands of postmodern theory, seem an impossible task. Fictional or dramatic modes of reporting, while possessing certain advantages over the dry prose style of realist texts, may lead authors to abandon methodological caution, tending to cover what is in fact a strong authorial presence. An alternative to attempts at de-emphasizing authorial presence is to accept it more fully and to present a strong story, supported with good evidence about the way of life reported, within a fallibilistic framework that seeks to empower readers to make their own judgements about the credibility of the story told.

There are signs that, as Marcus (1994) has put it, the 'fatal attraction' (1994: 563) of postmodern debate has now been overcome (how quickly we slip in and out of fashions!) so that 'we are already in a post-"post" period – post-poststructuralism, post-postmodernism, and so on' (1994: 563). As in many previous revolutions, the postrevolutionary phase is not simply a return to the past, but is a more confident return to a type of realist reporting that is methodologically self-aware without being excruciatingly so. Evidence now figures more powerfully in support of conclusions and authors are back in fashion.

Recent examples of this post-postreporting form, which is related to the ethnographic realist tradition while also being a significant advance on this, can now be found in a variety of journals and reports. I would like to end this book as it started, with some examples. Without pretending to review what is still an emerging form, I have chosen a recent issue of the journal *Theory, Culture and Society* for two particularly good examples of such subtle realist, methodologically aware reporting styles. After presenting these and highlighting certain features which I believe to be generally desirable in reporting research, I discuss the role of aesthetic judgement in evaluating the quality of research texts, taking Goffman as an example from which much can be learned.

Reporting the American city

The art of the hustler   The first example of 'post-post' realist research reporting is by Wacquant (1998), who presents 13 pages of transcription of an interview with Rickey, a 'hustler' in a 'Black American Ghetto' (1998: 1). This is preceded by an equal amount of other text, juxtaposing material that describes the physical appearance and statistical profile of inner-city Chicago with the story of how Wacquant met Rickey, giving some of Rickey's biographical details, making some comments on the position of women in the 'ghetto' and presenting a brief extract from the autobiography of Malcolm X. The interview itself is directly preceded by some comments about the difficulties and distortions that arise in attempts to transcribe 'black English street vernacular' (1998: 17) as well as an acknowledgement that the transcript is 'edited and *constructed*' (1998: 16, Wacquant's italics). The text deliberately announces its break with traditional ethnographic reporting forms by this collage-like juxta-positioning of different forms of text, and the presentation of a tran-script which takes up half the piece, ending not with a section marked 'Conclusion' or 'Discussion' but with the transcript itself. This signals its importance by occupying a location traditionally reserved for the auth-orial summary, rather than being relegated to an appendix as 'data'.

The transcript itself is organized to display themes identified by Wacquant, though expressed in Rickey's words, such as 'We was Poor, but We was Always Together' (1998: 17) to indicate his perception of his early life, or 'They Kill Ya at the Drop of a Dime' (1998: 18) to indicate the casual quality of the violence that Rickey presents as being endemic. Here is an extract from this last section:

LW: During this time, when you were growin' up, did you ever witness a killing?

Rickey: Yeah, aw man! lotta times! Jus' matter of fact, jus' week an' a half ago, I witnessed two homicides. [*Very matter of fact, slowly*] Guy got shot in the head, died, they chased the guy down, killed him ya know.

LW: In the projects?

> *Rickey*: By Ida B. Wells, yeah. Broad daylight, jus' like this here – matter fact, it was a lil' brighter, 'cause the sun was shinin'. It happens, it's jus' it happens man! Go to the fun'ral tha's it. Jus' move on. You have to change to get they money, or whatever, you know. Tha's how you know, sometimes I be aroun' certain spots like gamblin' spots an' stuff like tha' an' guys, man *they kill ya at the drop of a dime*, they jus' kill ya' and later on the night, they go buy a six-pack [*of beer*], ya know: it's jus' tha', tha's the mentality tha' they have. (1998: 18–19)

A conventional objection might be to raise questions of empirical representativeness when generalizations are made from this single case. Yet Wacquant does a certain amount to persuade us that Rickey's way of life is likely to be typical of many in this setting, presenting in the supporting text observations about hustling as a general pattern of existence, of which Rickey can be seen as an example: 'the hustler, of which he offers a compact personalized incarnation, is . . . a *generic figure that occupies a central position* in the social and symbolic space of the black American ghetto' (1998: 11). Wacquant, unlike Richardson (see Chapter 11) who will not tell us about the social structural conditions of Louisa May's life for fear of contaminating her text with sociology, is not shy of trying to persuade readers of the truth of his own commentary on the meaning of Rickey's life, arguing that it is an adaptation to the carceral realities of ghetto life:

> Rickey is not a social anomaly or the representative of a deviant micro-society: rather he is the *product of the exacerbation of a logic of economic and racial exclusion* that imposes itself ever more stringently on all residents of the ghetto. (1998: 11)

Like many classic sociological ethnographies in the realist tradition (for example Whyte's study of *Street Corner Society*), Wacquant seeks to explicate the world view of the underdog to an otherwise uncomprehending middle-class policy-making elite.

A night in a shooting gallery   In the same issue is a report by Bourgois (1998), which announces its difference from conventional research reporting by containing no list of references to other authors – although mention is made of the ideas of another author at a single point in the text (1998: 62). A noticeable feature of academic writing over recent years has been the lengthening of reference lists. Go to the library shelves and consult any journal containing reports of social research from the 1950s or before: you will see that many articles contain just one or two references, some none at all. Roth (1957) for example (discussed in Chapter 9) contains no reference to other works, which does not stop him from pointing out the relevance of his findings for key theoretical concepts (ritual, magic) of his discipline. Still later, Glaser and Strauss's (1964a) article, in which they first expounded their theory of social loss, contains no references. In the same year, the article in which they first explained their theory of awareness contexts (1964b) contained just nine references. These articles by Glaser and Strauss announced the birth of key concepts, based on research work, within the relevant field. Compare these reference counts with one more recent article on awareness contexts (Schou, 1993) which contains a relatively modest 21 references, another (Seale et al., 1997) that contains 36. I pick up at random a journal from my shelf and turn to a report of a qualitative research study (Skelton, 1998) and find that it contains 44 references. One immediately before this (Charles et al., 1998) contains 81.

One might seek to explain the growth of referencing by the point that knowledge on all topics has expanded. Computer searching, downloading and importing of references into articles has developed alongside this, meaning that the physical labour involved has been mechanized. Yet it is also a textual strategy to persuade readers of writers' authority to speak, an increasingly anxious preoccupation in research writing. Peppering the text with references can impose a cloud between reader and writer, deferring critical evaluation, perhaps, until the reader has equalled the reading achievements of the writer. Yet it is clear that many works to which authors refer have not been closely read by them. I know this from experience of seeing other authors refer to my own studies, claiming to see things in them that I, frankly, cannot find.

So Bourgois strips away this cloud of referencing and presents his data and ideas, as it were, defenceless. This in itself feels like a marker of honesty. It may also be a marker of confidence in his own voice, a sign that he is aware that he has something worthwhile to say.

The majority of the article is an account, written in a style reminiscent of a detective fiction, of his night spent in a (heroin) 'shooting gallery' in East Harlem, accompanying addicts to this place of temporary refuge, talking with and observing their activity. The first 24 pages of the 29-page article consist of the narrative of this experience, in which he first describes the organization of sales events:

> We were greeted at the corner by an eager, emaciated 'steerer' advertising that 'Knockout' – a well-established local brand – was 'open, workin', and 'pumpin' Man! I'm telling you it's smokin'. We hurried our stride toward the three-man Knockout team in the middle of the block, which was composed of a 'pitcher' who actually makes the hand-to-hand sale and his two look-outs, who also double as bodyguards and touters. (1998: 38)

After a lengthy description of the procedures followed at this sales site, Bourgois goes to another location, the 'shooting gallery' where the proprietor ('Doc') hosts the setting, treating Bourgois to candy, popcorn and beer as his 'guest of honour' (1998: 59). He notes:

Our tasty mix of snacks all processed by completely legal multinational corporations paralleled the gallery's cocaine-versus-heroin speedball pleasure principle of maximizing sensory input through contradictory chemicals: salt versus sugar alloyed in fat. (1998: 59)

Here, Bourgois is using a rhetorical device common in ethnography (see Atkinson, 1990), juxtaposing the rationality of people in the study setting with that of the official world, in an attempt to valorize the underdog perspective, pointing out its organized and orderly character, a kind of shadow version of capitalist enterprise. Bourgois's implied criticisms of officialdom occasionally surface elsewhere in the description, as where he observes that the most serious violence that he personally has suffered in this reputedly violent place has been at the hands of the police, or where he describes an abandoned school used as a sales site as one of 'many . . . city-owned sites of public sector decay' (1998: 38). Like Wacquant, then, Bourgois is following in the tradition of classic inner-city ethnographers, who sought to expose the social order of the 'slums' they studied and to relate this to social policy issues.

At one point, Bourgois also records that he tried to move his conversations with informants beyond the 'logistical particulars of their narcotized lifestyles' (1998: 59) to consider issues that might relate their lives to historical and structural aspects of mainstream America. He learned about the migration experiences from South to North of the parents of the people he was with, discovered that Doc's mother had moved out of South Carolina having seen her uncle lynched, that Doc could proudly recall an acquaintance with Malcolm X, insofar as he had been able to use the political gatherings generated by Malcolm X's political speeches as an opportunity to practise his pickpocketing skills:

Doc was proud of his professional skill as a pickpocket who used to 'work' sidewalk crowds rapt in attention before charismatic speakers. He most definitely did not consider himself to be a structural victim of a racist society. He was not interested in confirming a college professor's political-economy analysis of the victimization of the unemployed progeny of rural immigrants, and he certainly did not believe in visions of hopeful struggle or solidary liberation. His oppression is fully internalized and, almost like a neo-liberal ideologue, he takes full responsibility for his poverty, illiteracy and homelessness.

Realizing that Doc would abort my continued attempts to ferret out the systemic root causes for the devastations all around us, I shifted to personal questions about his relationship to substance abuse. Still suspicious of the bleeding-heart sympathy lurking beneath my questions, Doc cut me short once again with a laconic, 'I started shooting heroin at 14, now I'm 64'. (1998: 60)

It is only in the last five pages that Bourgois presents an explicit commentary on the significance of what he has seen, having allowed his story to 'speak for itself' in large part up until then, though clearly any narrative like this has a rhetorical, constructed character. His commentary reflects his perception that these self-destructive lives are determined in large part by an 'inner city apartheid' (1998: 61), involving 'no concerted attempt by the government to intervene in this obvious misery' (1998: 61). He points out that a character like Doc has become 'the most proximate agent for "black genocide" in his community' (1998: 61–2), echoing Wacquant's analysis. He observes the ignorance or indifference of the wider community to these facts and, finally, asserts that he 'remains firmly committed to ethnography as a key to understanding extreme social suffering' (1998: 62).

Here, then, is no timid, self-doubting account protected by an obscuring fog of jargon and reference lists. Though his story uses rhetorical devices to convey its effects, one does not need a literary analysis of these, or an extended confession to methodological anxieties, in order to form judgements about its credibility. His presence in the setting, and the nature of his relationships with informants, is clearly conveyed for readers to evaluate. Nor does he balk from presenting a powerful moral perspective, which is again one that readers can evaluate without needing any help from him. One might argue that neither of these authors is particularly fallibilistic in their presentations, but the clarity of his story telling – enhanced by the avoidance of academic baggage – itself makes it easy for readers to use their human judgement to critically evaluate his writing.

In 1986, in a text heralding the postmodern critique of ethnography, Clifford and Marcus wrote that 'To return to realism one must first have left it' (1986: 25). The work of writers such as Wacquant and Bourgois is indeed suggestive of such a return, which is a welcome prospect for the quality of research writing. A key strength of these accounts is that they have aesthetic appeal, dramatically drawing the reader into the worlds concerned, in a manner similar to a well-written fictional or dramatic account. This prompts the question of whether aesthetic values ought to be involved in judging the quality of research reports.

Aesthetics

In his assessment of textual radicalism of the sort described in the previous chapter (i.e. the works of Crapanzano, Dwyer, Richardson and Paget), Hammersley observes that these tend to 'mislead or confuse audiences' because they 'obscure the line of argument' (1995b: 95), failing to present sufficient evidence for the general argument and, indeed, failing to make the general argument clear. Indeed, how could this be otherwise in an 'authorless' text that, in theory at least, sets its face against the presentation of an overarching argument? Hammersley's solution is to argue for a degree of standardization in the reporting of qualitative research, even to the extent that is common in natural science or quantitative social research. The focus of the study, cases investigated, methods used, claims made and evidence supporting claims should all be covered, preferably in that order. He does not rule out the presentation of evidence by using unusual forms, such as fictional constructions of typical characters, but says that these should be subordinate to the headings above. Hammersley's final observation, though, sounds a note of caution: 'Above all, these techniques must not be used to suppress critical reflection on the part of readers, *or to invite aesthetic appreciation*' (1995: 98; my italics).

There is, however, an opposite point of view which claims that aesthetic qualities are central to good-quality research reporting; in other words, that truth and beauty may well go together rather than spoiling each other's pitch. Salner (1989), for example, argues that 'judging the validity of human science research requires that we incorporate aesthetic criteria' (1989: 57). For Salner, the aesthetic is that which 'takes what is *already known* (tacitly) and makes us consciously or explicitly aware of it' (1989: 57). Kvale (1989a), in the same volume, is critical of the downplaying of the 'aesthetic dimension of truth' (1989a: 89), arguing that in mathematics 'elegance and beauty have a stronger position when it comes to determining truth value' (1989a: 89). Both Salner and Kvale draw on Polkinghorne's (1989) discussion of Kant's separation of three independent realms of knowledge (theoretical, practical, aesthetic), which has led to the view that aesthetic judgements are subjective statements of personal preference, of a different order to those involved in scientific reasoning. By contrast, Polkinghorne seeks to reunify scientific thinking with the aesthetic.

The opposition between these philosophers and Hammersley is in fact more apparent than real. This is shown if we come down a little from the level of abstraction at which the philosophical debate occurs and specify what might be meant, in practical terms, by attending to the aesthetic dimensions of research reporting, which I believe is valuable for researchers to do without necessarily sacrificing that rationality and fallibilism which Hammersley wishes to promote. Silverman's (1997a) discussion is helpful in identifying two key aspects of aesthetic quality in research writing. First, there is the issue of tacit knowledge, also raised as we saw by Salner. Second, there is the issue of clarity which Silverman, among other things, associates with a minimalist approach, seeking like Wittgenstein to avoid speaking about questions that are ultimately unanswerable and to express clearly the thoughts that remain. He expresses distaste for high-sounding theoretical language, and a preference for that which is clear and simple.

This is a different approach to the role of the aesthetic than that followed by the postmodern textual experimenters reviewed in the previous chapter. In Silverman's eyes, no blurring of the boundaries between fact and fiction, truth and fantasy, is implied. There is simply the claim that the expression of truth tends in any case to have a beautiful quality. This can involve writers showing readers what they half knew already, and by making such tacit knowledge explicit, bringing new objects into the sphere of rational discourse. Or it can involve the economical expression of things that need saying, rather than a cloud of jargon that obscures the fact that a writer has no very clear message.

Humour in Goffman

As an example of a piece of research writing that possesses both qualities, although in some other respects it is lacking in features desirable in research writing, we can turn to one of Goffman's reports, for which I draw on Fine and Martin's (1995) perceptive analysis of humour in Goffman's work. Humour, of course, is a genre uniquely suited to exposing the assumptions that underlly common-sense reasoning. The best humour provokes a spark of self-recognition in the audience, as the humorist makes explicit what we already half know. This is precisely Goffman's strength.

Fine and Martin note that sarcasm, satire and irony are all used in Goffman's *Asylums* (1961). Sarcasm is used to criticize the world view of psychiatry in the first place simply by 'bracketing' its claims, suggesting that psychiatric rationales for the actions taken by mental hospital staff are provisional, with no clear evidence in favour of them. Thus, in describing the mortification of self-identity that occurs as inmates enter the institution, he mentions that 'We very generally find staff employing *what are called* admission procedures' (Goffman 1961: 16; Fine and Martin's italics). Cutting metaphors are also employed to cast the institution in a hostile light: 'A total institution is like a finishing school, but one that has many refinements and is little refined' (1961: 41–2). Alternatively, the quality of argument is sometimes sarcastic, as here where the word 'engaging' in the quote that follows denotes hostility towards the phenomenon described:

> In mental hospitals we find the engaging phenomenon of the staff using stereotyped psychiatric terminology in talking to each other or to patients but chiding patients for being 'intellectualistic' and for avoiding the issues when they use this language, too. (1961: 97)

Satire, which can be understood as a playful distortion of the familiar, is also incorporated in Goffman's writing, involving the portrayal of the 'underlife' of the institution which at times involves inmates turning official versions of events on their heads:

> Some patients even managed to find hidden values in insulin shock therapy: patients receiving insulin shock were allowed in bed all morning in the

insulin ward, a pleasure impossible in most other wards, and were treated quite like patients by nurses there. (1961: 223)

Irony, involving the use of 'incongruity to suggest a disjunction between reality and expectations' (Fine and Martin, 1995: 186), is also a feature of *Asylums*:

> The punishment of being sent to a worse ward is described as transferring a patient to a ward whose arrangements he can cope with, and the isolation cell or 'hole' is described as a place where the patient will be able to feel comfortable with his inability to handle his acting-out impulses. Making a ward quiet at night through the forced taking of drugs, which permits reduced night staffing, is called medication or sedative treatment. Women long since unable to perform such routine medical tasks as taking bloods are called nurses and wear nursing uniforms; men trained as general practitioners are called psychiatrists. (1961: 381)

A humorous note in fact imbues most of Goffman's writings. In *Asylums* it is used to make a point, as we have seen. Elsewhere, though, it is sometimes present purely to grasp the attention of the reader, indicating a generally wry frame of mind that will take nothing on trust, irreverent towards tradition. Consider, for example, the opening sentence of *Stigma*:

> The Greeks, who were apparently strong on visual aids, originated the term *stigma* to refer to bodily signs designed to expose something unusual and bad about the moral status of the signifier. (1990: 11; first published 1963)

There is nothing significant about the comment on visual aids, except that it is a funny thought, automatically debunking any desire to regard classical Greek culture in a hallowed light. The sentence grabs the attention, and makes one want to read more. This is use of the aesthetic not to give force to insights (as in the other Goffman extracts) but simply as a writerly device for announcing a stylish essay.

Goffman, then, is an attractive writer and we need seriously to consider the charge (implied by Hammersley's point) that the aesthetic appeal of his work may blind the reader to methodological flaws. (One might also apply this charge to Wacquant and Bourgois.) Goffman is not a particularly fallibilistic writer of research reports. He is notoriously brief in his discussions of methodology. In fact, some of his greatest works rely on second-hand evidence rather than the observational experiences he claims as the basis for *Asylums*. We do not know much about the representativeness of the asylum that Goffman studied, or about the people within it with whom he interacted. It is possible that more humane institutions existed, or pockets of genuinely therapeutic practice within the asylum he studied. Indeed, the wave of mental hospital closures prompted in part by his report have been regretted by some who appreciate the genuine sense of asylum from a hostile community that is provided by institutional life (Scheper-Hughes and Lovell, 1986).

Fine and Martin (1995), following this line of criticism, provide a cutting analysis of the deficiencies of Goffman's approach to research:

> To Goffman, the goal is to discover how the world is 'subjectively experienced' by the patient. To the reader, the book represents anything but. The essays represent how a 'sane' Goffman would *himself* experience a large mental hospital if he was incarcerated against his will. Readers learn precious little about how patients experience their own world or, at the least, how they report this experience. (1995: 170)

There are few direct quotes from patients' words in Goffman's text. The voice is almost entirely his. In this sense, one can say that the rhetorical power of his writing style is misleading in encouraging readers to believe an account that gives insufficient space to the voice of the 'Other' with which Danforth, Dwyer and Crapanzano (see Chapter 11) are concerned. Yet it seems feasible to combine some of the literary style of Goffman, who uses humour so effectively in the aid of clarity and in promoting the shock of recognition, with a more fallibilistic and informative reporting of methodological procedures. Goffman's style is too self-confident to serve as a model for contemporary practice, but we can learn much from him nevertheless. Aesthetic appeal, as Hammersley warns, can cloud critical judgement, but one should not then reject the attempt to write in an attractive and immediate way that does not always follow a set pattern of reporting conventions.

Summary and conclusion

I have presented an argument in this chapter and the last for the cautious use of literary forms such as fiction and drama, as well as more subtle aspects of the writer's art such as the use of humour, to enhance the immediacy of research reporting. In this respect, I am arguing that researchers should attend to aesthetic qualities of their work in the interests of good communication. Caution is nevertheless also appropriate, since the use of forms normally associated with fictional genres, especially if linked to radical epistemological positions such as one finds within constructivist or postmodern thought, can lead authors to abandon responsibility for fallibilistic reporting, in favour of an approach that privileges particularistic views.

The work of writers like Wacquant and Bourgois show us that it is possible to dispense with conventional reporting forms and still present a strong story. This is fashioned by the author's interpretive work, which at the same time gives voice to research participants and is reasonably fallibilistic. These writers appear to trust their readers' critical faculties.

This chapter also demonstrates one of the general themes of this book, that the quality of research is as likely to be improved by close examination of a variety of research practices, as much as by study of purely methodological accounts. This is why I have tried to present numerous extended examples wherever possible in the second part of this book, the first part being devoted to a more conventional discussion of methodological principles. Making principled methodological choices during research work is a different matter from following through particular methodological procedures, worked out in the abstract, or in relation to particular research experiences, but inappropriately applied as universal rules. This is not to say that anything goes in research, but that methodological awareness can support many forms of good-quality research practice which methodologists are unable to predict.

KEY POINTS

- A strong authorial presence and a return to realist reporting are back in fashion.

- This can involve new textual forms without abandoning a commitment to fallibilism and reflexive methodological accounting.

- Attention to the aesthetic qualities of research texts is an important contributor to quality, though this stops short of using aesthetic criteria to judge credibility.

Appendix A: Criteria for the Evaluation of Qualitative Research Papers

1 *Are the methods of the research appropriate to the nature of the question being asked?*

- Does the research seek to understand processes or structures, or illuminate subjective experiences or meanings?
- Are the categories or groups being examined of a type which cannot be preselected, or the possible outcomes cannot be specified in advance?
- Could a quantitative approach have addressed the issue better?

2 *Is the connection to an existing body of knowledge or theory clear?*

- Is there adequate reference to the literature?
- Does the work cohere with, or critically address, existing theory?

Methods

3 *Are there clear accounts of the criteria used for the selection of subjects for study, and of the data collection and analysis?*

4 *Is the selection of cases or participants theoretically justified?*

- The unit of research may be people, or events, institutions, samples of natural behaviour, conversations, written material, etc. In any case, while random sampling may not be appropriate, is it nevertheless clear what population the sample refers to?
- Is consideration given to whether the units chosen were unusual in some important way?

5 *Does the sensitivity of the methods match the needs of the research questions?*

- Does the method accept the implications of an approach which respects the perceptions of those studied?
- To what extent are any definitions or agendas taken for granted, rather than being critically examined or left open?
- Are the limitations of any structured interview method considered?

6 *Has the relationship between fieldworkers and subjects been considered, and is there evidence that the research was presented and explained to its subjects?*

- If more than one worker was involved, has comparability been considered?
- Is there evidence about how the subjects perceived the research?
- Is there evidence about how any group processes were conducted?

7 *Was the data collection and record keeping systematic?*

- Were careful records kept?
- Is the evidence available for independent examination?
- Were full records or transcripts of conversations used if appropriate?

Analysis

8 *Is reference made to accepted procedures for analysis?*

- Is it clear how the analysis was done? (Detailed repetition of how to perform standard procedures ought not to be expected.)
- Has its reliability been considered, ideally by independent repetition?

9 *How systematic is the analysis?*

- What steps were taken to guard against selectivity in the use of data?
- In research with individuals, is it clear that there has not been selection of some cases and ignoring of less interesting ones? In group research, are all categories of opinion taken into account?

10 *Is there adequate discussion of how themes, concepts and categories were derived from the data?*

- It is sometimes inevitable that externally given or predetermined descriptive categories are used, but have they been examined for their real meaning or any possible ambiguities?

11 *Is there adequate discussion of the evidence both for and against the researcher's arguments?*

- Is negative data given? Has there been any search for cases which might refute the conclusions?

12   *Have measures been taken to test the validity of the findings?*

- For instance, have methods such as feeding them back to the respondents, triangulation, or procedures such as grounded theory been used?

13   *Have any steps been taken to see whether the analysis would be comprehensible to the participants, if this is possible and relevant?*

- Has the meaning of their accounts been explored with respondents? Have apparent anomalies and contradictions been discussed with them, rather than assumptions being made?

Presentation

14   *Is the research clearly contextualized?*

- Has all the relevant information about the setting and subjects been supplied?
- Are the variables being studied integrated in their social context, rather than abstracted and decontextualized?

15   *Are the data presented systematically?*

- Are quotations, fieldnotes etc. identified in a way which enables the reader to judge the range of evidence used?

16   *Is a clear distinction made between the data and their interpretation?*

- Do the conclusions follow from the data? (It should be noted that the phases of research – data collection, analysis, discussion – are not usually separate and papers do not necessarily follow the quantitative pattern of methods, results, discussion.)

17   *Is sufficient of the original evidence presented to satisfy the reader of the relationship between the evidence and the conclusions?*

- Though the presentation of discursive data is always going to require more space than numerical data, is the paper as concise as possible?

18   *Is the author's own position clearly stated?*

- Is the researcher's perspective described?
- Has the researcher examined his or her own role, possible bias and influence on the research?

19   Are the results credible and appropriate?

- Do they address the research question(s)?
- Are they plausible and coherent?
- Are they important, either theoretically or practically, or trivial?

Ethics

20   Have ethical issues been adequately considered?

- Has the issue of confidentiality (often particularly difficult in qualitative work) been adequately dealt with?
- Have the consequences of the research – including establishing relationships with the subjects, raising expectations, changing behaviour etc. – been considered?

Source: British Sociological Association Medical Sociology Group, 1996

Appendix B: Discussion Exercises

Many of these exercises involve the application of general ideas or techniques to the conduct of specific research studies. These exemplars might be drawn from research studies you have done, or are doing, or published studies of your choice. Try to stay with the same exemplars across a number of these exercises if you can. Choose exemplars that illustrate a variety of methods (for example interviews, observation, ethnography, discourse analysis etc.).

Chapter 1   Why quality matters

Seek out and read two studies that represent different 'moments' in the history of qualitative research. For example, choose a study that involves grounded theorizing and another where the author situates him or herself within postmodernism.

How do the studies differ in their conception of what makes a good research study? How might each author apply these criteria to the other's work?

Chapter 2   Two critiques of research as science

Exercise 1   Taking a research project that you are planning to do, consider the extent to which this is likely to be relevant to the political or practical projects of the people studied. How will it help them improve their lives? Could it serve any other purpose?

Exercise 2   Consider a research project that you have written up, or a published research project that you have read. In what ways is this different from a fictional work that a writer might have produced with the aim of portraying the way of life analysed in the report? What textual strategies does the report share with fictional forms?

Chapter 3   Trust, truth and philosophy

Exercise 1   Choose a research study in an area of work where you have some knowledge of existing literature and assess it in the light of the following questions:

(a) How consistent are the findings with what is already known?
(b) What evidence is supplied to support the credibility of the conclusions and how persuasive is this?
(c) What relevance might the study have for political or practical affairs?

Exercise 2 To what extent should social researchers be influenced by philosophical considerations? What might be gained by such an involvement? What might the disadvantages be?

Chapter 4   Guiding ideals

Exercise 1 Choose a study you know or have done yourself. Use the criteria list in Appendix A to assess its quality. What does the list miss out? How could it be improved?

Exercise 2 In relation to a specific study, consider whether its quality would be improved by attention to the issues raised under the 'positivist' headings of measurement validity, internal and external validity and reliability. To what extent could the interpretivist criteria outlined in the chapter be applied to the study? Do these lead you to consider different issues from those raised under the 'positivist' headings?

Chapter 5   Converging on a point?

Exercise 1 In relation to a specific study, assess whether the authors have used any form of triangulation (data, investigator, theory or methodological) and for what purposes. If used, has it enhanced the credibility of the report? If not used, how might these have been used and what would the effects have been?

Exercise 2

(a) Tape record a few minutes of a conversation between two or more people.
(b) Ask each participant, out of the hearing of the other(s), to summarize what they believe was going on during the talk. Tape record what they say.
(c) Play back the recordings made at (b) to the other participant(s) in the conversation. Where do the accounts agree? Where do they disagree? How feasible is it in an exercise like this to get a single true account?

Exercise 3 In relation to a specific study, assess whether the authors have used any form of member validation (see Table 5.1) and for what purposes. If used, has it enhanced the credibility of the report? If not used, how might this have been used and what would the effects have been?

Exercise 4 This exercise assumes that you have written up a research study of some aspect of human behaviour and still have access to the people involved.

(a) Choose one or more participants in the research study and show them a segment of data in which you record their deeds or words. Ask them to judge whether it is an accurate record.

(b) Now ask them to read your final report (or some edited summary) and to say whether this is an accurate record.
(c) What difficulties were there in conducting the exercise? What did it tell you about the adequacy of your data record/account? Are any further lines of inquiry suggested by the responses you have gathered?

Chapter 6   Accounting for contradiction

Exercise 1   In relation to a specific research study, assess the extent to which the author(s) have searched for and/or accounted for things that contradict the emerging account. What more might have been done to pursue such negative instances? How might this have improved the quality of the study?

Exercise 2   Identify either the explicit or the implicit causal claims made in a particular research study. How might these have been extended by means of analytic induction?

Chapter 7   Grounding theory

Exercise 1   Choose a specific research study and ask of it:

(a) How well are the concepts grounded in data; how adequately are central claims supported by evidence?
(b) What strategies from grounded theorizing might the researcher have pursued in order to generate a more 'saturated' or 'thick' theoretical account? Consider here theoretical sampling decisions that might have been taken, or comparisons that might have been made.

Exercise 2   Grounded theorizing involves an attempt to construct an account that is well defended against threats to its truth status. To what extent does this allow for alternative voices? Is this a desirable feature of qualitative research?

Chapter 8   Generalizing from qualitative research

Exercise 1   Take a particular research study and establish what can be learned from it in guiding action in, or understanding the dynamics of, other settings. What has the researcher done to improve the chances of this being done? What might the researcher have done to take this further?

Exercise 2   Under what circumstances can the urge to generalize from research studies become an 'act of despotism' (Lyotard, 1993)?

Chapter 9   Using numbers

Exercise 1   Examine the report of a qualitative research study to identify (a) instances where actual numbers are used and (b) instances where quantitative words (e.g. 'many', 'some') are used. Then answer the following questions:

(a) If numbers have been used, how has this affected the quality of the study? How adequate would the study have been without the numbers?
(b) Where quantitative words have been used, how might actual numbers, if substituted, have affected the quality of the study?
(c) Which of the uses of numbers listed in the chapter were not used? What would the researcher have needed to do to use each of these methods? Would this have enhanced the quality of the study?

Exercise 2   Assess the view that quantitative research and qualitative research involve such fundamentally different starting assumptions, paradigms or theories that they cannot be usefully combined.

Chapter 10   Reliability and replicability

Exercise 1   This exercise requires you to work with others on some qualitative data, such as some interview transcripts.

(a) Without discussing your ideas with others in your group, read one part of the data transcript (for example a single interview) and draw up a list of key themes that you perceive in the data.
(b) Compare the themes you have identified with those of others in your group. What are the similarities and differences?
(c) Take four or five themes from those identified by members of the group and, working individually again, apply them to some new data (for example a second interview) by marking parts of the transcript which you believe exemplify each theme.
(d) Compare what you have done with others in the group. What difficulties are there in consistently applying the themes? Does inconsistency matter?

Exercise 2   Take a published qualitative research study as an example and identify what the researcher has done to establish reliability and enable replication. What more might have been done? Would this have improved the quality of the study?

Chapter 11   Reflexivity and writing

Exercise 1   Examine a 'confessional tale' from one of the numerous published collections in which researchers give accounts of how they conducted a research project.

(a) Which elements are likely to help you assess the quality of the research study involved?
(b) Which elements appear irrelevant for this purpose?
(c) What other matters might have been included to assist such an evaluation?

Exercise 2   This group exercise requires the transcript of an interview.

(a) Each member of the group should construct a poem from the words and phrases contained in the interview transcript which in their opinion best convey the perspective of the person interviewed.

(b) Compare poems and ask: how do these representations of the interviewees' perspectives differ? What advantages do such poems have in reporting the perspectives of interviewees?

Chapter 12   Reinstating the author

Exercise 1   Assess the aesthetic quality of a particular research report, focusing for example on the quality of the writing style and its dramatic or literary appeal. Does this assist you or hinder you in judging the credibility and plausibility of the researcher's conclusions?

Exercise 2   Evaluate my argument that research is a craft skill, relatively autonomous of philosophy and theory, so that it can be carried out without an exclusive commitment to a particular philosophical or theoretical position.

Exercise 3   Evaluate my argument that the quality of qualitative research practice is enhanced if researchers engage with relevant philosophical and theoretical debates contained in methodological texts. What arguments could there be for *not* engaging in this way?

References

Altheide, D.L. and Johnson, J.M. (1994) 'Criteria for assessing interpretive validity in qualitative research', in Denzin, N.K. and Lincoln, Y.S. (eds), *Handbook of Qualitative Research*. Thousand Oaks, CA: Sage. pp. 485–99.

American Psychological Association (1954) 'Validity. Technical recommendations for psychological tests and diagnostic techniques', *Psychological Bulletin* (supplement), 13–28.

Arber, S. and Ginn, J. (1991) *Gender and Later Life: a Sociological Analysis of Resources and Constraints*. London: Sage.

Armstrong, D. (1983) *The Political Anatomy of the Body: Medical Knowledge in Britain in the Twentieth Century*. Cambridge: Cambridge University Press.

Armstrong, D. (1987) 'Silence and truth in death and dying', *Social Science and Medicine*, 24 (8): 651–7.

Armstrong, D., Gosling, A., Weinman, J. and Marteau, T. (1997) 'The place of inter-rater reliability in qualitative research: an empirical study', *Sociology*, 31 (3): 597–606.

Arney, W.R. and Bergen, B.J. (1984) *Medicine and the Management of Living: Taming the Last Great Beast*. Chicago: University of Chicago Press.

Asad, T. (ed.) (1973) *Anthropology and the Colonial Encounter*. London: Ithaca Press.

Atkinson, P. (1990) *The Ethnographic Imagination: Textual Constructions of Reality*. London: Routledge.

Atkinson, P. (1992) *Understanding Ethnographic Texts*. London: Sage.

Barker, E. (1984) *The Making of a Moonie: Choice or Brainwashing?* Oxford: Basil Blackwell.

Barrett, M. (1991) *The Politics of Truth*. Cambridge: Polity.

Barton, A.H. (1955) 'The concept of property-space in social research', in Lazarsfeld, P.F. and Rosenberg, M. (eds), *The Language of Social Research*. Glencoe, Ill.: Free Press. pp. 40–53.

Bateson, G. and Mead, M. (1942) *Balinese Character: a Photographic Analysis*. New York: New York Academy of Sciences.

Baudrillard, J. (1988) *America*. London: Verso.

Becker, H.S. (1963) *Outsiders: Studies in the Sociology of Deviance*. New York: Free Press.

Becker, H.S. (ed.) (1970a) *Sociological Work: Method and Substance*. Chicago: Aldine.

Becker, H.S. (1970b) 'Problems of inference and proof in participant observation', in Becker, H.S. (ed.), *Sociological Work: Method and Substance*. Chicago: Aldine. pp. 25–38.

Becker, H.S. (1970c) 'Fieldwork evidence', in Becker, H.S. (ed.), *Sociological Work: Method and Substance*. Chicago: Aldine. pp. 39–62.

Becker, H.S. (1970d) 'On methodology', in Becker, H.S. (ed.), *Sociological Work: Method and Substance*. Chicago: Aldine. pp. 3–24.

Becker, H.S. (1998) *Tricks of the Trade: How to Think about Your Research while You're Doing it*. Chicago: University of Chicago Press.

Becker, H.S. and Geer, B. (first published 1957) 'Participant observation and interviewing: a comparison', in McCall, G. and Simmons, J.L. (eds) (1969), *Issues in Participant Observation*. New York: Addison-Wesley. pp. 322–31.

Becker, H.S., Geer, B., Hughes, E. and Strauss, A. (1961) *Boys in White: Student Culture in a Medical School*. Chicago: University of Chicago Press.

Bell, B. and Newby, H.W. (1977) *Doing Sociological Research*. London: Allen and Unwin.

Ben-Ari, E. (1995) 'On acknowledgments in ethnographies', in Van Maanen, J. (ed.), *Representation in Ethnography*. Thousand Oaks, CA: Sage. pp. 130–64.

Bhaskar, R. (1989) *Reclaiming Reality*. London: Verso.

Blaikie, N.W.H. (1991) 'A critique of the use of triangulation in social research', *Quality and Quantity*, 25: 115–36.

Blaikie, N. (1993) *Approaches to Social Enquiry*. Cambridge: Polity.

Blease, D. and Bryman, A. (1986) 'Research in schools and the case for methodological integration', *Quality and Quantity*, 20: 157–68.

Bloor, M. (1976) 'Bishop Berkeley and the adenotonsillectomy dilemma', *Sociology*, 10 (1): 43–61.

Bloor, M. (1978) 'On the analysis of observational data: a discussion of the worth and uses of inductive techniques and respondent validation', *Sociology*, 12 (3): 545–57.

Bloor, M. (1997) 'Techniques of validation in qualitative research: a critical commentary', in Miller, G. and Dingwall, R. (eds), *Context and Method in Qualitative Research*. London: Sage. pp. 37–50.

Blumer, H. (1969) *Symbolic Interactionism*. Englewood Cliffs, NJ: Prentice-Hall.

Boelen, W.A.M. (1992) 'Street Corner Society: Cornerville revisited', *Journal of Contemporary Ethnography*, 21: 11–15.

Booth, C. (1886–1902) *The Life and Labour of the People of London* (17 volumes). London: Macmillan.

Bourgois, P. (1998) 'Just another night in a shooting gallery', *Theory, Culture and Society*, 15 (2): 37–66.

Brady, I. (ed.) (1983) 'Speaking in the name of the real: Freeman and Mead on Samoa', *American Anthropologist*, 85 (4): 908–48.

British Sociological Association Medical Sociology Group (1996) 'Criteria for the evaluation of qualitative research papers', *Medical Sociology News*, 22 (1): 69–71.

Brown, G. (1973) 'Some thoughts on grounded theory', *Sociology*, 7: 1–16.

Brown, G. and Harris, T. (1978) *Social Origins of Depression*. London: Macmillan.

Bryman, A. (1988) *Quantity and Quality in Social Research*. London: Unwin Hyman.

Buchanan, D.R. (1992) 'An uneasy alliance: combining quantitative and qualitative research methods', *Health Education Quarterly*, 19: 117–35.

Buckingham, R.W., Lack, S.A., Mount, B.M., Maclean, L.D. and Collins, J.T. (1976) 'Living with the dying: use of the technique of participant observation', *Canadian Medical Association Journal*, 115: 1211–15.

Burman, E. and Parker, I. (eds) (1993) *Discourse Analytic Research*. London: Routledge.

Cain, M. and Finch, J. (1981) 'Towards a rehabilitation of data', in Abrams, P., Deem, R., Finch, J. and Rock, P. (eds), *Practice and Progress: British Sociology 1950–1980*. London: George Allen and Unwin. pp. 105–19.

Campbell, D.T. (1969) 'Reforms as experiments', *American Psychologist*, 24: 409–29.

Campbell, D.T. and Fiske, D.W. (1959) 'Convergent and discriminant validation by the multitrait-multimethod matrix', *Psychological Bulletin*, 56 (2): 81–105.

Campbell, D.T. and Stanley, J.C. (1966) *Experimental and Quasi-experimental Design for Research*. Chicago: Rand McNally.

Cannell, C.F. and Kahn, R.O. (1954) 'Interviewing', in Lindzey, G. and Arondson, E. (eds), *The Handbook of Social Psychology*. New York: Addison-Wesley.

Charles, C., Redko, C., Whelan, T., Gafni, A. and Reyno, L. (1998) 'Doing nothing is no choice: lay constructions of treatment decision-making among women with early-stage breast cancer', *Sociology of Health and Illness*, 20 (1): 71–95.

Cicourel, A.V. (1964) *Method and Measurement in Sociology*. New York: Free Press.

Cicourel, A.V. (1974) *Cognitive Sociology*. New York: Free Press.

Clifford, J. (1986) 'Introduction: partial truths', in Clifford, J. and Marcus, G.E. (eds), *Writing Culture: the Poetics and Politics of Ethnography*. Berkeley: University of California Press. pp. 1–26.

Clifford, J. and Marcus, G.E. (eds) (1986) *Writing Culture: the Poetics and Politics of Ethnography*. Berkeley: University of California Press.

Clough, P.T. (1992) *The End(s) of Ethnography*. Thousand Oaks, CA: Sage.

Cobb, A.K. and Hagemaster, J.N. (1987) 'Ten criteria for evaluating qualitative research proposals', *Journal of Nursing Education*, 26 (4): 138–43.

Coffey, A. and Atkinson, P. (1996) *Making Sense of Qualitative Data Analysis: Complementary Strategies*. Thousand Oaks, CA: Sage.

Coffey, A., Holbrook, B. and Atkinson, P. (1996) 'Qualitative data analysis: technologies and representations', *Sociological Research On-line*, 1, 1 http://www.soc.surrey.ac.uk/socresonline

Cook, T.D. and Campbell, D.T. (1979) *Quasi-experimentation: Design and Analysis Issues for Field Settings*. Chicago: Rand McNally.

Corbin, J. (1987) 'Women's perceptions and management of a pregnancy complicated by chronic illness', *Health Care for Women International*, 84: 317–37.

Cornwell, J. (1984) *Hard Earned Lives*. London: Tavistock.

Cornwell, J. (1988) 'A case study approach to lay health beliefs: reconsidering the research process', in Eyles, J. and Smith, D. (eds), *Qualitative Methods in Human Geography*. Oxford: Blackwell. pp. 219–32.

Crapanzano, V. (1980) *Tuhami: Portrait of a Moroccan*. Chicago: University of Chicago Press.

Cressey, D.R. (1950) 'The criminal violation of financial trust', *American Sociological Review*, 15, 738–43.

Cressey, D.R. (1953) *Other People's Money: a Study in the Social Psychology of Embezzlement*. Belmont, CA: Wadsworth.

Cronbach, L.J. and Meehl, P.E. (1955) 'Construct validity in psychological tests', *Psychological Bulletin*, 52: 281–302.

Crotty, M. (1998) *The Foundations of Social Research: Meaning and Perspective in the Research Process*. London: Sage.

Danforth, L. (1982) *The Death Rituals of Rural Greece*. Princeton: Princeton University Press.

Denzin, N.K. (1970) *The Research Act in Sociology*, 1st edn. London: Butterworth.

Denzin, N.K. (1978) *The Research Act: a Theoretical Introduction to Sociological Methods*, 2nd edn. New York: McGraw-Hill.

Denzin, N.K. (1988a) 'Qualitative analysis for social scientists', *Contemporary Sociology*, 17 (3): 430–2.

Denzin, N.K. (1988b) 'Blue velvet: postmodern contradictions', *Theory, Culture and Society*, 5: 461–73.

Denzin, N.K. (1989) *The Research Act: a Theoretical Introduction to Sociological Methods*, 3rd edn. Englewood Cliffs, NJ: Prentice Hall.

Denzin, N.K. (1994) 'Postmodernism and deconstructionism', in Dickens, D.R. and Fontana, A. (eds), *Postmodernism and Social Inquiry*. London: UCL Press. pp. 182–202.

Denzin, N.K. (1996) 'The facts and fictions of qualitative inquiry', *Qualitative Inquiry*, 2 (2): 230–41.

Denzin, N.K. (1997) *Interpretive Ethnography: Ethnographic Practice for the 21st Century*. Thousand Oaks, CA: Sage.

Denzin, N.K. and Lincoln, Y.S. (1994) *Handbook of Qualitative Research*. Thousand Oaks, CA: Sage.

Dingwall, R. (1992) 'Don't mind him – he's from Barcelona: qualitative methods in health studies', in Daly, J., McDonald, I. and Willis, E. (eds), *Researching Health Care*. London: Routledge. pp. 161–75.

Dingwall, M. (1997a) 'Conclusion: the moral discourse of interactionism', in Miller, G. and Dingwall, R. (eds), *Context and Method in Qualitative Research*. London: Sage. pp. 198–205.

Dingwall, M. (1997b) 'Accounts, interviews and observations', in Miller, G. and Dingwall, R. (eds), *Context and Method in Qualitative Research*. London: Sage. pp. 51–65.

Dingwall, R. and Murray, T. (1983) 'Categorisation in Accident Departments: "Good" Patients, "Bad" Patients and Children', *Sociology of Health and Illness*, 5 (2): 121–48.

Douglas, J. (1967) *The Social Meanings of Suicide*. Princeton: Princeton University Press.

Durkheim, E. (1970, first published 1897) *Suicide: a Study in Sociology*. London: Routledge and Kegan Paul.

Durkheim, E. (1976, first published 1915) *The Elementary Forms of the Religious Life*. London: Allen and Unwin.

Durkheim, E. (1982) *The Rules of Sociological Method*. London: Macmillan.

Durkin, T. (1997) 'Using computers in strategic qualitative research', in Miller, G. and Dingwall, R. (eds), *Context and Method in Qualitative Research*. London: Sage. pp. 92–105.

Dwyer, K. (1982) *Moroccan Dialogues: Anthropology in Question*. Baltimore, MD: Johns Hopkins University Press.

Emerson, R.M. (1981) 'Observational fieldwork', *Annual Review of Sociology*, 7: 351–78.

Emerson, R.M. and Pollner, M. (1988) 'On the uses of members' responses to researchers' accounts', *Human Organisation*, 47: 189–98.

Evans-Pritchard, E.E. (1940) *The Nuer*. Oxford: Oxford University Press.

Feyerabend, P. (1975) *Against Method*. London: New Left Review Editions.

Fielding, N. (1993) 'Ethnography', in Gilbert, N. (ed.), *Researching Social Life*. London: Sage. pp. 154–71.

Fielding, N. and Fielding J.L. (1986) *Linking Data*. London: Sage.

Filmer, P., Phillipson, M., Silverman, D. and Walsh, D. (1972) *New Directions in Sociological Theory*. London: Collier Macmillan.

Fine, G.A. and Martin, D.D. (1995) 'Humor in ethnographic writing: sarcasm, satire, and irony as voices in Erving Goffman's *Asylums*', in Van Maanen, J. (ed.), *Representation in Ethnography*. Thousand Oaks, CA: Sage. pp. 165–97.

Fitzpatrick, R. and Boulton, M. (1996) 'Qualitative research in health care: 1: the scope and validity of methods', *Journal of Evaluation in Clinical Practice*, 2: 123–30.

Fontana, A. (1994) 'Ethnographic trends in the postmodern era', in Dickens, D.R. and Fontana, A. (eds), *Postmodernism and Social Inquiry*. London: UCL Press. pp. 203–23.

Foucault, M. (1967) *Madness and Civilization: a History of Insanity in the Age of Reason*. London: Tavistock.

Foucault, M. (1977) *Discipline and Punish*. London: Allen Lane.

Foucault, M. (1992, first published 1970) *The Order of Things: an Archaeology of the Human Sciences*. London: Routledge.

Fox, N.J. (1992) *The Social Meaning of Surgery*. Buckingham: Open University Press.

Frake, C.O. (1961) 'The diagnosis of disease among the Subanun of Mindanao', *American Anthropologist*, 63: 113–32.

Frake, C.O. (1964) 'Notes on queries in ethnography', *American Anthropologist*, 66: 132–45.

Freeman, D. (1983) *Margaret Mead and Samoa*. Cambridge, MA: Harvard.

Freilich, M. (1970) *Marginal Natives*. New York: Wiley.

Game, A. (1991) *Undoing the Social: Towards a Deconstructive Sociology*. Buckingham: Open University Press.

Gans, H.J. (1967) *The Levittowners*. London: Allen Lane.

Geertz, C. (1988) *Works and Lives: the Anthropologist as Author*. Stanford, CA: Stanford University Press.

Geertz, C. (1993, first published 1973) *The Interpretation of Cultures*. London: Fontana.

Geuss, R. (1981) *The Idea of a Critical Theory: Habermas and the Frankfurt School*. Cambridge: Cambridge University Press.

Giddens, A. (1979) *Central Problems in Social Theory*. London: Macmillan.

Giddens, A. (1990) *The Consequences of Modernity*. Cambridge: Polity.

Giddens, A. (1991) *Modernity and Self-identity: Self and Society in the Late Modern Age*. Cambridge: Polity.

Gill, R. (1993) 'Justifying injustice: broadcasters' accounts of inequality in radio', in Burman, E. and Parker, I. (eds), *Discourse Analytic Research*. London: Routledge. pp. 75–93.

Glaser, B.G. (1978) *Theoretical Sensitivity: Advances in the Methodology of Grounded Theory*. Mill Valley, CA: Sociology Press.

Glaser, B.G. (1992) *Emergence versus Forcing: Basics of Grounded Theory Analysis*. Mill Valley, CA: Sociology Press.

Glaser, B.G. and Strauss, A.L. (1964a) 'The social loss of dying patients', *American Journal of Nursing*, 64 (6): 119–21.

Glaser, B.G and Strauss, A.L. (1964b) 'Awareness contexts and social interaction', *American Sociological Review*, 29: 669–79.

Glaser, B.G. and Strauss, A.L. (1966) *Awareness of Dying*. London: Weidenfeld and Nicolson.

Glaser, B.G. and Strauss, A.L. (1967) *The Discovery of Grounded Theory: Strategies for Qualitative Research*. Chicago: Aldine.

Glaser, B.G. and Strauss, A.L. (1968) *Time for Dying*. Chicago: Aldine.

Goffman, E. (1961) *Asylums*. Garden City, New York: Anchor.

Goffman, E. (1990, first published 1963) *Stigma: Notes on the Management of Spoiled Identity*. Harmondsworth: Pelican.

Goodenough, W.H. (1964) 'Cultural anthropology and linguistics', in Hymes, D. (ed.), *Language, Culture and Society*. New York: Harper and Row. pp. 36–9.

Graham, H. and Oakley, A. (1981) 'Competing ideologies of reproduction: medical and maternal perspectives on pregnancy', in Roberts, H. (ed.), *Women, Health and Reproduction*. London: Routledge and Kegan Paul. pp. 50–72.

Green, J. (1998) 'Effectiveness in health promotion: the role of qualitative evaluation studies. Notes from a case study of Accident Alliances', unpublished paper.

Guba, E.G. and Lincoln, Y.S. (1989) *Fourth Generation Evaluation*. Newbury Park, CA: Sage.

Guba, E.G. and Lincoln, Y.S. (1994) 'Competing paradigms in qualitative research', in Denzin, N.K. and Lincoln, Y.S. (eds), *Handbook of Qualitative Research*. Thousand Oaks, CA: Sage. pp. 105–17.

Gubrium, J.F. and Holstein, J.A. (1997) *The New Language of Qualitative Method*. Oxford: Oxford University Press.

Hacking, I. (1982) 'Language, truth and reason', in Hollis, M. and Lukes, S. (eds), *Rationality and Relativism*. Oxford: Basil Blackwell. pp. 48–66.

Hacking, I. (1990) *The Taming of Chance*. Cambridge: Cambridge University Press.

Hammersley, M. (1991) 'A note on Campbell's distinction between external and internal validity', *Quality and Quantity*, 25: 381–7.

Hammersley, M. (1992a) 'The paradigm wars: reports from the front', *British Journal of Sociology of Education*, 13 (1): 131–43.

Hammersley, M. (1992b) *What's Wrong with Ethnography: Methodological Explorations*. London: Routledge.

Hammersley, M. (1995a) 'Theory and evidence in qualitative research', *Quality and Quantity*, 29: 55–66.

Hammersley, M. (1995b) *The Politics of Social Research*. London: Sage.

Hammersley, M. (1997) 'Qualitative data archiving: some reflections on its prospects and problems', *Sociology*, 31 (1): 131–42.

Hammersley, M. and Atkinson, P. (1983) *Ethnography: Principles in Practice*, 1st edn. London: Routledge.

Hammersley, M. and Atkinson, P. (1995) *Ethnography: Principles in Practice*, 2nd edn. London: Routledge.

Hammersley, M. and Gomm, R. (1997) 'Bias in social research', *Sociological Research Online*, 2, 1: http://www.soc.surrey.ac.uk/socresonline.

Harding, S. (1986) *The Science Question in Feminism*. Milton Keynes: Open University Press.

Hindess, B. (1973) *The Use of Official Statistics: a Critique of Positivism and Ethnomethodology*. London: Macmillan.

Holmes, L. (1983) 'A tale of two studies', *American Anthropologist*, 85 (4): 930–6.

Holmes, T.H. and Rahe, R.H. (1967) 'The social readjustment rating scale', *Journal of Psychosomatic Research*, 11: 213–18.

Huberman, A.M. and Crandall, D.P. (1982) 'Fitting words to numbers: multisite/multimethod research in educational dissemination', *American Behavioral Scientist*, 26 (1): 62–83.

Hyman, H. (1955) *Survey Design and Analysis*. New York: Free Press.

Jayaratne, T.E. (1983) 'The value of quantitative methodology for feminist research', in Bowles, G. and Duelli Klein, R. (eds), *Theories of Women's Studies*. London: Routledge and Kegan Paul.

Jeffery, R. (1979) 'Normal rubbish: deviant patients in casualty departments', *Sociology of Health and Illness*, 1 (1): 90–107.

Jenkins, R. (1983) *Lads, Citizens and Ordinary Kids: Working Class Youth Life-Styles in Belfast*. London: Routledge and Kegan Paul.

Jick, T.D. (1979) 'Mixing qualitative and quantitative methods: triangulation in action', *Administrative Science Quarterly*, 24: 602–11.

Kelle, U. (1997) 'Theory building in qualitative research and computer programs for the management of textual data', *Sociological Research Online*, 2, 2: http://www.soc.surrey.ac.uk/socresonline

Kelle, U. (ed.) (1995) *Computer-aided Qualitative Data Analysis: Theory, Methods, Practice*. London: Sage.

Kelle, U. and Laurie, H. (1995) 'Computer use in qualitative research and issues of validity', in Kelle, U. (ed.), *Computer-aided Qualitative Data Analysis: Theory, Methods, Practice*. London: Sage. pp. 19–28.

Kerlinger, F.N. (1964) *Foundations of Behavioral Research*. London: Holt, Rinehart and Winston.

Kirk, J. and Miller, M. (1986) *Reliability and Validity in Qualitative Research*. Newbury Park, CA: Sage.

Kuckharz, U. (1995) 'Case-oriented quantification', in Kelle, U. (ed.), *Computer-aided Qualitative Data Analysis: Theory, Methods, Practice*. London: Sage. pp. 158–66.

Kvale, S. (1989a) 'To validate is to question', in Kvale, S. (ed.), *Issues of Validity in Qualitative Research*. Lund: Studentlitteratur. pp. 73–92.

Kvale, S. (ed.) (1989b) *Issues of Validity in Qualitative Research*. Lund: Studentlitteratur.

Lather, P. (1993) 'Fertile obsession: validity after poststructuralism', *Sociological Quarterly*, 34 (4): 673–93.

Layder, D. (1998) *Sociological Practice: Linking Theory and Social Research*. London: Sage.

Lazarsfeld, P.F. and Rosenberg, M. (1955) *The Language of Social Research: a Reader in the Methodology of Social Research*. Glencoe, Ill.: Free Press.

LeCompte, M. and Goetz, J. (1982) 'Problems of reliability and validity in ethnographic research', *Review of Educational Research*, 52 (1): 31–60.

Lee, R.M. and Fielding, N.G. (1995) 'Users' experience of qualitative data analysis software', in Kelle, U. (ed.), *Computer-aided Qualitative Data Analysis: Theory, Methods, Practice*. London: Sage. pp. 29–40.

Lewis, O. (1951) *Life in a Mexican Village: Tepoztlan Restudied*. Urbana, IL: University of Illinois Press.

Lincoln, Y.S. and Denzin, N.K. (1994) 'The fifth moment', in Denzin, N.K. and Lincoln, Y.S. (eds), *Handbook of Qualitative Research*. Thousand Oaks, CA: Sage. pp. 575–86.

Lincoln, Y.S. and Guba, E. (1985) *Naturalistic Enquiry*. Beverly Hills, CA: Sage.

Lindesmith, A. (1947) *Opiate Addiction*. Bloomington: Principia Press.

Llobera, J. (1998) 'Historical and comparative research', in Seale C.F. (ed.) *Researching Society and Culture*. London: Sage. pp. 72–81.

Lofland, J. (1971) *Analysing Social Settings: a Guide to Qualitative Observation*. Belmont, CA: Wadsworth.

Long, S.O. and Long, B.D. (1982) 'Curable cancers and fatal ulcers: attitudes toward cancer in Japan', *Social Science and Medicine*, 16: 2101–8.

Lyotard, J.F. (1993) 'Answering the question: what is postmodernism?', in Docherty, T. (ed.), *Postmodernism: A Reader*. London: Harvester Wheatsheaf. pp. 38–46.

Malinowski, B. (1922) *Argonauts of the Western Pacific*. New York: E.P. Dutton.

Malinowski, B. (1967) *A Diary in the Strict Sense of the Term*. New York: Harcourt, Brace and World.

Marcus, G.E. (1994) 'What comes (just) after 'post'? The case of ethnography', in Denzin, N.K. and Lincoln, Y.S. (eds), *Handbook of Qualitative Research*. Thousand Oaks, CA: Sage. pp. 563–74.

Marsh, C. (1982) *The Survey Method: the Contribution of Surveys to Sociological Explanation*. London: Allen and Unwin.

Maynard, M. (1994) 'Methods, practice and epistemology: the debate about feminism and research', in Maynard, M. and Purvis, J. (eds), *Researching Women's Lives from a Feminist Perspective*. London: Taylor and Francis. pp. 10–26.

Maynard, M. and Purvis, J. (1994) 'Doing feminist research', in Maynard, M. and Purvis, J. (eds), *Researching Women's Lives from a Feminist Perspective*. London: Taylor and Francis. p. 109.

McKeganey, N. (1996) 'Measurement in qualitative work', talk given at Goldsmiths College, London on 29th May.

McKeganey, N., Abel, M. and Hay, G. (1996) 'Contrasting methods of collecting data on injectors' risk behaviour', *AIDS Care*, 8 (5): 557–63.

McKeganey, N., Abel, M., Taylor, A., Frischer, M., Goldberg, D. and Green, S. (1995) 'The preparedness to share injecting equipment: an analysis using vignettes', *Addiction*, 90: 1253–60.

Mead, M. (1942, first published 1930) *Growing up in New Guinea: a Study of Adolescence and Sex in Primitive Societies*. Harmondsworth: Penguin.

Mead, M. (1943, first published 1928) *Coming of Age in Samoa: a Study of Adolescence and Sex in Primitive Societies*. Harmondsworth: Penguin.

Medawar P. (1991, first published 1963) 'Is the scientific paper a fraud?', in Medawar, P. (ed.), *The Threat and the Glory*. Oxford: Oxford University Press.

Melia, K.M. (1996) 'Rediscovering Glaser', *Qualitative Health Research*, 6 (3): 368–78.

Merton, R.K. (1968) *On Theoretical Sociology*. New York: Free Press.

Miles, M. and Huberman, A. (1994) *Qualitative Data Analysis: an Expanded Sourcebook*. Thousand Oaks, CA: Sage.

Millen, D. (1997) 'Some methodological and epistemological issues raised by doing feminist research on non-feminist women', *Sociological Research Online*, 2, 3: http://www.soc.surrey.ac.uk/socresonline

Mills, C.W. (1959) *The Sociological Imagination*. Oxford: Oxford University Press.

Mishler, E.G. (1990) 'Validation in inquiry-guided research: the role of exemplars in narrative studies', *Harvard Educational Review*, 60 (4): 415–42.

Mitchell, J.C. (1983) 'Case and situational analysis', *Sociological Review*, 31 (2): 187–211.

Morgan, D. (1981) 'Men, masculinity and the process of sociological enquiry', in Roberts, H. (ed.), *Doing Feminist Research*. London: Routledge and Kegan Paul. pp. 83–113.

Mulkay, M.J. (1985) *The Word and the World: Explorations in the Form of Sociological Analysis*. London: George Allen and Unwin.

Novack, D.H., Plumer, R., Smith, R.L., Ochitill, H., Morrow, G.R. and Bennett, J.M. (1979) 'Changes in physicians' attitudes toward telling the cancer patient', *Journal of the American Medical Association*, 241: 897–900.

Oakley, A. (1981) 'Interviewing women a contradiction in terms?', in Roberts, H. (ed.), *Doing Feminist Research*. London: Routledge. pp. 30–61.

Oakley, A. (1989) 'Who's afraid of the randomised controlled trial? Some dilemmas of the scientific method and "good" research practice', *Women and Health*, 15 (4): 25–59.

Paget, M.A. (1995) 'Performing the text', in Van Maanen, J. (ed.), *Representation in Ethnography*. Thousand Oaks, CA: Sage. pp. 222–44.

Pelto, P.J. and Pelto, G.H. (1978) *Anthropological Research: the Structure of Inquiry*. Cambridge: Cambridge University Press.

Peräkylä, A. (1995) *AIDS Counselling: Institutional Interaction and Clinical Practice*. Cambridge: Cambridge University Press.

Peräkylä, A. (1997) 'Reliability and validity in research based on tapes and transcripts', in Silverman, D. (ed.), *Qualitative Research: Theory, Method and Practice*. London: Sage. pp. 201–20.

Polkinghorne, D.E. (1989) 'Changing conversations about human science', in Kvale, S. (ed.), *Issues of Validity in Qualitative Research*. Lund: Studentlitteratur. pp. 13–46

Pomerantz, A. (1980) 'Telling my side: "limited access" as a "fishing device"', *Sociological Inquiry*, 50: 186–98.

Popper, K.R. (1963) *Conjectures and Refutations*. London: Routledge and Kegan Paul.

Popper, K.R. (1972) *Objective Knowledge*. Oxford: Clarendon Press.

Porteous, J. (1988) 'Topocide: the annihilation of place', in Eyles, J. and Smith, D. (eds), *Qualitative Methods in Human Geography*. Oxford: Blackwell. pp. 75–93.

Potter, J. and Wetherell, M. (1987) *Discourse and Social Psychology: Beyond Attitudes and Behaviour*. London: Sage.

Potter, J. and Wetherell, M. (1994) 'Analyzing discourse', in Bryman, A. and Burgess, R.G. (eds), *Analyzing Qualitative Data*. London: Routledge. pp. 47–66.

Pratt, J., Bloomfield, J. and Seale, C.F. (1982) *Option Choice: a Question of Equal Opportunity*. Windsor: NFER/Nelson.

Ragin, C.C. (1987) *The Comparative Method: Moving beyond Quantitative and Qualitative Strategies*. Berkeley and Los Angeles: University of California Press.

Ragin, C.C. (1995) 'Using qualitative comparative analysis to study configurations', in Kelle, U. (ed.), *Computer-aided Qualitative Data Analysis: Theory, Methods, Practice*. Thousand Oaks, CA: Sage. pp. 177–89.

Redfield, R. (1930) *Tepoztlan: a Mexican Village*. Chicago: Chicago University Press.

Reinharz, S. (1992) *Feminist Methods in Social Research*. Oxford: Oxford University Press.

Richardson, L. (1992) 'The consequences of poetic representation', in Ellis, C.

and Flaherty, M. (eds), *Investigating Subjectivity*. Thousand Oaks, CA: Sage. pp. 125–37.

Richardson, L. (1994) 'Nine poems: marriage and the family', *Journal of Contemporary Ethnography*, 23: 3–14.

Richardson, L. (1996) 'Ethnographic trouble', *Qualitative Inquiry*, 2 (2): 227–9.

Riessman, C.K. (1993) *Narrative Analysis*. Newbury Park, CA: Sage.

Robinson, W.S. (1951) 'The logical structure of analytic induction', *American Sociological Review*, 16: 812–18.

Roller, E., Mathes, R. and Eckert, T. (1995) 'Hermeneutic-classificatory content analysis: a technique combining principles of quantitative and qualitative research', in Kelle, U. (ed.), *Computer-aided Qualitative Data Analysis: Theory, Methods, Practice*. London: Sage. pp. 167–76.

Rosaldo, R. (1993, first published 1989) 'Introduction: grief and a headhunter's rage', in Rosaldo, R. (ed.), *Culture and Truth: the Remaking of Social Analysis*. London: Routledge. pp. 1–21.

Rose, G. (1982) *Deciphering Social Research*. London: Macmillan.

Rosenberg, M. (1968) *The Logic of Survey Analysis*. New York: Basic Books.

Rossman, G.B. and Wilson, B.L. (1994) 'Numbers and words revisited: being "shamelessly eclectic"', *Quality and Quantity*, 28: 315–27.

Roth, J. (1957) 'Ritual and magic in the control of contagion', *American Sociological Review*, 22: 310–14.

Rowntree, B.S. (1901) *Poverty: a Study of Town Life*. Basingstoke: Macmillan.

Russell, D. (1986) *The Secret Trauma: Incest in the Lives of Girls and Women*. New York: Basic Books.

Sacks, H., Schegloff, E.A. and Jefferson, G. (1974) 'A simple systematics for the organization of turn-taking for conversation', *Language*, 50: 696–735.

Salner, M. (1989) 'Validity in human science research', in Kvale, S. (ed.), *Issues of Validity in Qualitative Research*. Lund: Studentlitteratur. pp. 47–72.

Schatzman, L. and Strauss, A. (1973) *Field Research: Strategies for a Natural Sociology*. Englewood Cliffs, NJ: Prentice Hall.

Scheff, T. (1997) 'Part/whole morphology: unifying single case and comparative methods', *Sociological Research Online*, 2, 3: http://www.soc.surrey.ac.uk/socresonline.

Schegloff, E.A. (1968) 'Sequencing in conversational openings', *American Anthropologist*, 70: 1075–95.

Scheper-Hughes, N. and Lovell, A.M. (1986) 'Breaking the circuit of social control: lessons in public psychiatry from Italy and Franco Basaglia', *Social Science and Medicine*, 23 (2): 159–78.

Schou, K.C. (1993) 'Awareness contexts and the construction of dying in the cancer treatment setting: "micro" and "macro" levels in narrative analysis', in Clark, D. (ed.), *The Sociology of Death*. Oxford: Blackwell and *The Sociological Review*. pp. 238–63.

Schutz, A. (1944) 'The stranger: an essay in social psychology', *American Journal of Sociology*, 49 (6): 499–507.

Schutz, A. (1970, first published 1953) 'Concept and theory formation in the social sciences', in Emmet, D. and MacIntyre, A. (eds), *Sociological Theory and Philosophical Analysis*. London: Macmillan. pp. 1–19.

Schwandt, T.A. (1996) 'Farewell to criteriology', *Qualitative Inquiry*, 2 (1): 58–72.

Seale, C.F. (1995) 'Heroic death', *Sociology*, 29 (4): 597–613.

Seale, C.F. (1996) 'Living alone towards the end of life', *Ageing and Society*, 16: 75–91.

Seale, C.F. (ed.) (1998a) *Researching Society and Culture*. London: Sage.

Seale, C.F. (1998b) *Constructing Death: the Sociology of Dying and Bereavement*. Cambridge: Cambridge University Press.

Seale, C.F. (1999) 'Using computers to analyse qualitative data', in Silverman, D. (ed.), *Doing Qualitative Research*. London: Sage.

Seale, C.F. and Silverman, D. (1997) 'Ensuring rigour in qualitative research', *European Journal of Public Health*, 7: 379–84.

Seale, C.F., Addington-Hall, J. and McCarthy, M. (1997) 'Awareness of dying: prevalence, causes and consequences', *Social Science and Medicine*, 45 (3): 477–84.

Secker, J., Wimbush, E., Watson, J. and Milburn, K. (1995) 'The use of qualitative methods in health promotion research: some criteria for quality', *Health Education Journal*, 54 (1): 74–87.

Selvin, H.C. and Stuart, A. (1966) 'Data dredging procedures in survey analysis', in Bynner, J. and Stribley, K.M. (eds), *Social Research: Principles and Procedures*. Harlow: Longman/Open University Press. pp. 278–84.

Sieber, S. (1979) 'The integration of fieldwork and survey methods', *American Journal of Sociology*, 78 (6): 1353–59.

Silverman, D. (1984) 'Going private: ceremonial forms in a private oncology clinic', *Sociology*, 18: 191–202.

Silverman, D. (1985) *Qualitative Methodology and Sociology*. Aldershot: Gower.

Silverman, D. (1989) 'Telling convincing stories: a plea for cautious positivism in case-studies', in Glassner, B. and Moreno, J.D. (eds), *The Qualitative–Quantitative Distinction in the Social Sciences*. Netherlands: Kluwer. pp. 57–77.

Silverman, D. (1993) *Interpreting Qualitative Data: Methods for Analysing Talk, Text and Interaction*. London: Sage.

Silverman, D. (1997a) 'Towards an aesthetics of research', in Silverman, D. (ed.), *Qualitative Research: Theory, Method and Practice*. London: Sage. pp. 239–53.

Silverman, D. (1997b) *Discourses of Counselling: HIV Counselling as Social Interaction*. London: Sage.

Silverman, D. (1998a) 'The quality of qualitative health research: the open-ended interview and its alternatives', *Social Sciences in Health*, 4 (2): 104–17.

Silverman, D. (1998b) 'Analysing conversation', in Seale, C.F. (ed.), *Researching Society and Culture*. London: Sage. pp. 261–74.

Skelton, A. (1998) 'The hidden curriculum of patient education for low back pain in general practice', *Sociology of Health and Illness*, 20 (1): 96–111.

Smith, A.G. and Robbins, A.E. (1982) 'Structured ethnography: the study of parental involvement', *American Behavioral Scientist*, 26 (1): 45–61.

Smith, J.K. (1984) 'The problem of criteria for judging interpretive inquiry', *Educational Evaluation and Policy Analysis*, 6 (4): 379–91.

Smith, J.K. and Heshusius, L. (1986) 'Closing down the conversation: the end of the qualitative-quantitative debate among educational enquirers', *Educational Researcher*, 15: 4–12.

Snow, D.A. and Morrill, C. (1993) 'Reflections on anthropology's ethnographic crisis of faith', *Contemporary Sociology*, 22: 8–11.

Strauss, A.L. (1987) *Qualitative Analysis for Social Scientists*. Cambridge: Cambridge University Press.

Strauss, A.L. and Corbin, J. (1990) *Basics of Qualitative Research: Grounded Theory Procedures and Techniques*. Newbury Park, CA: Sage.

Strong, P.M. (1979) *The Ceremonial Order of the Clinic*. London: Routledge and Kegan Paul.

Surbone, A. (1992) 'Truth telling to the patient', *Journal of the American Medical Association*, 268: 1661–2.

Swanborn, P.G. (1996) 'A common base for quality control criteria in quantitative and qualitative research', *Quality and Quantity*, 30: 19–35.

Trow, M. (first published 1957) 'Comment on "Participant observation and interviewing: a comparison"', in McCall, G. and Simmons, J.L. (eds) (1969), *Issues in Participant Observation*. New York: Addison-Wesley. pp. 332–8.

Turner, B.A. (1981) 'Some practical aspects of qualitative data analysis: one way of organising the cognitive processes associated with the generation of grounded theory', *Quality and Quantity*, 15: 225–47.

Turner, R.H. (1953) 'The quest for universals in sociological research', *American Sociological Review*, 18: 604–11.

Tyler, S.A. (1986) 'Post-modern ethnography: from document of the occult to occult document', in Clifford, J. and Marcus, G. (eds), *Writing Culture: The Poetics and Politics of Ethnography*. Berkeley: University of California Press. pp. 122–40.

Van Maanen, J. (1988) *Tales of the Field: on Writing Ethnography*. Chicago: University of Chicago Press.

Van Maanen, J. (1995) *Representation in Ethnography*. Thousand Oaks, CA: Sage.

Voysey, M. (1975) *A Constant Burden: the Reconstitution of Family Life*. London: Routledge and Kegan Paul.

Wacquant, L. (1998) 'Inside the zone: the social art of the hustler in the Black American ghetto', *Theory, Culture and Society*, 15 (2): 1–36.

Waitzkin, H. (1979) 'Medicine, superstructure and micropolitics', *Social Science and Medicine*, 13A: 601–9.

Walter, T. (1994) *The Revival of Death*. London: Routledge.

Webb, E.J., Campbell, D.T., Schwartz, R.D. and Sechrest, L. (1966) *Unobtrusive Measures: Non-reactive Research in the Social Sciences*. Chicago: Rand McNally.

Weber, M. (1949) *The Methodology of the Social Sciences*. New York: Free Press.

West, P. (1990) 'The status and validity of accounts obtained at interview: a contrast between two studies of families with a disabled child', *Social Science and Medicine*, 30 (11): 1229–39.

Whyte, W.F. (1976) 'Research methods for the study of conflict and cooperation', *American Sociologist*, 11 (4): 208–16.

Whyte, W.F. (1981, first published 1943) *Street Corner Society: the Social Structure of an Italian Slum*, 3rd edn. Chicago: University of Chicago Press.

Whyte, W.F. (1996a) 'Qualitative sociology and deconstructionism', *Qualitative Inquiry*, 2 (2): 220–6.

Whyte, W.F. (1996b) 'Facts, interpretations, and ethics in qualitative inquiry', *Qualitative Inquiry*, 2 (2): 242–4.

Wiener, C.L. (1975) 'The burden of rheumatoid arthritis: tolerating the uncertainty', *Social Science and Medicine* 9: 97–104.

Williams, M. and May, T. (1996) *Introduction to the Philosophy of Social Research*. London: UCL Press.

Wolfe, T. (1973) 'The new journalism', in Wolfe, T. and Johnson, E.W. (eds), *The New Journalism: an Anthology*. New York: Harper and Row. pp. ix–52.

Yardley, L. (ed.) (1997) *Material Discourses of Health and Illness*. London: Routledge.

Yin, R.K. (1989) *Case Study Research: Design and Methods*. Thousand Oaks, CA: Sage.

Zelditch, M. (1962) 'Some methodological problems of field studies', *American Journal of Sociology*, 67: 506–76.

Znaniecki, F. (1934) *The Method of Sociology*. New York: Rinehart.

Index

Lightning Source UK Ltd.
Milton Keynes UK
UKOW041837110412

190506UK00001B/13/A